MEDIA DISCOURSE

Norman Fairclough

Edward Arnold
A member of the Hodder Headline Group
LONDON NEW YORK SYDNEY AUCKLAND

First published in Great Britain in 1995 by
Edward Arnold, a division of Hodder Headline PLC
338 Euston Road, London NW1 3BH
175 Fifth Avenue, New York, NY10010

Distributed exclusively in the USA by
St Martin's Press Inc.,
175 Fifth Avenue,
New York, NY10010

British Library Cataloguing in Publication Data
A catalogue entry for this book is available from the British Library

Library of Congress Cataloging-in-Publication Data
Fairclough, Norman, 1941–
    Media discourse/Norman Fairclough.
        p.   cm.
    Includes bibliographical references (p. 206) and index.
    ISBN 0–340–63222–4. — ISBN 0–340–58889–6
    1. Mass media and language.   I. Title.
P96.L34F35   1995
302.23—dc20   95–17679
                                                                    CIP

ISBN 0 340 58889 6 (Pb)
ISBN 0 340 63222 4 (Hb)

1 2 3 4 5   95   96   97   98   99

Composition by Phoenix Photosetting, Chatham, Kent
Printed and bound in Great Britain by J. W. Arrowsmith, Bristol

CONTENTS

ACKNOWLEDGEMENTS

My thanks to those who have looked at and commented on a draft version of this book – Alan Bell, Mike Birch, Gunther Kress, Theo van Leeuwen, Mary Talbot – or commented on presentations based upon Chapters 8 and 9 – Andrew Tolson and colleagues at Queen Margaret College, Edinburgh, and those who attended a seminar on critical discourse analysis at the London Institute of Education in April 1994. My thanks also to students, visitors and colleagues in the Department of Linguistics at Lancaster University, and to participants in many fascinating interdisciplinary meetings, for a stimulating intellectual environment. To Simon and Matthew for their precocious critical media awareness. And above all to Vonny.

Thanks are due to the following for permission to reproduce copyright material: The British Broadcasting Corporation for extracts from *Medicine Now, High Resolution,* and *Today* (all Radio 4). Mirror Syndication International for extracts from the *Daily Mirror*, 7 October 1992 and 14 January 1993. The *Guardian* for an extract, 7 October 1992. Rex Features Ltd for extracts from the *Sun*, 24 May 1985 and 14 January 1993.

Note on transcriptions

The transcriptions of broadcast talk in this book are in some cases the author's, in other cases taken from a variety of published sources. Transcriptions generally do not divide speech into sentences, and omit the punctuation found in written text. Other transcription conventions vary – in, for instance, the extent to which they reproduce hesitations.

The following conventions will be found here:

Pauses: represented as dots between words, like . this. Longer pauses are shown by two . . or three . . . dots, or by giving the pause as parts of a second, e.g. (0.5).

Hesitations: e, em, e:, e:m, or e:r, with the colon marking an elongated syllable.

Simultaneous talk by two speakers is indicated by a square bracket.

1

MEDIA AND LANGUAGE: SETTING AN AGENDA

Four events took place in roughly the first half of 1994, while I was working on this book: Silvio Berlusconi's Forza Italia won the Italian general election, in the UK Tony Blair was elected leader of the Labour Party, between one and two million Hutu refugees fled from Rwanda into Zaïre in the space of a few days, and Rupert Murdoch made a week-long trip to Delhi. It was generally recognized that Forza Italia was a media creation (Berlusconi founded the party in January, it won the election in March) and that Berlusconi's victory was largely the result of his control of the Italian media – he owns three television channels with a 40 per cent share of the audience, a national newspaper, and Italy's biggest publishing company. Long before the Labour leadership contest even officially opened, most of the British media had already chosen Tony Blair as the successor to the late John Smith. Blair's campaign was orchestrated by Labour's own 'spin doctor' Peter Mandelson, and his attractiveness as a media personality was seen (whatever his other virtues) as a major qualification for the job. In mid-July the civil war in Rwanda, which had received patchy coverage before, suddenly became the lead item on television news (and in other media) for days on end, with extensive, shocking coverage of suffering and death amongst the massive numbers of Hutu refugees. And Murdoch's visit to Delhi was linked to his acquisition of access to five satellite television channels beamed at 2.5 billion people in fifty countries – more than two-thirds of the world's population. The common theme of these events is the power of the mass media. The power of the media to shape governments and parties, to transform the suffering of the South (rooted in exploitation by the North) into the entertainment of the North, to beam the popular culture of North America and western Europe into Indian agricultural communities which still depend upon bullock-power. The power to influence knowledge, beliefs, values, social relations, social identities. A signifying power (the power to represent things in particular ways) which is largely a matter of how language is used, but not only that: what made Rwanda 'good television' for a short period in July 1994 was above all the availability of high-quality film of the appalling human suffering.

This book has several objectives. The first is to set out a framework for analysing media language which readers can use for themselves to pursue their own interests in mass media. I hope to persuade readers with a background in language studies of the particular fascinations associated with analysing media language. And I hope to persuade readers with a background in media studies of the value of analysing mass media linguistically and in terms of discourse (I use 'discourse' for language use seen in a particular way, as a form of social practice – see further below). The substantively linguistic and discoursal nature of the power of the media is one good argument for doing so. But I must stress that the approach to language adopted here is a novel one, which links in well with issues which have been widely taken up in recent media studies, such as intertextuality, genre mixing, and identity.

A second objective is to argue a particular case: I hope to convince readers that analysis of media language should be recognized as an important element within research on contemporary processes of social and cultural change, a theme which is attracting growing interest in the social sciences. I have in mind, for instance, research on a claimed transition from 'modern' to 'postmodern' society or from 'high modern' to 'late modern' society, research on shifts in cultural values (e.g. in the direction of individualism or a 'promotional culture') and the constitution of social identities, on 'detraditionalization' and changes in power relations and authority relations, and so forth (see, for example, Beck 1992, Featherstone 1991, Giddens

1991, Lash 1990, Wernick 1991). Given the focal position of the mass media in contemporary social systems, there can be little argument about their relevance to the study of sociocultural change. What will be less obvious to most social scientists, and more contentious, is that analysis of the *language* of the mass media can make a substantive contribution to such research. I hope to establish this in this book – and my argument is again dependent upon a novel approach to language analysis which rejects the arid formalism of past approaches. A third objective, as I have already implied, is to highlight the linguistic and discoursal nature of media power.

I shall be focusing upon the language of what we might call public affairs media – news, documentary, magazine programmes, dealing with politics, social affairs, science, and so forth. Many of my examples are taken from the British media – the press, radio and television – in the period 1992–3, and there are also some from the USA and Australia. In the course of the book I shall refer to quite a number of samples of media language, and I want to begin here with four short examples which will give readers a sense of some of the main concerns of the book, and provide a basis for the more theoretical discussion later in this chapter.

The first is from the beginning of an edition of the BBC current affairs programme *Panorama*, concerned with the reprocessing in Britain of nuclear fuel from overseas (BBC1, 10 August 1992). The reporter, John Taylor, is pictured facing the camera, leaning against the rail of a launch, with the ship referred to in the text at anchor in the background:

> In the coming week this ship, the *Shikishimi*, will put to sea to guard a deadly cargo on a dangerous voyage around the world. Its cargo will be plutonium, one of the world's most toxic substances, and the raw material of nuclear weapons. It will herald the start of an international trade in plutonium centred around British Nuclear Fuel's reprocessing plant at Sellafield. Critics say each shipment could be a floating Chernobyl. Tonight *Panorama* asks: is the plutonium business worth the risk?

This extract is followed by the usual *Panorama* opening sequence including the programme logo (a revolving globe) and signature tune, and a sequence of images representing nuclear risk (including the explosion of a nuclear bomb, and someone testing for radioactivity with a Geiger counter).

Apart from the last sentence, which contains a question (*is the plutonium business worth the risk?*), the extract consists of declarative sentences – statements. (I shall use as little linguistic terminology as possible, and the terms I do use are explained as we go along.) The first three sentences are statements about what will happen in the future. Despite the fact that future events are contingent on many things and therefore uncertain, these are firm, categorical statements – that is the effect of using the auxiliary verb *will* – and there is no qualification or 'hedging' (no 'probably' or 'maybe'). These categorical statements are part of how a relationship between the reporter and the audience, and social identities for reporter and audience, are established at the outset of the programme. The reporter is projected as a figure of authority, someone who knows (has 'the facts'), and someone who has the right to tell. The authoritativeness of the language works together with the authoritativeness of the image – a well-known reporter directly addressing the audience on-camera – and of the delivery, which is measured, emphatic (the reporter using movements of head and hands to support vocal emphasis) and serious. The audience is projected as receptive, waiting to be told, wanting to know.

But this is only part of the story, for reporter/audience identities and relations are more complex. In addition to the knowledgeable reporter informing the interested citizen, there is an element – more muted in this example than the next one – of the media artist entertaining the viewer as consumer. This is evident in certain rhetorical, attention-grabbing features: the direct question at the end, the metaphor of *a floating Chernobyl* which links reprocessing to the nuclear *cause célèbre* of Chernobyl in a witty and memorable phrase. It is also evident in the choice of genre: the decision to represent the issue of the 'international trade in plutonium' as a narrative, a story, about a projected voyage of an individual ship – not something that has happened (as in most stories) but something that is expected to happen. This story, with pictures of the actual ship, makes for a more dramatic and entertaining account than a description of the planned trade in general terms within an expository genre, which might have been selected.

In any representation, you have to decide what to include and what to exclude, and what to 'foreground' and what to 'background'. In this case, certain details which you might have expected to be backgrounded or excluded altogether – on the grounds that they are common knowledge which a *Panorama* audience might be expected to share – have been foregrounded: describing the cargo as *deadly* and the voyage as *dangerous*, mentioning that plutonium is *one of the world's most toxic substances* and *the raw material of nuclear weapons*. This detail generates a sense of alarm, underlined by the reporter's delivery which stresses the words *deadly*, *dangerous* and *toxic*. It is sensationalist. It also helps to build up a negative, critical view of the trade early in the programme, as indeed does representing it as a *trade* and a *business* rather than, say, as a *transfer* between countries. Notice also that the trade is *centred around* the reprocessing plant at Sellafield (already another *cause célèbre*), rather than, say, *involving* Sellafield, or *between* Sellafield and Japan. The sentence beginning *Critics say* . . . is interesting from this point of view. Given that the programme has apparently already joined the critics, perhaps the role of *critics say* is a 'modal' one, to mitigate and disclaim responsibility for a damning judgement by attributing it to unspecified others. The indirectness and implicitness of the critical stance towards the 'trade' perhaps shows a tension and trade-off between the evenhandedness required of the reporter in his more traditional information-giving, authoritative role, and the more sensationalist demands upon the reporter as entertainer. Tension between the objectives of giving information and entertaining is widespread in the contemporary media.

This brief example shows how analysis of the language of media texts – by which I mean what is said in broadcasts as well as what is written in the press – can illuminate three sets of questions about media output:

1. How is the world (events, relationships, etc.) represented? *representation*
2. What identities are set up for those involved in the programme or story (reporters, audiences, 'third parties' referred to or interviewed)? *identities*
3. What relationships are set up between those involved (e.g. reporter–audience, expert–audience or politician–audience relationships)? *relations*

I shall refer from now on to *representations*, *identities* and *relations*. A useful working assumption is that any part of any text (from the media or from elsewhere) will be simultaneously representing, setting up identities, and setting up relations.

My second example comes from an edition of the ITV current affairs programme *This Week* entitled 'Vigilante!' (10 September 1992), which dealt with vigilante groups in Britain enacting their own justice where they perceive the law to be ineffective. The programme opens with a 'trailer' which gives brief versions of the vigilante stories to be covered, followed by the usual *This Week* opening visual sequence and signature tune, then the programme title 'Vigilante!' imposed on a still picture of a silhouetted man carrying what appears to be an axe handle. My extract comes after this. On the left I have given a rough representation of visual images in the extract, and on the right the language (reporter voice-over).

IMAGES	LANGUAGE
Pictures of hills and valleys, sound of choir	As the coalmines of South Wales fall silent, the blackened hills and valleys grow green again. It's a picture of peace. But in the
Groups of people converge on house, shouting	village of Penwyn, in July, an ugly scene was played out following the violent death of an elderly spinster. When two teenage girls from the neighbourhood were charged with murder, a mob of several hundred local people converged on
Crowd in front of houses, gestures and shouts	the houses where the parents of the accused lived. (*Long pause filled with shouting.*) The dead woman's complaints of harassment had apparently gone unheeded. The crowd were enraged by reports she'd been so brutally killed that she could only be
Missiles picked up and thrown at windows, sounds of breaking glass, crowd shouting and cheering	identified by her fingerprints. (*Long pause filled with shouting.*) A shower of missiles drove the families from their homes. The police could do nothing but help them to safety.

This extract takes one step further the tendency in the earlier one for reporter and audience identities and relations to be on the entertainer–consumer model. The genre is past-event narrative, and the story is told through a combination of words and what the programme identifies as a filmed reconstruction of the incident. The extract, and indeed the programme as a whole, is on the borderline between information and entertainment, and between fact and fiction. The visual narrative of the film, in which the crowd is played by actors, is dramatic fiction.

The images have primacy over the words in the sense that the events related happen first visually (e.g. we see a missile thrown before we hear *a shower of missiles*). (See Barthes 1977 and van Leeuwen 1991 on variable relationships between words and images.) The linguistic account provides an interpretation of the images, identifying the people in the crowd, the house and its inhabitants, but also shifting between narrating events and providing setting and background for them, often in the same sentence. An important part of this is providing explanations of the crowd's behaviour.

There are also apparent inconsistencies between words and images. The images show, first, groups of angry-looking people walking purposefully along shouting, then a crowd of angry people shouting and gesticulating in front of the lighted window of a house, then some of them hurling missiles at the window, and glass breaking. Responsibility for the violence is clear and unmitigated in the film. In the linguistic account, responsibility is less clearly attributed, and is mitigated. There are just three clauses (simple sentences) which recount the incident itself. What is interesting is both the way these are formulated, and the way they are positioned in the account. The first (*an ugly scene was played out*) is vague about who did what to whom, the third (*A shower of missiles drove the families from their homes*) transforms the action of throwing missiles into an entity, a shower of missiles, and does not indicate who actually did it. Only in the second (*a mob of several hundred local people converged on the houses*) is the crowd represented as actually taking action, and then it is 'converging on' (which implies a *controlled* action that does not entirely square with the behaviour of a 'mob') rather than 'attacking' the house.

What I'm suggesting is that the linguistic account is rather restrained in blaming the crowd. True, it is referred to damningly as 'a mob', but two sentences later it is referred to more neutrally as 'the crowd'. What is significant about the positioning of these event clauses is that they are separated by background explanatory clauses. This both slows down the story and reduces the impact of the violence; it also mitigates the actions of the crowd by framing them with a great deal of interpretative, explanatory material. There is, in short, an ambivalence in the representation here which accords, I think, with an ambivalence in the programme as a whole: it does not wish to defend unlawful violence, but it presents the vigilantes as normally decent people frustrated by the ineffectiveness of the law. The notion of 'good television' perhaps favours the image of frightening violence in the film, which is unambivalent, but which can be partly 'balanced' by mitigating language. Once again, there is a tension between information and entertainment.

My next example is from a programme in a BBC education series on engineering, called *The Works*. Produced in collaboration with the Engineering Training Authority, the series was designed to 'show engineers in a creative light', mainly to secondary-school pupils. The programme, entitled 'Slippery When Wet' (BBC2, 1 September 1992), is concerned with liquids. The extract comes immediately after the series opening sequence, which is done in a 'pop video' style, with a fast-changing sequence of technical and scientific images accompanied by loud synthesized music.

> A liquid: a substance that can change its shape, but cannot be expanded or compressed. These properties give liquids a special part to play in the triumph of technology. Half the weight of this massive aircraft is liquid, mostly kerosene, but also water, hydraulic oil, engine oil, toilets, detergents, booze, and of course passengers, who are also two-thirds liquid. It's a miracle it can fly at all. But without fluids, it wouldn't work.

The language here is produced by an unidentified reporter in voice-over. It is accompanied by highly complex interlocking images, music and sound effects which give the programme a style which is quite different from traditional forms of television science. During the course of this short extract, there are images of: a drop of water falling in slow motion into a puddle, what appear to be blow-ups of water molecules, liquid pouring into a vat, oil pouring into a glass, part of an engine rotating at high speed, toothpaste being spread on to a toothbrush, a hand 'painting out' the rotating engine to reveal an aircraft taking off. At transitions between these images, they are superimposed upon one another in several cases. Most of them are accompanied by appropriate sound effects, and through most of the sequence there is music. The overall result is noisy, fast-moving, bewildering, and certainly attention-grabbing, an unusually entertaining form of broadcast science, providing a different resolution of the information–entertainment tension from that of the last example.

The extract also illustrates another, related, tension, between public and private: science and technology are part of public, institutional life, as indeed is the whole business of producing television programmes – but those programmes are received and consumed overwhelmingly in private contexts, in the home, within the family. Public life and private life involve different ways of using language, and we find this tension realized in a combination, within the extract, of private and public language. The private element is actually most striking in features of the extract which are not apparent in the transcription: accent and delivery. The reporter has a Tyneside accent. This is an accent which is more common among characters in broadcast drama than amongst political, science or education broadcasters; for most people, it is associated with private life rather than public life. The effect here is to weaken the boundary between the public and the private, mixing the public world of science and technology with a voice from ordinary life. The delivery is also strikingly conversational in rhythm, intonation and stress. The mixture of public and private is also evident in the transcription. The language in part has a semi-technical character: terms like *substance, properties* and *fluids* are part of scientific vocabulary, and the provision of formal definitions (like the definition of a liquid at the beginning) is a scientific but not an ordinary language practice. Notice, however, that there is no specialist vocabulary which a reasonably well-educated person might not understand. But there is also some conversational language: *booze, wouldn't work*, describing the aircraft as *massive* (the word is also foregrounded by being emphatically stressed), and the idiomatic formula *it's a miracle it can . . .* (*fly*, in this case). We can describe this as a case of *conversationalization* of the public language of science and technology (on conversationalization in public language, see Fairclough 1994).

My final example is taken from the *Today* programme which is broadcast every weekday morning on BBC Radio 4. The particular programme I am using was broadcast during the 1992 UK general election campaign (8 April 1992). The presenter, Brian Redhead (BR), is asking representatives of each of the three main political parties (Conservative, Labour, Liberal Democrat) why an imaginary 'floating voter' should support them.

> BR: now our floating voter turns to you Brian Gould and he says look (BG: yeah) I don't really fancy another Conservative government I think we've had enough of that but I can't really bring myself to vote for you because you've been out of office for so long you haven't got the experience if you get in the City might say do this lot know enough to run the country I'm nervous that a vote for you would mean a vote for some kind of flight from the pound
> (answer from Brian Gould, question from BR to Des Wilson, and answer from Des Wilson omitted)
> BR: Des Wilson thank you now . imagine this floating voter actually is a mate of all three of you . knows you personally . and has sat up he's a different bloke altogether this one's been here through the whole

election he's listened to every blooming broadcast (one of panel: lucky chap) he's fed up to the back teeth (one of panel: haven't we all) . and he rings you up and he says the same question to each of you and I just want a quick answer from each if you would . he says . hey Chris . e:m . your campaign has been dreadful . I mean you've just underestimated the intelligence of the electorate and particularly of me . what would you why did you get it wrong

Conversationalization is much more marked in this case. The presenter is constructed as an ordinary bloke talking to ordinary people, sharing with them a common 'lifeworld' (Habermas 1984), a commonsense world of ordinary experience. One conversational feature is the direct representation of the talk of others, including an attempt to imitate the voice of the (real or imaginary) original. Indeed, this whole item is built around the presenter's simulation of the voice of the floating voter. Conversationalization is also realized in a variety of linguistic features. Most obvious are items of colloquial vocabulary (*fancy, mate, bloke, blooming*) and the colloquial idiom *fed up to the back teeth*. Notice also that *altogether* is used in a distinctively conversational way, in close associa- tion with *different*, placed after a noun, meaning 'completely'. The extract includes the colloquial use of the demonstrative pronoun *this* to refer to someone previously mentioned (e.g. *imagine this floating voter actually is a mate of all three of you*). There is also a feature of conversational narrative in the use of narrative present tense (e.g., from earlier in this interview, *he comes back to you Chris Patten and he says*).

These examples have identified two tensions affecting contem- porary media language:

- the tension between information and entertainment
- the tension between public and private.

They are indicative of two tendencies:

- the tendency of public affairs media to become increasingly con- versationalized
- its tendency to move increasingly in the direction of entertainment[1] – to become more 'marketized'.

Of course, a large part of media output is clearly designed as enter- tainment (drama, soap operas, comedy shows, quiz shows, and so forth), so what is involved here can be thought of as a shift in the internal structure of the media, a relaxation of the boundary between public affairs and entertainment within the media. This shift can be seen in more general terms as part of an intensified 'marketization' of the media: because of increasing commercial pressures and competition, media are being more fully drawn into operating on a market basis within the 'leisure' industry, and one part of that is greater pressure to entertain even within public affairs output.

Marketization is a process affecting not only mass media. One feature of Thatcherism in Britain and parallel political regimes in other countries is that more and more domains of social life have been forced to operate on a more explicitly market basis – educational institutions including schools and universities, the health service, and sections of the arts amongst them. Economic change has been accompanied by cultural change, which has led some to refer to contemporary societies as 'consumer' or 'promotional' cultures (Featherstone 1991, Wernick 1991). Like many others, I regard these developments as matters for concern. In the case of the media, for instance, is the commercial imperative (especially in television) to constantly entertain (Postman 1987), almost without regard to the nature of the programme, compatible with the tradition of public service broadcasting? If audiences are constructed, and competed for, as consumers, even in news and current affairs programmes, does this not negate the claims of broadcasting to constitute a public sphere (Habermas 1989) in which people, as citizens, are drawn into serious debate on the issues of the day? And if the media is not sustaining a political public sphere, where else can it be constructed in our mediatized society? (Perhaps the 'networking' associated with, for instance, anti-road-building campaigns indicates that there are other possibilities.) I return to these questions in Chapter 3.

Conversationalization, also, is affecting many other domains in addition to the mass media – it is evident in interactions between professionals (in a wide sense) and their publics or 'clients' in medicine, education, politics and many other domains. A large-scale merging of private and public practices is indeed a hallmark of contemporary social life. I referred above to the particular structural properties of mass-media communication which favour conversationalization – the contradiction between the public nature of media production and the private nature of media consumption (Cardiff 1980, Scannell 1992). But there are also, as in the case of the shift towards entertainment, more general social and cultural changes at issue. We might see these in terms of tradition as an organizing principle within societies becoming problematic (Giddens 1991), which entails problems with relationships based upon authority, an opening up and democratization of social relations, a new public prestige for 'ordinary' values and practices, popular culture, including 'ordinary' conversational practices.

We might also see a link between conversationalization and marketization (the shift towards the consumer model and entertainment). According to one view (Abercrombie 1991), the emphasis has shifted in contemporary economies from production to consumption, and this has entailed a change in authority relations which favours consumers over producers, and a more general shift in social relations in favour of ordinary people and their practices, culture and values, including conversational language. While I certainly do see a connection between the two tensions and between the two tendencies, I shall treat them here as distinct, if overlapping.

I have highlighted two aspects of the relationship between the mass media and other parts of the network of social institutions they operate within: their relationship to ordinary life (the 'lifeworld') and the family on the one hand, their relationship to business and commerce on the other. (The latter is a partly internal relationship, in the sense that the mass media increasingly *are* seen as business.) I see the mass media as operating within a social *system* (Blackwell and Seabrook 1993), which makes it important not to isolate particular aspects such as these two tendencies from the way the media are shaped by, and in turn contribute to shaping, the system overall. I have already signalled a concern with the question of power: the question of how the mass media affect and are affected by power relations within the social system, including relations of class, gender, and ethnicity, and relations between particular groups like politicians or scientists and the mass of the population. These issues have been extensively discussed in media studies in terms of *ideology* (Hall 1977, Hall *et al.* 1978), and a major issue is how media language might work ideologically (Fowler *et al.* 1979, Hodge and Kress 1979). Representations, identities and relations are of relevance to answering this question: the ideological work of media language includes particular ways of representing the world (e.g. particular representations of Arabs, or of the economy), particular constructions of social identities (e.g. the construction in particular ways of the scientific experts who feature on radio or television programmes), and particular constructions of social relations (e.g. the construction of relations between politicians and public as simulated relations between people in a shared lifeworld).

Two connected questions about the tensions and tendencies I have highlighted are how they affect power relations within the social system, and how they work ideologically. In respect of marketization, the increasing construction of audiences as consumers and the increasing pressure on producers to entertain can be seen as part of a normalization and naturalization of consumer behaviour and consumer culture which also involves advertising and the representation of people across the whole range of programmes (quiz shows, soap operas, sport, drama, news, and so forth). There is considerable diversity of voices, but these diverse voices are so ordered that overwhelmingly the system, with respect to consumption and consumerism, is constantly endorsed and re-endorsed. Also, because marketization undermines the media as a public sphere as I suggested above, there is a diversion of attention and energy from political and social issues which helps to insulate existing relations of power and domination from serious challenge – people are constructed as spectators of events rather than participating citizens.

On the other hand, there is a major ambivalence in the case of conversationalization. To put the issue rather baldly, do conversationalized discourse practices manifest a real shift in power relations in favour of ordinary people, or are they to be seen as merely a strategy on the part of those with power to more effectively recruit people as audiences and manipulate them socially and politically? Fowler (1991: 57) takes the latter view: 'the ideological function of conversation is to naturalize the terms in which reality is represented'. What he presumably has in mind is the sort of example we have in the extract from the *Today* programme: *you haven't got the experience if you get in the City might say do this lot know enough to run the country I'm nervous that a vote for you would mean a vote for some kind of flight from the pound.* This presupposes that sudden international movements of capital are judgements on issues like government competence, rather than judgements on prospects for profit. Notice the embedding of talk here: the whole of this sequence is in the voice of the floating voter, which has embedded within it the voice of 'the City', and these are in turn embedded in the presenter's voice in the extract. Interestingly, all these voices are conversationalized in similar ways. This not only helps naturalize the ideological presupposition noted above, it also ideologically presupposes, in itself, that the presenter, the floating voter, and the City all belong to the same lifeworld, the same world of ordinary experience, along with the audience.

But conversationalization cannot, I think, be simply dismissed as ideological: it might be ideologically invested or appropriated and indeed often is, but it does nevertheless represent some degree of cultural democratization. For example, in the extract from *The Works* above, conversationalization helps to democratize technology, making it more accessible to people, raising the status of the language and experience of ordinary life by recasting science in their terms to a degree, and rejecting the élitism and mystification which go along with science as authorized specialists talking technical language. Similar remarks might be made, for example, about conversationalization in politics. There is a real ambivalence about conversationalization, not simply a matter of its being sometimes ideological and sometimes democratic. The fact that conversationalization is so widely appropriated ideologically gives an aura of insincerity to even the most innocent and exemplary instances of it. Conversely, even where it is most clearly ideologically appropriated, the implicit claims it makes about common experience and equality put these issues on the public agenda – in certain circumstances, even hollow claims may be challenged and redeemed in a way that would not happen if they were not made at all. For instance, politicians can find themselves (in Shakespearean terms) 'hoist with their own petard': if they claim to be ordinary, they may find themselves evaluated as ordinary people and found wanting, and unable to resort to traditional resources of political mystique and charisma to protect themselves. In a very limited sense, politicians are now more in the hands of ordinary people, no matter how shallow their populist political rhetoric, even if this 'people power' is systematically manipulated by the media.

I understand ideology as 'meaning in the service of power' (Thompson 1984, 1990) – ideologies are propositions that generally figure as implicit assumptions in texts, which contribute to producing or reproducing unequal relations of power, relations of domination. They may be implicit, for instance, in the presuppositions (taken-for-granted assumptions) of texts. Following work in French discourse analysis (Pêcheux 1982, Williams forthcoming), I see presuppositions as 'preconstructed' elements within a text, elements that are constructed beforehand and elsewhere. This links ideology to the presence of other, prior texts within a text (see Chapter 5). Ideologies are also implicit in the naturalized ways of organizing particular types of interaction (e.g. the ways talking turns are organized in interviews). To show that meanings are working ideologically it is necessary to show that they do indeed serve relations of domination in particular cases. A useful methodological principle is that the analyst should always ask of any text whether and how it is working ideologically, but expect answers to vary: ideology is more of an issue for some texts than for others.

Exploring whether a particular implicit proposition or a set of propositions are working ideologically is one issue within a general set of questions that can be asked whenever one representation is selected over other available ones, or whenever identities or relations are constructed in one way rather than another. The questions are (a) what are the social origins of this option? where and who does it come from? (*whose* representation is it, for instance?) (b) what motivations are there for making this choice? (c) what is the effect of this choice, including its effects (positive or negative) upon the various interests of those involved?

It is possible to assess the importance of particular representations, relations or identities for relations of domination without getting involved in questions about truth. The question of whether a taken-for-granted proposition helps produce or reproduce relations of domination is independent of judgements about its truth or falsity. Nevertheless, critical analysis cannot be indifferent to questions of truth (Dews 1987, Norris 1992), whether it is a matter of how reports falsify by omitting part of what was done or said (Herman and Chomsky 1988), or a matter of false ideological presuppositions. For example, if a text presupposes that women are less intelligent than men or black people than white people, it is an important part of the analysis to point out that the ideological assumption is false.

Some readers may be persuaded of the case for investigating questions of power and ideology and the tensions between public and private and information and entertainment in the mass media, but not see the point of doing so with a focus upon language, and particularly with a focus on what may seem irrelevant fine detail of the language of a rather small number of texts. It is true that analysis of language tends to get very detailed about very few texts, but that points to the need to see language analysis as one of a range of types of analysis which need to be applied together to the mass media, including complementary forms of analysis which can generalize across large quantities of media output (e.g. forms of content analysis as well as forms of cultural and sociological analysis). But analysis of language has certain advantages over other forms of analysis. The tensions and contradictions I have referred to are manifest in the heterogeneity of textual meanings and forms. Texts provide usually temporary and short-lived ways of resolving the dilemmas into which people are put by the tensions and contradictions which frame those texts. Textual analysis can give access to the detailed mechanisms through which social contradictions evolve and are lived out, and the sometimes subtle shifts they undergo.

One objection that some media analysts may have to language analysis is that it puts undue emphasis on the analysis of texts. The trend in media studies has been away from analysis of texts and towards analysis of reception of texts by audiences (Allen 1992,

Corner *et al.* 1990), though there are signs of a partial return towards texts (Brunsdon 1990). This was a reaction against analyses of media texts which postulated meanings and effects, including ideological effects, without taking any account of how texts are actually received by audiences. Media reception research has suggested that texts do not have unitary meanings, but are quite variously interpreted by different audiences and audience members, and may be quite various in their effects. I fully accept the importance of reception studies for understanding meanings and effects. But reception studies sometimes lead to a disregard for the text itself, which I do not accept. It strikes me as self-evident that although readings may vary, any reading is a product of an interface between the properties of the text and the interpretative resources and practices which the interpreter brings to bear upon the text. The range of potential interpretations will be constrained and delimited according to the nature of the text (Brunsdon 1990). If this is so, text analysis remains a central element of media analysis, though it needs to be complemented by analysis of text reception as well as by analysis of text production.

Language analysis, then, can help anchor social and cultural research and analysis in a detailed understanding of the nature of media output. But only language analysis of a particular sort is capable of making such a contribution. A rather arid, formalist analysis of language, in abstraction from social context, still tends to dominate many departments of linguistics. That sort of approach cannot be the basis for effective interdisciplinary work on the media. My view is that we need to analyse media language as *discourse*, and the linguistic analysis of media should be part of the discourse analysis of media. Linguistic analysis focuses on texts, in a broad sense: a newspaper article is a text, but so too is a transcription of a radio or television programme. But discourse analysis is concerned with practices as well as texts, and with both *discourse practices* and *sociocultural practices*. By discourse practices I mean, for instance, the ways in which texts are produced by media workers in media institutions, and the ways in which texts are received by audiences (readers, listeners, viewers), as well as how media texts are socially distributed. There are various levels of sociocultural practice that may constitute parts of the context of discourse practice. I find it helpful to distinguish the 'situational', 'institutional' and 'societal' levels – the specific social goings-on that the discourse is part of, the institutional framework(s) that the discourse occurs within, and the wider societal matrix of the discourse. Discourse analysis can be understood as an attempt to show systematic links between texts, discourse practices, and sociocultural practices. A detailed explanation of this view of discourse analysis will be found in Chapter 3.

Let me say a little more about what is meant by *text* in this framework. A first point is that I am using the word as it is often used by linguists, for both spoken and written language – a transcription of a broadcast is a text as well as a newspaper article. Second, in the case of television it makes sense to include visual images and sound effects as parts of texts, and to see linguistic analysis as part of what has recently been called 'social semiotic' analysis (Hodge and Kress 1988, Kress and van Leeuwen 1990). Also, written texts in contemporary society are increasingly becoming visual as well as linguistic texts, not only in the sense that newspapers, for instance, combine words with photographs and with maps and diagrams, but also because considerations of layout and visual impact are increasingly salient in the design of a written page.

Third, the framework takes a 'multifunctional' view of texts, drawn from the 'systemic' theory of language. Halliday (1978) argues that what he calls the 'ideational', 'interpersonal' and 'textual' functions of language are always simultaneously at work in any text, and even in any particular sentence or clause. This ties in with my suggestion earlier that representations, relations and identities are always simultaneously at issue in a text: the ideational function of language is its function in generating representations of the world; the interpersonal function includes the functioning of language in the constitution of relations, and of identities. (The textual function relates to the constitution of texts out of individual sentences – this will be discussed later in Chapter 6.) The value of such a view of texts is that it makes it easier to connect the analysis of language with fundamental concerns of social analysis: questions of knowledge, belief and ideology (representations – the ideational function), questions of social relationships and power, and questions of identity (relations and identities – the interpersonal function). Representations are a long-standing concern in debates about bias, manipulation, and ideology in the media, but identities and relations have received less attention. The wider social impact of media is not just to do with how they selectively represent the world, though that is a vitally important issue; it is also to do with what sorts of social identities, what versions of 'self', they project and what cultural values (be it consumerism, individualism or a cult of personality) these entail. And it is to do with how social relationships are defined, especially social relationships between the mass of the population who constitute audiences for the most popular media output and people like politicians, scientists, church leaders, and broadcasters themselves.

Another and related strength of a systemic view of text is that it sees texts as sets of options. A text selects particular options from the systems of options – the potential – available. On one level, these are selections amongst available language forms, from the lexical and grammatical potential: one word rather than another, or one grammatical construction rather than another (e.g. a passive rather than an active sentence, or a declarative rather than an interrogative or an imperative sentence – see Quirk *et al.* 1972). But these formal choices constitute choices of meaning, the selection of options from within the meaning potential – how to represent a particular event or state of affairs, how to relate to whoever the text is directed at, what identities to project. And these choices are in turn linked to choices at a different level: what genres to draw upon in producing (or interpreting) a text, what discourses to use (see below). Such a view of text encourages analysts to be sensitive to absences from the text – the choices that were not made but might have been – as well as presences in it, as well as to weigh presences against possible alternatives (e.g. how else might this have been put?). One should not, however, be misled by the language of 'choices' and 'options'; this is a framework for analysing the variability of language and its social determinants and effects, and self-conscious linguistic choice is a relatively marginal aspect of the social processes of text production and interpretation.

I should also mention here an important aspect of the analysis of 'discourse practice' in the framework for discourse analysis sketched out above: intertextual analysis. This will be explained in Chapter 4.

The term *discourse* is widely and sometimes confusingly used in various disciplines (Fairclough 1992a, Foucault 1978, van Dijk 1985). It is helpful to distinguish two main senses. One is predominant in language studies: discourse as social action and interaction, people interacting together in real social situations. The other is predominant in post-structuralist social theory (e.g. in the work of Foucault): a discourse as a social construction of reality, a form of knowledge. My use of the term 'discourse' subsumes both of these, and indeed sets out to bring them together. The first sense is most closely associated with the interpersonal function of language, and with the concept of genre (see Chapter 5, pages 85 ff.). The second sense is most closely associated with the ideational function of language, and with discourses – notice that in addition to being used as an abstract noun for this general view of language in social use, discourse is used as a count noun (*a discourse, several discourses*) as a category (alongside 'genre') within the intertextual analysis of texts (see Chapter 5).

In the discourse perspective on media language which I have sketched out above, the analysis of texts is not treated in isolation from the analysis of discourse practices and sociocultural practices. However, since this book is about media language, the *focus* will be on texts rather than practices. Also, the focus will be on linguistic aspects of texts, rather than other semiotic aspects such as visual images in television. I shall, however, be alluding throughout, though selectively, to the interconnection between the texts that are in focus and other dimensions of the framework.

Chapters 2 to 7 will present a view of media discourse and a framework for analysing it, and Chapters 8 and 9 will deal with case-studies of particular types of media discourse. Chapter 2 will review some of the most important previous work on media discourse, and provide a set of desiderata for a satisfactory critical analysis of the subject. Chapters 3 and 4 sketch out a social theory of media discourse, with an account of communication in the mass media in Chapter 3, and a description of the critical discourse analysis framework which I use in the book in Chapter 4. Chapter 5 is concerned with intertextual analysis of media texts, understood both in terms of how media texts transform and embed within themselves other texts, and in terms of how they draw upon and combine together available discourses and genres. Chapters 6 and 7 deal with the linguistic analysis of media texts, with Chapter 6 focusing upon representational aspects of texts, and Chapter 7 focusing upon aspects of texts that have to do with relations and identities. Chapter 8 is a case study of one television programme, *Crimewatch UK*, and Chapter 9 is a study of political discourse in the media.

2

APPROACHES TO MEDIA DISCOURSE

My main objective in this chapter is to give a selective account of previous work on media discourse. Let me emphasize that this will cover only one part of the literature I shall be drawing upon in this book: I shall also be using material from media studies, social theory, and elsewhere. Nor will the chapter attempt an exhaustive account of the media discourse literature; I shall focus upon work which I have found particularly fruitful in developing my own analytical framework. I discuss the following approaches in turn: linguistic and sociolinguistic analysis, conversation analysis, semiotic analysis, critical linguistics and social semiotics, social-cognitive analysis, and cultural–generic analysis. Separating the approaches in this way is helpful for presentational purposes, but in fact there is a great deal of cross-fertilization between them, and many analysts combine them. (In describing these approaches, I shall sometimes use terms which are not fully explained until Chapter 4. If these are unfamiliar, readers may find it helpful to return to parts of this chapter after reading Chapter 4.) The chapter concludes with a set of desiderata for an adequate critical discourse analysis of media discourse, compiled on the basis of the review of approaches, which sets the scene for the presentation in Chapter 4 of the framework I shall use in the rest of the book.

Linguistic and sociolinguistic analysis

Ways in which language is used in the media may be of interest to linguists for their own sake, as evidence, for instance, of particular types of grammatical structure or particular intonation patterns. For example, newspaper headlines have distinctive syntactic properties which make them a grammatical oddity, and have long attracted the attention of linguists (Mardh 1980, Straumann 1935). Media language has also been analysed sociolinguistically, notably by Bell (1991). Bell's work is unusual in that he is a practising journalist as well as a sociolinguist. A number of the studies he has carried out use linguistic and sociolinguistic analysis in ways which illuminate the sociocultural analysis of news media, and I shall refer to them again in Chapter 3. But much of his work is typical of 'variationist' sociolinguistics in focusing upon correlations between variable linguistic features and variable aspects of social context. In Bell (1984), for example, he shows how the degree to which word-final-consonant clusters are simplified in the language of radio reporters (giving, for instance, *Wes' Coas' coal* as a pronunciation of *West Coast coal*) varies between different New Zealand radio stations according to the main occupational profiles of their audiences (whether they are mainly manual, skilled, office or professional workers). The strength of this work is its attention to linguistic detail, to the form and 'texture' of texts. (I use the term 'texture' to refer broadly to the 'form' as opposed to the 'content' of texts – see Fairclough 1992b.) But this element in Bell's work operates with a rather narrow conception of social aspects of media, and does not attempt to show systematic linkages between language and sociocultural context.

Conversation analysis

Conversation analysis has been developed by a group of sociologists known as 'ethnomethodologists'. Ethnomethodology is an interpretative approach to sociology which focuses upon everyday life as a skilled accomplishment, and upon 'methods' which people use for producing it (Garfinkel 1967). Some ethnomethodologists take a particular interest in conversation and methods that people use for producing and interpreting it (Atkinson and Heritage 1984). Conversation analysts have concentrated mainly upon informal conversation between equals (e.g. telephone conversation), though more recent work has given attention to institutional types of discourse (Button and Lee 1987), including media discourse.

To illustrate the approach, I refer to studies of media interview carried out by Heritage (1985), Greatbatch (1986) and Hutchby (1991). Heritage focuses upon the 'formulations' used by interviewers in the course of news interviews. This is one of his examples:

> INT: Would you be happy to see Prince Charles become King of Wales?
> MAN: Well I couldn' I – you know I just couldn't care tuppence who comes King and who don't like (0.5)
> INT: You don't think it makes any difference to you.

A formulation (such as the interviewer's second contribution here) is a widely used device interviewers use to summarize what interviewees have said. Formulations typically stress certain aspects of what has been said rather than others, and often elaborate what has been said by drawing out its implications. That happens here: the interviewee didn't *say* that it made no difference to him, but he did arguably imply it. Heritage sees formulation as a technical device which interviewers use to manage interviews within the constraints under which they are forced to operate. One constraint is the presence of a listening audience: formulations are a way of ensuring the audience is constantly kept in the picture by clarifying what interviewees say, drawing out implications, etc. Another is the requirement on interviewers to maintain a 'stance of formal neutrality': alternative formulations provide a covert means of evaluating what is said, making things easier or more difficult for interviewees, pushing the direction of the interview one way rather than another.

Heritage's view of properties of news interviews emphasizes technical solutions to institutional problems. This is a valuable perspective because it shows how discursive practices are rooted in institutional structures and practices (one could fruitfully extend this 'back' to the political economies of institutions – see Chapter 3). But it is not adequate on its own: to make sense of contemporary interviewing practices, one needs to recognize how they are shaped by, and help shape, wider social and cultural shifts. Heritage emphasizes the normative side of news interviews, what news interviews have in common – their 'tacit ground rules'. But news interview is not a unitary genre: there is considerable, culturally patterned, variation not only historically (1953 interviews were generally very different from 1993 interviews) but also in contemporary broadcasting, depending upon the medium, type of programme, and particular style of the interviewer. Greatbatch (1986) gives limited recognition to this variability. One of the ground rules of interviewing, normatively, is that interviewees should confine themselves to answering questions, but as he points out they don't always do so: sometimes they answer the question and then introduce topics of their own, sometimes they introduce topics of their own first and then answer the question, sometimes they don't answer the question at all. One of Greatbatch's examples is:

> INT: D'you quite like him?
> EH: Well er I – think in politics you see: i – it's not a *question* of going about *lik*ing people or no:t, it's a question of *deal*ing with people.
> And e:r I've always been able to deal perfectly well with Mister Wilson and er – indeed he has with me.

The interviewee (EH) does not answer the interviewer's question, but begins by denying its relevance, says what he thinks the relevant question is, and talks about that. However, Greatbatch considers such examples as violations of the rule that interviewees should confine themselves to answering questions: what he is interested in is when interviewers sanction such violations, and when they tolerate them. What this violational view misses is that some types of news interview are now *routinely* seen as occasions where interviewees talk about their own topics, subject to the weaker requirement that they at least coherently link them to the interviewer's questions. This is not violative behaviour but part of a culturally significant shift in genre whose further ramifications have been analysed by Tolson (1991 – see the discussion of his work in the section on cultural-generic analysis below).

Conversation analysis actually shares with linguistic and sociolinguistic analysis strengths in the detailed description of organizational properties of media language. It has extended the resources of descriptive linguistics through its analysis of the organization of interaction (turn-taking, topic-control, formulation, etc.), though at the same time it ignores many of the features which a linguistic description would attend to. The focus is very much upon relational aspects of conversation – the achievement of interaction – and questions of representation and associated linguistic features are given relatively little attention. It is also resistant to linking properties of talk with higher-level features of society and culture – relations of power, ideologies, cultural values.

Semiotic analysis

By contrast, semiotic analysis does treat analysis of texts as a key component of cultural analysis of media. I refer specifically here to Hartley's important study of news discourse (Hartley 1982, see also Fiske and Hartley 1978). Hartley's focus is upon the semiotic codes and conventions which underlie both linguistic and visual aspects of news stories. Analysis of visual codes attends to different modes of presentation on television – the 'talking head' (newsreader or correspondent looking directly at the camera), use of graphics and still photographs, various types of 'actuality' or film report (film with voice-over, the 'stake-out' with the reporter talking directly to camera, the 'vox pop' with a member of the public talking to an unseen reporter) – as well as the framing of pictures, camera movements (pans and zooms) and the sequencing of shots. The assumption is that choices among options available within visual codes – including technical options relating to the camera-work – carry social meanings (see also Tuchman 1978).

Hartley analyses a range of language-related codes and conventions, including categorization of stories into a small number of major topics, the effect of news values (as an 'ideological code') on the treatment of topics, the assumption of consensus and the handling of dissent, audience address – the operation of broadcasters as 'mediators' who translate news into the common-sense terms of audiences, use of a conversational communicative style, the structuring of news stories. A focus typical of semiotic analysis is upon ideologically potent categories and classifications which are implicit in news texts, and upon alternative or competing categories which are absent, 'suppressed'. For instance, it is a common observation that news stories are personalized: the category of individual personality is widely evoked in news stories, whereas the category of social (and especially class) subject is correspondingly suppressed. Or again, many oppositions which appear on the surface of a text – for instance between government and unions, management and strikers, western allies and foreign dictators – can be assimilated to an underlying opposition between 'us' and 'them'.

One very important achievement of this work is establishing that analysis of texts is a significant part of sociocultural analysis of media, by linking properties of texts to ideologies, power relations and cultural values. This general objective is taken up in critical approaches to linguistics and discourse analysis, which operate however with a linguistically grounded conception of text. An obvious limitation of semiotic analysis in comparison with the linguistically oriented approaches (linguistic, sociolinguistic, critical linguistic, social-cognitive and cultural-generic analysis) is that it does not systematically attend to detailed properties of the texture of texts.

Critical linguistics and social semiotics

'Critical linguistics' is a type of discourse analysis which was developed by a group based at the University of East Anglia in the 1970s (Fowler *et al.* 1979, Hodge and Kress 1979). Media discourse is one of its main concerns (Fowler 1991, Trew 1979a, 1979b). Critical linguistics is based upon 'systemic' linguistic theory (Halliday 1978, 1985). It brings to analysis of media discourse systemicist views of the text already introduced in Chapter 1: the view of the text as multifunctional, always simultaneously representing the world (ideational function) and enacting social relations and identities (interpersonal function); seeing texts as built out of choices from within available systems of options in vocabulary, grammar, and so forth. Discourse is seen as 'a field of both ideological processes and linguistic processes, and . . . there is a determinate relation between these two kinds of process' (Trew 1979b); specifically, the linguistic choices that are made in texts can carry ideological meaning.

Some of the most revealing analyses concern representation and the ideational function, how events and the people and objects involved in them are represented in the grammar of clauses (simple sentences). The basic premiss is that coding events in language entails choices among the models – the distinct process and participant types – which the grammar makes available, and that such choices are potentially ideologically significant. For example, on a BBC Radio 4 *Today* programme (11 March 1993) the following comment was made about 'cheap' Russian fish being 'dumped' on the British market: 'the funny thing is it's not transferring itself to the consumer at terribly low prices at all'. This might have been worded as, for instance, 'the dealers involved in the distribution of the fish are overcharging the consumer', coding the pricing of the fish as an action process with a responsible agent (*the dealers*). Instead, we have the distribution of the fish coded with an action process verb (*transfer*) used reflexively, and the process of pricing is transformed into a state (*at terribly low prices*). Responsibility and agency are elided. If there were a systematic tendency in news reports for such choices of process and participant types to leave agency and responsibility unspecified in this way, one might (depending upon the wider sociocultural context) see those choices as having ideological meaning. See Chapter 6, pages 109–16 for more detail.

I suggested that in the above example pricing was transformed from a process into a state. This sort of transformation is a 'nominal-ization', changing a process into a nominal (i.e. noun-like) entity. Another type of transformation is the shift of an active sentence into a passive (e.g. from *they are dumping fish on the market* to *fish is being dumped on the market*). The argument is that transformations such as nominalization and shifting into the passive may be ideologically motivated. For example, both allow the actor, the responsible agent, to be omitted and, as I have just suggested, systematic elision or back-grounding of agency may be an ideologically significant feature of texts.

Trew (1979a, 1979b) has done some particularly fruitful work on 'discourse in progress' in newspapers – the transformation of mater-ial from news agencies and other sources into news reports, and the transformations a story undergoes from one report to another, or from reports to in-depth analyses to editorials, over a period of time. He refers to the coverage of police shootings in Zimbabwe in 1975 in *The Times*. The headline of the first report (*RIOTING BLACKS SHOT DEAD BY POLICE AS ANC LEADERS MEET*) identifies the police as agent but in an informationally de-emphasized position in the middle of the headline, whereas the 'rioting' of those shot is foregrounded (being placed at the beginning).

> RIOTING BLACKS SHOT DEAD BY POLICE AS
> ANC LEADERS MEET
> Eleven Africans were shot dead and 15 wounded when Rhodesian police opened fire on a crowd of about 2,000 in the African Highfield township of Salisbury this afternoon.
>
> (Trew 1979a: 94)

In the lead (first) paragraph, an agentless passive is used (*were shot dead and . . . wounded*), and the police are explicitly present only as agents of *opened fire on a rioting crowd*, rather than as the ones who shot dead the people. In an editorial, the event is transformed into *The rioting and sad loss of life in Salisbury* for which 'factionalism' is said to be responsible – the police as responsible agent is elided. These are part of a more complex series of transformations over time which background police responsibility, and which are ideological as well as linguistic processes: they assimilate problematic events to preconstructed ideological frames for representing political relations in southern Africa. The linguistic processes involve rewordings as well as grammatical changes – notice *loss of life* replacing *shot dead*. Such ideological-linguistic processes are also processes of struggle, in which choosing to represent an event in one way may also be refusing to represent it in other currently available ways. For further development of this concept of transformation, see Hodge and Kress (1979, 1988, 1992). See also the discussion of transformations of texts across 'intertextual chains' of discursive practices in Fairclough (1992a).

Critical linguistics emphasizes the role of vocabulary choices in processes of categorization. For example, a study of gender discrimination in media reporting might consider how differences in the vocabulary used to refer to women and men assimilates people to pre-existing categorization systems of an ideologically powerful sort. Are women, for instance, systematically represented in terms of their family roles (as 'wives' or 'mothers') or in terms of their sexual interest to men? It is fruitful to combine such questions with analysis of process and participant types: what sorts of participants in what sorts of processes do women/men predominantly function as – for instance, are both equally likely to function as actors in action processes? and where they do function as actors, what particular categories of process are involved (is it, for instance, smiling and screaming, or debating and voting?). See Fowler 1991 chapter 6 for an analysis along these lines.

A clause which codes an event (ideationally) in terms of a particular type of process will also assess (interpersonally) the truth or probability of the proposition so encoded, and the relationship between producer and addressee(s). The concept of 'modality' is used in a very general way to cover features of texts which 'express speakers' and writers' attitudes towards themselves, towards their interlocutors, and towards their subject-matter' (Fowler *et al.* 1979: 200). Choices of pronouns, modal auxiliaries, speech acts, and many others, are included within modality.

The limitations of critical linguistics have been quite widely discussed, even by those involved and their sympathizers (Fowler 1987, Kress 1989, Richardson 1987). In terms of the text–practice distinction I introduced in Chapter 1, the focus is upon text and (especially in the case of Trew) productive practices, but texts tend to be interpreted by the analyst without reference to the interpretative practices of audiences. Media studies has shifted its emphasis away from text analysis to audience reception (recall the discussion of this issue in Chapter 1), and this has not surprisingly led to criticism. In terms of sociocultural practice, there tends to be a rather monolithic view of the role of media in ideological reproduction which understates the extent of diversity and change in media practices and media discourse. Although there is attention to inter-personal (especially relational) aspects of texts, the emphasis is perhaps rather too one-sidedly on representations, and I would argue that issues of social identity ought to be foregrounded more than they are. Although there are elements of intertextual analysis of the constitution of texts in terms of discourses and genres, this is underdeveloped compared with linguistic and above all grammatical analysis. And the linguistic analysis is very much focused upon clauses, with little attention to higher-level organization properties of whole texts. Mention of these limitations is not meant to minimize the achievement of critical linguistics – they largely reflect shifts of focus and developments of theory in the past twenty years or so. See Hodge and Kress (1992) for a recent attempt to 'update' the critical linguistics work of the 1970s.

A number of critical linguists have been involved in developing the somewhat different approach of 'social semiotics' (Hodge and Kress 1988, Kress and van Leeuwen 1990). In contrast with critical linguistics, there is an interest in visual semiosis as well as language (which makes it particularly useful in analysis of television). Also, productive and interpretative practices have become a major concern, there is an orientation towards struggle and historical change in discourse, and towards the development of a theory of genre (van Leeuwen 1987, 1993) and the intertextual analysis of texts. I shall draw upon some of this work and describe it more fully in later chapters.

Van Dijk: the 'social-cognitive' model

In a series of studies, van Dijk (1988a, 1988b, 1991) has developed a framework for analysing news (especially in newspapers) as discourse which is similar in some ways to the view of discourse taken in this book (and sketched out in Chapter 1). Discourse is conceptualized in terms of three dimensions or perspectives (which I have called text, discourse practice and sociocultural practice), and a focus on discourse practice is seen as providing a way of linking textual analysis to sociocultural analysis. Van Dijk's work, like social semiotics, has made the important transition from text analysis (which critical linguistics really still is) to discourse analysis. Beyond that common ground, there are significant differences, however. Van Dijk's analysis of practices of news production and news comprehension has a social-psychological emphasis on processes of social cognition – on how cognitive 'models' and 'schemata' shape production and comprehension – whereas I focus (here and in other publications) upon how socially available genres and discourses are drawn upon. Van Dijk's main motivation for linking media texts to context is to show in detail how social relationships and processes (e.g. the reproduction of racism) are accomplished at a micro-level through routine practices, whereas my major concern is to show how shifting language and discursive practices in the media constitute social and cultural change. See Chapter 4 for a detailed account of my approach.

Van Dijk's framework analyses news texts in terms of what he calls the 'structures of news', processes of news production, processes of news comprehension. The analysis aims to show relationships between texts, production processes and comprehension processes, and between these and the wider social practices they are embedded within. In analysing structures of news a distinction is made between the 'macro' and 'micro' structures of news discourse. The former relate to the overall content of a text – its 'thematic' structure – and the overall form of a text – its 'schematic' structure.

The concept of 'macrostructure' is central to the analysis of *thematic* structure: the macrostructure of a text is its overall organization in terms of themes or topics. It is a hierarchical organization, in the sense that we can identify the theme of a whole text (and sum it up as a single proposition), which can typically be spelt out in terms of a few rather less general themes, which can each in turn be spelt out in terms of even more specific themes, and so on. The *schematic* structure of a particular type of text is specified in terms of the ordered parts it is built out of. Thus van Dijk suggests that a news report typically has a headline, a lead, an 'events' element which covers the main events of the story, and perhaps an element which gives verbal reactions to the story, and a comment element (these last two elements do not always occur as distinct sections). Each element of schematic structure corresponds to a more general theme in the thematic structure. The headline of a news report formulates the overall theme of a text. An important feature of the schematic structure of a text type are principles governing the way it orders thematic content. In the case of news reports, there is a powerful 'relevance principle' which requires more general information to come first, to be followed by more detailed information. Thus the initial headline and lead elements of news reports typically contain more general information.

The 'microstructures' of news discourse are analysed in terms of semantic relations between propositions – coherence relations of causality, consequence and so forth. Microanalysis also identifies syntactic and lexical characteristics of newspaper style, and rhetorical features of news report, such as features which give reports an aura of factuality.

The concepts of 'macrostructure' and 'schematic structure' are at the centre of analysis of news production and comprehension, as well as analysis of news structures. These wholistic structures are seen to generate texts, and the interpretation of texts involves identifying the wholistic structures which underlie them. Such structures are intrinsic to the mental models of events and situations which reporters bring to bear in interpreting events and source texts, models which reporters try to convey to audiences in the way they write reports, and models which audiences (readers etc.) draw upon in interpreting reports. This cognitive perspective helps to specify how exactly the 'news values' that have been identified as shaping news coverage influence the way particular reports are produced. It also sheds light on how the texts which journalists get from news agencies and other sources are transformed in producing a report, on the forms in which news reports are memorized, and on the longer-term effects they are likely to have on perception, cognition and action.

This is a powerful integrated framework for news discourse analysis. Nevertheless, for my purposes it has a number of limitations. First, the focus is on representations; social relations and identities in news discourse – and the interpersonal function of language – receive little attention. Second, texts are analysed linguistically but not intertextually, in terms of their constitution through configurations of discourses and genres. A central feature of my approach is the claim that linguistic analysis needs to be complemented by intertextual analysis (see Fairclough 1992b, and Chapters 4 and 5). A third and related point is that van Dijk's work gives a one-sided emphasis to news-making practices as stable structures which contribute to the reproduction of relations of domination and racist ideologies, which backgrounds the diversity and heterogeneity of practices.

Cultural-generic analysis

Some British studies of media discourse have drawn upon work in cultural studies associated with the Centre for Contemporary Cultural Studies (at the University of Birmingham) to explore the cultural and social import of ways in which media genres such as interview or 'chat' are currently evolving (Montgomery 1990, Tolson 1990). They take what Raymond Williams called a 'cultural materialist' view of genre, seeing an innovation in genre as 'an articulation, by technical discovery, of changes in consciousness which are themselves forms of consciousness of change' (Williams 1981: 142), and regarding analysis of generic form as itself a mode of cultural analysis. An important feature of this approach is that it simultaneously attends to interaction (and relational features of texts) and representation (see also van Leeuwen 1993). It draws upon work by Goffman (1981) on how radio announcers address audiences and the orientation in conversation analysis towards the ongoing accomplishment of social relationships in talk, as well as a Hallidayan multifunctional view of text (see Mancini 1988).

Montgomery's study of 'Our Tune', which I discuss in more detail in Chapter 5, will serve as an example (Montgomery 1991). 'Our Tune' was a very popular slot in a BBC Radio 1 show, in which the DJ (Simon Bates) summarized readers' letters in narrative form. Following the method of Labov (1972), Montgomery gives an account of the generic structure of 'Our Tune' narratives in terms of components, some obligatory and some optional, which occur in a particular (though not totally rigid) order. In accordance with common practice in narrative analysis, Montgomery distinguishes the analysis of the story material from the analysis of its discursive presentation. The latter involves those aspects of the narrative which bring about the transformation of a private letter into a public narrative, and those aspects which are oriented towards audience reception of the story. Tensions which characterize media culture are negotiated in the discursive presentation of this genre. For instance, the tension between the public nature of media output and the private circumstances of media reception (Scannell 1992 – see also the discussion on this issue in Chapter 1) is concretely manifested 'in a subtle blend of institutional and audience voices – private discourses in a public space, public therapy on personal experience'. 'Our Tune' also tries to concretely negotiate the constant tension in broadcasting between pressures to inform and pressures to entertain by achieving balance between an entertaining narrative style which draws upon fictional models (such as magazine stories), and a commitment to truthfully recounting listeners' stories. These examples point to the intertextual analysis of texts as often hybrid configurations of genres and discourses which are realized in heterogeneous linguistic features.

The cultural-generic approach tried to relate changes in broadcast genres to the evolution of the 'public sphere' of broadcasting (Habermas 1989). Scannell (1992) has characterized the 'communicative ethos' of broadcasting, emergent since the early days of radio, in terms of the emergence of patterns of programming and a communicative style which accommodates to the private, domestic conditions of media reception. Broadcasting genres have developed simulated versions of informal conversational language (recall the discussion in Chapter 1). Montgomery (1988) has investigated one conventional feature, direct address of audiences, which is realized textually in second-person pronouns, interrogative clauses, imperative clauses, and so forth. He shows how audiences are constructed as complex and differentiated through the shifting direct address of different sections of them. Such examples suggest that features of genre are relevant to the construction of publics and of the public sphere itself. Tolson, in a study of the evolution of interview genre in documentary and talk shows, has argued that the generic evolution of interview talk indicates a fragmentation of audiences, and marks the demise of the 'general public' within the public sphere of broadcasting. Tolson's work also shows how experimentation in the mixing of broadcasting formats (talk, variety, comedy) and associated genres in intertextually complex and hybrid texts links to wider tendencies in cultural change. These include the general cultural validation of individualism (manifested in the 'personality system' of the media), and the 'reflexivity' which has been taken as a general feature of contemporary culture (Giddens 1991). Reflexivity shows up as, for instance, 'self-reflexive metadiscourse' on the part of talk show participants about television, about their own personalities as constructs, about the apparent revelation of one's 'real self' in talk shows as just a game.

Desiderata for a critical analysis of media discourse

In the final section of this chapter, I want to pull together from the review of the literature a list of desiderata for an adequate critical analysis of media discourse. This list will then provide a basis for the elaboration of my own analytical framework in Chapter 4, and help clarify how that framework relates to the literature. I should add that no single book could reasonably hope to meet all these desiderata, the list should rather be interpreted as pointing towards a pro-gramme of research.

1. One focus of analysis should be on how wider changes in society and culture are manifest in changing media discourse practices. The selection of data should correspondingly reflect areas of vari-ability and instability as well as areas of stability. (Cultural-generic analysis. Compare conversation analysis, critical linguistics, social-cognitive analysis.)
2. The analysis of media texts should include detailed attention to their language and 'texture' (compare linguistically oriented approaches with semiotics). It should also include detailed analysis of visual images and sound effects (compare semiotics and social semiotics with the other approaches.)
3. Text analysis should be complemented by analysis of practices of text production and text consumption (compare social-cognitive analysis with the other approaches), including attention to trans-formations which texts regularly undergo across networks of discourse practices (compare critical linguistics and social-cognitive analysis with other approaches).
4. Analysis of texts and practices should be mapped on to analysis of the institutional and wider social and cultural context of media practices, including relations of power and ideologies (compare semiotic analysis, critical linguistics and cultural-generic analysis with linguistic and sociolinguistic analysis and with conversation analysis).
5. Text analysis should include both linguistic analysis and intertex-tual analysis in terms of genres and discourses. It should be recog-nized that texts are commonly hybrid intertextually with mixtures of genres and discourses, and that such hybridity is manifest in heterogeneous linguistic features. (Compare cultural-generic analysis and social semiotics with other approaches.)
6. Linguistic analysis of texts should be conceived multifunctionally, and be oriented towards representation and the constitution of relations and identities as simultaneous processes in texts, and the important relationships between them. (Compare cultural-generic analysis and to a degree critical linguistics with other approaches.)

7. Linguistic analysis of texts involves analysis at a number of levels, including phonic, lexical, grammatical, and macrostructural/ schematic. (Compare social-cognitive analysis with conversation analysis or critical linguistics.)
8. The relationship between texts and society/culture is to be seen dialectically. Texts are socioculturally shaped but they also constitute society and culture, in ways which may be transformative as well as reproductive. (Compare more recent with earlier critical approaches.)

3

COMMUNICATION IN THE MASS MEDIA

The overall objective of Chapters 3 and 4 is to develop a social theory of media discourse. Chapter 3 gives a general account of communication in the mass media, while Chapter 4 gives a more focused theoretical account of media discourse and a framework for critically analysing it. The analytical framework, briefly alluded to already in Chapter 1, is a version of 'critical discourse analysis' (Fairclough 1989, 1992a, 1993). The theory set out in these two chapters will be elaborated in greater detail, with examples, in Chapters 5–7, and will form the basis for later chapters. Chapters 3 and 4 therefore have a key theoretical and methodological role in the book as a whole.

It will perhaps be helpful to approach the question of what is distinctive about mass communication in the first part of the chapter through a comparison between communicative events in the media and another type of communicative event. I shall refer for contrast to medical consultation between doctors and patients (Fairclough 1992a, Mishler 1984). And given the diversity of media output, it will help to have in mind one particular type of output. I have already indicated that the book is centred upon news, current affairs and documentary, and in this chapter I shall be alluding mainly – though not exclusively – to television documentary (see the excellent study in Silverstone 1985).

Mass communication has certain special properties which distinguish it from other forms of communication, and which are partly attributable to the nature of the technologies which it deploys (Thompson 1990). These properties will be my first concern. But in addition to such questions of medium and technology, an account of communication in the mass media must consider the economics and politics of the mass media: the nature of the market which the mass media are operating within, and their relationship to the state, and so forth. It is also important to attend to institutional aspects of media, including practices of media text production within the institutions of the press, radio and television, but also practices of media text consumption and reception within the family and the home. A further consideration is the wider sociocultural context of mass media communication, the social and cultural structures, relations, practices and values which frame the mass media, shape mass media communication, and are shaped by it.

The properties of mass communication

Communicative events differ in their time–space parameters. Whereas, for example, a medical consultation takes place with all participants (centrally, doctor and patient) present together at a particular time and place, a communicative event in the media, such as a television documentary, involves major temporal and spatial disjunctions. The fundamental point is that the time and place of production of a mass communication text is different from the time and place of consumption, when an audience views or hears or reads it. Indeed, a mass communication text is likely to be consumed in various sorts of place and at various times, especially now with the widespread use of video machines. And even the production of such texts is often spatially and temporally disjoined – for instance, a documentary may take eighteen months to make and involve filming in several countries. Satellite technology and the associated globalization of mass media, and the global domination of North American and European media conglomerates, give a further twist to the temporal and spatial disjunctions of the media, in the sense that spatial and temporal disjunctions are now often also major cultural disjunctions – for instance, material produced in the USA or Europe may be seen by audiences in India and South-East Asia.

These properties of temporal and spatial setting mean that a communicative event in the mass media can actually be seen as a *chain* of communicative events. In the case of a television documentary, for instance, there is not only the actual broadcast but also the communicative events which constitute the production of the documentary (a complex chain in its own right), and the viewing of the documentary. The actual broadcast is in a sense a deficient communicative event in that there is no direct communication between broadcasters and audience. The chain can be extended to include the source communicative events (such as political speeches or interviews) which are transformed into the documentary on the one hand, and subsequent communicative events (conversations, reviews, etc.) in which the documentary itself is a transformed source. (See below the discussion of sources in the section on practices of production and consumption.) Notice that such a chain connects the public domain to the private domain: programmes are produced in the public domain using predominantly public domain source materials (e.g. political events), but they are consumed in the private domain, mainly in the home and within the family. A crucial property of the mass media is that they 'mediate' in this way between the public and the private domains.

In fact the media have had a major impact on the boundaries between public and private life and institutions, redrawing them in fundamental ways (Scannell 1992, Thompson 1990), as I indicated in Chapter 1. Public events such as coronations or parliamentary debates which were hitherto accessible only to those who attended them have become accessible for universal private consumption by being broadcast. Conversely, private events such as the private lives of public figures (e.g. the British royal family) or the private grief of bereaved parents have become public events meriting the status of 'news'. The media have helped restructure people's expectations about the boundary between what Goffman (1969) called 'front' and 'back' region behaviour – behaviour for public consumption, versus behaviour in private contexts. One example of this is the way in which cameras have come to dwell upon the grief-stricken and tear-stained faces of bereaved people in television news broadcasts.

The media have tried to bridge the gap between the public conditions of media production and the private conditions of consumption by evolving a 'communicative ethos' and a 'communicative style' (Scannell 1992) which adjust towards the priorities, values and practices of private life. This includes the development of a 'public-colloquial' language (Leech 1966), a public language for use in the media which is modelled to varying degrees and in varying ways upon the practices of informal, colloquial, conversational speech. This is an important development which has already been referred to and which will figure at various points in this book. (See the section on the sociocultural context below for further discussion.)

Mass communication differs from other forms of communication in the technologies it draws upon, which make possible its characteristic temporal and spatial disjunctions. A medical consultation is a face-to-face communication involving interaction through spoken language and non-verbal communication (posture, gesture, expression, touch). It is transient, whereas a television or radio programme crucially is recorded in a permanent and reproducible form (Benjamin 1970). The written notes which a doctor makes obviously do not aim to represent the whole consultation; a consultation *may* be recorded, and may even become a media event by being broadcast, but these possibilities are not inherent properties of the genre. A television documentary, by contrast, can be stored indefinitely, it can be reproduced in any number of copies, and be used and reused for a variety of purposes at different times and in different places. It can be produced, distributed and consumed as a cultural commodity (see the discussion of economics below).

⁁There are obvious but important differences between different types of media in their channels of communication and the technologies they draw upon. The press uses a visual channel, its language is written, and it draws upon technologies of photographic reproduction, graphic design, and printing. Radio, by contrast, uses an oral channel and spoken language and relies on technologies of sound recording and broadcasting, whilst television combines technologies of sound- and image-recording and broadcasting. The relationship between the oral and visual channels in television is a major issue which merits detailed attention case by case. In contrast with film, television can be characterized in broad terms as verbally anchored, with images mainly being used to support words (Ellis 1982: 129).

These differences in channel and technology have significant wider implications in terms of the meaning potential of the different media. For instance, print is in an important sense less personal than radio or television. Radio begins to allow individuality and personality to be foregrounded through transmitting individual qualities of voice. Television takes the process much further by making people visually available, and not in the frozen modality of newspaper photographs, but in movement and action. It is a technology which harmonizes with our contemporary culture's focus on individualism and its orientation towards personality (see the section on the sociocultural context below). Television as a technology also favours action rather than contemplation, and foregrounds the present. Even where programmes are prerecorded, the illusion of liveness and immediacy is maintained. Rapid cutting between images generates action and excitement, while close-up shots of people ('talking heads') reduce social distance and convey an egalitarian ethos. The condensed thirty-second combination of sounds and images in a high-budget television commercial can stand as an archetype of the capabilities of the medium, and indeed the dominant cultural form in television – used as the basis of news programmes and soap operas alike – is a sequence of disconnected short segments no longer than five minutes in duration (on these and other properties of television, see Ellis 1982).

▲Different types of communication involve different categories of participant. In the case of medical consultations, the main participants are obviously doctors and patients, though there may be others (e.g. a nurse, or a relative of the patient). The categories of participant in the media follow from the character of mass communication discussed above in mediating between public and private domains. The main categories of participants in television documentaries, for instance, are reporters (a category of mediators), audience, and various categories of public domain 'third party' who may be involved – politicians, trade unionists, scientists and experts of various other types, academics, and so forth. There is also, interestingly, another important category of third party in contemporary media, which emanates from the private domain – ordinary people who may act as witnesses or represent typical behaviours or reactions (commonly referred to as 'vox pop', an abbreviated form of the Latin for 'voice of the people'). It is not simply the identification of participants that is of analytical interest; a key question is how participant identities and relations are constructed in various types of programme. (See the section on sociocultural context below.)

An obvious and important feature of media events is the mass nature of audiences. A television documentary is, in principle, available to the great majority of the population; there are powerful economic imperatives towards audience maximization, particularly in prime-time television (see the section on the economics of media below), and audiences of around 12 million people in Britain, for instance, are not unusual. Audience size underscores the potential influence and power of the media, and the interest that the state may have in attempting to control it (see the section on politics below). Moreover, media communicative events are sorts of monologues, which is also of course germane to questions about the power of mass media: audiences cannot directly contribute to the communication. Whereas doctor and patient alternate in speaker and listener roles in a medical consultation, media audiences only listen (or view or read). Terms like 'communication' or 'interaction' are in a sense misnomers, a point Thompson (1990: 228) makes in calling media discourse 'mediated quasi-interaction'. Media producers lack the simultaneous feedback from audiences which is readily available in what people say, fail to say, and in the ways in which they act and look in medical consultations. As a consequence, producers postulate and construct 'ideal' audiences partly on the basis of guesses about audience response drawn from experience and various types of indirect evidence (such as programme ratings or market research). There is much debate in this connection about questions of manipulation, cultural domination and imperialism (especially where the cultural gap between producer and audience is wide), and ideology.

All forms of mass communication give rise to questions about access. In mediated quasi-interaction, the issue of which categories of social agent get to write, speak and be seen – and which do not – assumes considerable importance. There is no technical reason why communities of various sorts (trade union branches, people living on an inner-city housing estate, people belonging to a minority culture) could not produce their own videos and have them broadcast as documentaries or news items. But this very rarely happens. Media output is very much under professional and institutional control, and in general it is those who already have other forms of economic, political or cultural power that have the best access to the media (see the discussion of sources on page 49). There do now appear to be various moves to open up access – or perhaps, to put it more cynically, to mitigate the unequal distribution of access. These include extensive use of vox pop, radio phone-in programmes in which members of the audience put questions to or even make comments on public figures, audience discussion programmes, and access programmes in which community groups or individuals *are* given space for their own material. But some commentators see these innovations as quite limited and marginal. Scannell (1992) notes, for instance, that whereas public persons are called upon for their opinions, private persons are generally called upon only for their experiences (though compare the views of Livingstone and Lunt 1994). Following

Enzensberger (1970), one might say that the social relations of the media inhibit the full exploitation of their potential as technologies.

Communicative events differ in the fields of social activity that they represent, and in how they represent them. A communicative event is itself a form of social practice, and what it represents are other social practices, and more often than not other communicative events. The question is, then, which (fields of) social practices and which communicative events are represented in particular types of communicative event. Medical consultations deal predominantly with social practices in private life, for instance with people's eating habits. Forms of mass communication such as television documentary, on the other hand, deal with a wide variety of social practices, mainly in the public domain, such as the social practices of politics, education or law. The idea of mass communication as an extended chain of communicative events is again helpful here, linking communicative events in the public domain to communicative events in the private domain of media reception and consumption.

The interesting question is, then, how public domain communicative events are transformed as they move along the chain. Following van Leeuwen (1993), we can ask how one type of communicative event 'recontextualizes' others – what particular representations and transformations it produces, and how these differ from other recontextualizations of the same events. The general point is that communicative events and social practices are recontextualized differently depending upon the goals, values and priorities of the communication in which they are recontextualized. This raises questions of truth, bias and manipulation which have been a major preoccupation in media analysis – see the section on the politics of media below. In the analysis of texts, such differences of representation can be specified in terms of the use of different 'discourses'. Notice that I am here using 'discourse' as a count noun, with a singular and plural ('a discourse', 'several discourses'): a discourse as a type of language associated with a particular representation, from a specific point of view, of some social practice. See also pages 18–19, and the analytical framework in Chapter 4.

A medical consultation is an operational, instrumental type of communication, concerned with getting things done. The patient brings a problem to the doctor for specialist help, the doctor tries to ascertain the precise nature of the problem, and to determine and prescribe a course of treatment. Media events are generally rather less clear-cut in terms of the purpose and nature of what is going on. In the case of a television documentary, for instance, on one level what is going on may be an educational and informative process: the programme is giving viewers a better understanding of some issue of current concern. Documentaries, however, tend also to be persuasive: they try to get viewers to see things in a particular way. And they also aim to be entertaining, to tell a good story as well as elaborating a convincing argument, and to produce a pleasing film (on the distinction between story and argument, see Silverstone 1985). Like other sorts of programme, they are subject to a complex of economic and political as well as cultural pressures.

The economics of media

The economics of an institution is an important determinant of its practices and its texts. The funding system for the National Health Service in Britain, for example, constrains the service doctors can provide for patients, and thereby shapes interactions between doctors and patients, and the texts that are produced: the possibilities for interaction are, for instance, severely reduced where doctors are limiting the duration of appointments to five minutes! Similarly, the intensely competitive commercial environment that the media operate in at present shape media practices and texts (Inglis 1990, Thompson 1990).

The press and commercial broadcasting are pre-eminently profit-making organizations, they make their profits by selling audiences to advertisers, and they do this by achieving the highest possible readerships or listener/viewer ratings for the lowest possible financial outlay. Even non-commercial broadcasting organizations such as the BBC are subjected to a parallel market logic: they are in competition with commercial broadcasting, and they rely upon their ratings to justify to the government and the public the licence fees which people are required to pay.

Media texts and programmes are from this perspective symbolic, cultural commodities, produced in what is effectively a culture industry, which circulate for profit within a market, and they are very much open to the effects of commercial pressures. The ratings battle leads both to an increase in types of programme with high audience appeal such as the 'soaps', and to attempts to increase the audience appeal of other types of programme such as news, current affairs and documentary. The process is often referred to as 'going down-market'. This typically involves, in broad terms, increasing emphasis on making programmes entertaining and correspondingly less emphasis on their informative or educative qualities (Postman 1987).

This affects both content and communicative style. For instance, considerations of what will make 'good television' (though this involves a complex of commercial and professional/aesthetic judgements) are likely to loom larger in the choice of topics for documentaries and in the ways in which topics are handled. The latter might include more dramatic forms of presentation drawing upon fictional models – as in the 'Vigilante!' extract discussed in Chapter 1 – a focus upon media presenters as 'personalities' and the particular types of personality that they cultivate, and the construction of an informal, conversational relationship between presenter and audience. Producers tend to see a shift towards the personal as increasing audience appeal – a focus, for instance, in news programmes on the grief of bereaved people – and the introduction of the topics of private life tends to go along with the simulation of the communicative styles of private life. But I shall argue shortly that market pressures are not the only cause of such developments in communicative style.

Patterns of ownership are also an important, if indirect, shaping influence upon media discourse. Ownership is increasingly in the hands of large conglomerates whose business is the culture industry, so that the media become more fully integrated with ownership interests in the national and international economy, intensifying their association with capitalist class interests. This manifests itself in various ways, including the manner in which media organizations are structured to ensure that the dominant voices are those of the political and social establishment (see the discussion of sources on page 49), and in the constraints on access to the media discussed earlier. It is also more pervasively present in a pro-capitalist 'ethos', as Williams (1975: 41) indicates in a statement about the global domination of television by US interests:

> The commercial character of television has then to be seen at several levels: as the making of programmes for profit in a known market; as a channel for advertising; and as a cultural and political form directly shaped by and dependent on the norms of a capitalist society, selling both consumer goods and a 'way of life' based on them, in an ethos that is at once locally generated, by domestic capitalist interests and authorities, and internationally organised, by the dominant capitalist power.

This pervasive ethos is manifest, and analysable, in media texts.

The politics of media

Broadcasting organizations in the UK have, as conditions on their licence to broadcast, public service obligations to provide impartial and balanced coverage of social and political news, and educational services. There is therefore a tension between the pressure to increase ratings through opting broadly for more entertainment, and the pressure to provide public service information and education. The tension is more evident in Britain, where the public service tradition of the BBC is a strong one, than in the USA, where broadcasting was commercially dominated from the start. But the public service tradition in Britain is now under threat even in the BBC, because it is obliged to enter a market where competitiveness has intensified, especially with the arrival of satellite and cable television and commercial radio.

Indeed, Habermas (1989) has pointed to a long-term demise of the media as an effective political public sphere, a space for rational debate and discussion of political issues, under the influence of a process of commercialization which goes back to the nineteenth century. He has referred to a 'refeudalization' of the mediatized public sphere, in which audiences become spectators rather than participants, and are addressed as consumers (of entertainment) rather than as citizens. The intensified commercialization of the media in the past few decades, especially since the advent of commercial television and radio, has led to similar analyses and a defence of the public service model (Garnham 1986). Scannell (1992) and Tolson (1991), however, argue that the mediatized political public sphere is evolving, not disappearing. Tolson contrasts an earlier 'paternalist' with a more recent 'populist' public sphere. Cardiff (1980) and Scannell (1992) have traced the evolution in broadcasting of a communicative ethos which is based upon an institutionalization of the conversational practices of the private domain. Tolson, by contrast, sees a public sphere with inner contradictions, vacillating between demands for information and for entertainment.

I find Tolson's formulation a helpful one and will work with it below. However, the concept of information needs to be treated with caution. A great deal of media analysis has pointed to informationally oriented aspects of media output (for instance in news programmes) being ideologically shaped. In particular, representations in media texts may be said to function ideologically in so far as they contribute to reproducing social relations of domination and exploitation. Ideological representations are generally implicit rather than explicit in

texts, and are embedded in ways of using language which are naturalized and commonsensical for reporters, audiences, and various categories of third parties – presuppositions and taken-for-granted
assumptions upon which the coherence of the discourse depends, or
the ordinary ways in which interviews are conducted.

I find it helpful to differentiate ideological aspects of discourse from
persuasive aspects, though both in different ways are political
aspects of discourse which problematize the idea of the media simply
'giving information'. A documentary, for instance, will typically
adopt a particular point of view on its topic and use rhetorical devices
to persuade audiences to see things that way too. Ideologies, by contrast, are not usually 'adopted' but taken for granted as common
ground between reporter and/or third parties and audience, without
recourse to rhetorical devices.

Where media analysis focuses upon ideological effects of media
discourse (critical linguistics, discussed in Chapter 2, is a case in
point), some form of complicity is suggested between the media and
dominant social classes and groups. But such complicity should not
be assumed. Rather, whether it exists and what forms it takes need to
be assessed case by case. The point is that while some sections of the
media can sometimes appear to be little more than tools of dominant
interests, the media overall are in a more complex and variable
relationship with such interests. There is sometimes direct conflict
between even mainstream media and government, or media and
capital. Where relationships of complicity do exist, they take a wide
variety of forms. There are cases of media moguls (people like Rupert
Murdoch, the late Robert Maxwell, or Conrad Black) directly manipu-
lating the media outlets they own in their own interests. There are
also instances in Britain of direct intervention by the state to control
media output – notoriously in the case of coverage of the crisis in
Northern Ireland – and in many other countries public broadcasting
is routinely controlled by the state. By contrast, the BBC in Britain has
rarely allowed itself to be *directly* politically manipulated – though it
did notoriously act as an instrument of the government during the
General Strike in 1926.

The state does have an interest in controlling media output. The
media, and especially television with its massive audiences, have
immense potential power and influence. This includes a mobilizing
power, as well as the ideological potential of the media (Enzensberger 1970). Recent examples which are often referred to are the influence in the USA of television coverage of the Vietnam war in
swinging public opinion against the war and forcing the American

withdrawal, the impact of television film of famine in Africa in forcing governments to at least give the appearance of doing more about 'Third World' poverty, and the effect of television coverage of the events of 1989 in the former socialist countries of eastern Europe on the mobilization of popular protest movements. Attempts at state control may be more or less direct. During the Gulf War, the military exercised tight control over the media, determined that the experience of the Vietnam war would not be repeated (Kellner 1992). Although in other circumstances the BBC may not suffer much direct censorship, it has at times been subject to intense monitoring and critique from government, notably in the Thatcher years of the 1980s, which must at least have an inhibiting effect, as do the relationships of mutual dependence, goodwill and trust which are built up between journalists and government ministers and officials within news-gathering networks (Tuchman 1978).

But in claiming that the media constitute a powerful ideological apparatus, one is not necessarily suggesting that they are subject to overt political manipulation on a large scale. The history of the BBC is an interesting case in point. Kumar (1977) points out that in the more unstable and competitive climate which has obtained since the beginning of the 1960s, the BBC has had to abandon its claim to be the voice of a national cultural consensus. Its voice – personalized in its announcers, newsreaders and presenters – has evolved in a populist direction, claiming common ground (the 'middle ground' and a shared 'common sense') with audiences, and often adopting a cynical, challenging and even aggressive stance to a variety of official institutions and personalities, including, for instance, government ministers. But the common-sense assumptions and presuppositions which the discourse of these key media personnel is built upon often have a heavily ideological character – naturalizing, taking as obvious, for instance, basic design features of contemporary capitalist society and its consumerist values. The cynicism and aggressiveness towards establishment figures is thus often at odds with the way in which the discourse naturalizes establishment (dominant) ideologies. Putting it differently, the opening up of social relations (realized in interpersonal aspects of language) is perhaps in contrast with the continuing closure of social representations (realized in the ideational aspects of language). (On the contrast between interpersonal and ideational functions of language, see further Chapter 4.)

The concept of ideology often implies distortion, 'false consciousness', manipulation of the truth in the pursuit of particular interests (see Chapter 1). The only way of gaining access to the truth is through representations of it, and all representations involve particular points of view, values, and goals. Accusations of 'bias' tend to overlook this. But this does not entail a relativism which sees all representations as equal. In media analysis one is always comparing and evaluating representations, in terms of what they include and what they exclude, what they foreground and what they background, where they come from and what factors and interests influence their formulation and projection, and so forth. 'The truth' in an absolute sense is always problematic, and a source of much fruitless argument. But representations can be compared in terms of their partiality, completeness, and interestedness, and conclusions can be arrived at – and constantly are arrived at – about the relative (un)truthfulness of representations. Needless to say, people always make such evaluations from particular positions and points of view, but these too can be compared in terms of how public-spirited or self-interested they are. Truth is a slippery business, but abandoning it altogether is surely perverse.

Ideological analysis of media has lost much of the prestige it had during the 1970s, partly because of a changing political climate and partly because of difficulties with this sort of analysis. It has been criticized for assuming ideological effects of texts upon audiences without actually investigating how audiences 'read' texts. Studies of audience reception have now become very popular, partly at the expense of ideological analysis (recall my comments on this in Chapter 1). Ideological analysis also tended to be reductionist in its approach to texts, which are never simply ideology. But there is a danger in the reaction against the ideological analysis of the 1970s that its important insights will be lost.

My view is that media discourse should be regarded as the site of complex and often contradictory processes, including ideological processes. Ideology should not be seen as a constant and predictable presence in all media discourse by definition. Rather, it should be a working principle that the question of what ideological work is being done is one of a number of questions which analysts should always be ready to ask of any media discourse, though they should expect the answers to be variable. Ideology may, for example, be a more salient issue for some instances and types of media discourse than for others. Media texts do indeed function ideologically in social control and social reproduction; but they also operate as cultural commodities in a competitive market (as I suggested earlier), are part of the business of entertaining people, are designed to keep people politically and socially informed, are cultural artefacts in their own right, informed by particular aesthetics; and they are at the same time caught up in – reflecting and contributing to – shifting cultural values and identities. There is obviously overlap between these various facets, but as well as differing in their relative salience between different media texts, they may involve different aspects of the forms and meanings of texts, and may result in texts which are contradictory in their forms and meanings.

Practices of media text production and consumption

A further dimension of communication in the mass media is the institutional practices associated both with the production of media texts and with the consumption of media texts. Processes of text production are managed through sets of institutional routines. Media organizations are characterized by routine ways of collecting and selecting material, and editing and transforming source material into finished texts (Bell 1991, Silverstone 1985, Tuchman 1978, van Dijk 1988a). The production of a text is a collective process, involving journalists, producers, and various categories of editorial staff, as well as technical staff. Bell estimates, for instance, that in a moderate-sized press newsroom up to eight people may contribute to the production of a story, and the story may correspondingly go through up to eight versions. Silverstone shows similar complexity in the production of documentary. The journalist's first draft may be changed by the chief reporter, the news editor, the editor, the chief sub-editor, a page sub-editor, a copy sub-editor, or the check sub-editor (Bell 1991: 44–6). Moreover, since a high proportion of source material is made up of news items already produced by news agencies, a given story may undergo a similiar process in each of several newsrooms before appearing in a newspaper or on a news broadcast.

Consequently, news, documentary, and other types of media discourse have a heavily *embedded* and *layered* character (Bell 1991: 50–5), in the sense that earlier versions are embedded within later versions, and constitute so many layers within them. At each stage in the construction of the story, earlier versions are transformed and recontextualized in ways which correspond to the concerns, priorities and goals of the current stage (recall my comments on representations in the previous section). But it is not simply earlier versions in the production process that are transformed, recontextualized and embedded in the final text: so too are the source communicative events which stories are ultimately based upon – the interviews, the political speeches, the policy documents, and so forth. The production of media texts can thus be seen as a series of transformations across what I earlier called a chain of communicative events which links source events in the public domain to the private domain consumption of media texts.

With respect to sources, one striking feature of news production is the overwhelming reliance of journalists on a tightly delimited set of official and otherwise legitimized sources which are systematically drawn upon, through a network of contacts and procedures, as sources of 'facts' and to substantiate other 'facts' (Tuchman 1978). These include government and local government sources, the police, employers' organizations and trade unions, scientific and technical experts from universities. Organizations which are not perceived as legitimate (for instance, what are defined as 'extreme' political groups or parties) are excluded or more rarely referred to. Ordinary people, including rank-and-file members of organizations, feature as offering typifications of reactions to news, but not as news sources – as Scannell (1992) puts it, they are entitled to their experiences but not their opinions. The result is a predominantly establishment view of the world, manifested textually in, for instance, ways in which the reporting of speech is treated. Herman and Chomsky (1988) suggest that where there is controversy, it is predominantly because there are divisions within the establishment. The narrowness and inherent conservatism of the network of legitimate sources can partly be attributed to the ways in which the media are economically embedded in and dependent upon the status quo in terms of ownership and profitability (recall discussion of the economics of media), and the dependence of journalists upon their sources constitutes an inbuilt limitation on their campaigning zeal.

The consumption of media texts is characterized by its own institutional practices and routines. Overwhelmingly, media texts are consumed in private domain contexts, in the home and in the context of family life. Research on media reception has shown the various ways in which media text consumption may be embedded within domestic life. Viewers may, for instance, in some cases give a television programme their full attention, while in other cases watching television may be an accompaniment to other domestic activities, such as eating. Or again, watching television may be a solitary activity or an activity engaged in collectively but in silence, or it may be embedded within, and be the topic of, conversation among viewers. Such variations are important in assessing the reception and effects of television. Reception studies have also emphasized the variability of

interpretations of, and responses to, television programmes: any discussion of 'the meaning' of a television programme needs to take
account of the variability of the meanings that may be attributed to it
by different categories of audience member.

It is fruitful to conceptualize media text consumption as well as its
production in terms of transformations across chained communicative events. Evidence for audience interpretations of media texts is
predominantly the talk and writing of audiences, and media texts are
transformed in°systematic ways into audience conversation (at
various distances in time and space from the original consumption of
the media text) and other types of audience discourse, written or
spoken. Such a perspective recognizes that the media constitute both
an important resource and topic for other types of discourse, and an
important formative influence upon them (Fairclough 1992b,
Thompson 1990).

Sociocultural context

One issue in discourse analysis is to what degree context is relevant to
investigation of discourse practices. Many analysts focus upon the
immediate situation of the communicative event (the 'context of
situation'), and maybe refer to some elements of institutional context,
but say little about the wider social and cultural context. My view is
that this wider contextual matrix must be attended to because it
shapes discourse practices in important ways and is itself cumulatively shaped by them. This is particularly clear in the case of the
media.

Factors of institutional context alone can only give a partial understanding of media practices. In Chapter 2 I discussed Heritage's
(1985) analysis of media interview, which gives a powerful account of
how features of interview design (such as the way formulations are
used) serve to cope with institutional constraints. What such an insti-
tutionally oriented analysis cannot explain is certain recent changes
in media interview which seem to be part of wider sociocultural
changes affecting contemporary societies. I have in mind, for
instance, the way in which political interviews have changed
between the 1950s and the present in Britain from very formal interactions between often anonymous reporters and public figures constructed in terms of their social status, to much more informal (often
conversational, sometimes combative) interactions between
presenters who are well-known media personalities in their own

right, and public figures who are also painstakingly constructed, by promotional apparatuses, as personalities (Tolson 1991). Whereas the relationship between interviewer and interviewee once faithfully reflected status-based authority differences, it is now much more open and negotiable, with politician and presenter often talking as equals. The personalities of presenters are in many cases fashioned from models in private life – as I suggested earlier, presenters often project themselves as inhabiting the same common-sense world as their audiences, using a communicative style partly based upon properties of conversation. In accordance with these changes, the discourse of political interviews has changed substantially.

The point is that such developments are not just features of media interview. Documentary has broadly shifted from a focus on general social issues in which people figured as representative of social types, to a concern to construct the people it represents as individuals with their own personalities (Corner 1991, Tolson 1990). And the shift towards greater informality and more conversation-like ('public-colloquial') discourse is a general one not only in the media but in many domains of public discourse, including medical consultations (Fairclough 1992a, Mishler 1984). They are part of general changes in social relations and cultural values which have been discussed in terms of individualism, 'detraditionalization' (Giddens 1991) and 'informalization' (Featherstone 1991), affecting relations of authority, relations between public and private domains of social life, and the construction of self-identity. The media are shaped by the wider society, but they also play a vital role in the diffusion of such social and cultural changes, and this should be one focus in analysis of media discourse. Obvious issues for attention here include changing constructions of gender relations, race relations, and class relations.

Changes in media discourse also reflect, and help to diffuse, contemporary 'promotional' (Wernick 1991) or 'consumer' culture, the way in which models of promotion (of goods, institutions, parties, personalities, and so forth) and consumption have spread from the domain of economic consumption to the public services, the arts, and the media. I have referred to the increasing salience of entertainment in various sorts of media output, and on how audiences are increasingly being constructed as consumers – with leisure being constructed as consumption – rather than as, say, citizens. Similarly, in government leaflets aimed at the public and dealing with such matters as welfare benefit rights, the influence of advertising and promotional genres is increasingly evident, with the public again being constructed as consumers rather than – or as well as – citizens, even though it is their civic rights that are at issue.

Media texts constitute a sensitive barometer of sociocultural change, and they should be seen as valuable material for researching change. Changes in society and culture manifest themselves in all their tentativeness, incompleteness and contradictory nature in the heterogeneous and shifting discursive practices of the media. The framework for critical discourse analysis introduced in Chapter 4 is designed to capture these properties of media discourse, and provide a resource for linking discourse analysis to social-scientific analysis of sociocultural change.

4

CRITICAL ANALYSIS OF MEDIA DISCOURSE

This chapter sketches out the framework which I shall use for analysing media discourse in the rest of the book, drawing upon the account given in Chapter 3 of communication in the mass media. This is a version of the theory of 'critical discourse analysis' which I have developed in previous publications (Fairclough 1989, 1992a, 1993). The chapter first briefly describes in general terms the theory of discourse I am operating with, and then focuses attention upon media discourse. The framework is described and then applied to an example.

Theory of discourse

Recent social theory has produced important insights into the social nature of language and how it functions in contemporary societies. Social theorists have tended to put such insights in abstract ways, without analysis of specific texts. To develop a form of discourse analysis which can contribute to social and cultural analysis, we need to combine these insights with traditions of close textual analysis which have developed in linguistics and language studies – to make them 'operational', practically usable, in analysis of specific cases. Some of the critical approaches discussed in Chapter 2 have begun to do this. Critical discourse analysis is an attempt to learn from them and improve on them, in line with the desiderata at the end of Chapter 2 (see Fairclough 1992a for a more detailed account).

Calling the approach 'critical' is a recognition that our social practice in general and our use of language in particular are bound up with causes and effects which we may not be at all aware of under normal conditions (Bourdieu 1977). Specifically, connections between the use of language and the exercise of power are often not clear to people, yet appear on closer examination to be vitally important to the workings of power. For instance, ways in which a conventional consultation between a doctor and a patient is organized, or a conventional interview between a reporter and a politician, take for granted a whole range of ideologically potent assumptions about rights, relationships, knowledge and identities. For example, the assumption that the doctor is the sole source of medically legitimate knowledge about illness, or that it is legitimate for the reporter – as one who 'speaks for' the public – to challenge the politician. Such practices are shaped, with their common-sense assumptions, according to prevailing relations of power between groups of people. The normal opacity of these practices to those involved in them – the invisibility of their ideological assumptions, and of the power relations which underlie the practices – helps to sustain these power relations.

'Discourse' (as I pointed out in Chapter 1) is a concept used by both social theorists and analysts (e.g. Foucault 1972, Fraser 1989) and linguists (e.g. Stubbs 1983, van Dijk 1985). Like many linguists, I shall use 'discourse' to refer to spoken or written language use, though I also want to extend it to include other types of semiotic activity (i.e. activity which produces meanings), such as visual images (photography, film, video, diagrams) and non-verbal communication (e.g. gestures). Recall the discussion of the 'social semiotics' approach in Chapter 2. In referring to use of language as discourse, I am signalling a wish to investigate it in a way that is informed by the social theory insights mentioned above, as a form of social practice.

Viewing language use as social practice implies, first, that it is a mode of action, as linguistic philosophy and the study of pragmatics have recognized (Austin 1962, Levinson 1983). It also implies that language is a socially and historically situated mode of action, in a dialectical relationship with other facets of the social. What I mean by a dialectical relationship is that it is socially shaped, but is also socially shaping – or socially *constitutive*. Critical discourse analysis explores the tension between these two sides of language use, the socially shaped and socially constitutive, rather than opting one-sidedly for one or the other.

Language use – any text – is always simultaneously constitutive of (1) social identities, (2) social relations and (3) systems of knowledge and belief (corresponding respectively to identities, relationships and representations in the terms introduced in Chapter 1). That is, any text makes its own small contribution to shaping these aspects of society and culture. In particular cases, one of the three might appear to be more important than the others, but it is a sensible working assumption that all three are always going on to some degree. Language use is, moreover, constitutive both in conventional ways which help to reproduce and maintain existing social identities, relations and systems of knowledge and belief, and in creative ways which help to transform them. Whether the conventional or the creative predominates in any given case will depend upon social circumstances and how the language is functioning within them.

The relationship between any particular instance of language use – any particular text – and available discourse types may be a complex and (in the terms of the last paragraph) creative one. It is always possible to find relatively straightforward instances of particular discourse types – a conventional and typical political interview on the radio, for instance. But many texts are not so simple. They may involve complicated mixtures of different discourse types – a political interview which is in part rather like a friendly conversation and in part like a political speech, for example. Given my concern in this book with changing discursive practices in the media, such complex texts are of particular interest.

The critical discourse analysis approach thinks of the discursive practices of a community – its normal ways of using language – in terms of networks which I shall call 'orders of discourse'. The order of discourse of a social institution or social domain is constituted by all the discursive types which are used there. The point of the concept of 'order of discourse' is to highlight the relationships between different types in such a set (e.g. in the case of a school, the discursive types of the classroom and of the playground): whether, for instance, a rigid boundary is maintained between them, or whether they can easily be mixed together in particular texts. The same question applies to relationships between different orders of discourse (e.g. those of the school and the home): do they commonly overlap and get mixed together in language use, or are they rigidly demarcated? Social and cultural changes very often manifest themselves discursively through a redrawing of boundaries within and between orders of discourse, and I shall be showing that this is true of the media. These boundaries are also sometimes a focus of social struggle and conflict. Indeed, orders of discourse can be seen as one domain of potential cultural hegemony, with dominant groups struggling to assert and maintain particular structuring within and between them.

It is useful to distinguish two main categories of discourse type, which are constituents of orders of discourse: genres, and discourses. A discourse is the language used in representing a given social practice from a particular point of view. Discourses appertain broadly to knowledge and knowledge construction. For instance, the social practice of politics is differently signified in liberal, socialist and Marxist political discourses; or again, illness and health are differently represented in conventional ('allopathic') and homoeopathic medical discourses. A genre, by contrast, is a use of language associated with and constituting part of some particular social practice, such as interviewing people (interview genre) or advertising commodities (advertising genre). Genres can be described in terms of their organizational properties – an interview, for instance, is structured in a quite different way from an advertisement. See Kress and Threadgold (1988) and van Leeuwen (1993).

The analysis of any particular type of discourse, including media discourse, involves an alternation between twin, complementary focuses, both of which are essential:

- communicative events
- the order of discourse.

On the one hand, the analyst is concerned with the particular, with specific communicative events, for instance a particular newspaper editorial or television documentary. The concern here is always with both continuity and change – in what ways is this communicative event normative, drawing upon familiar types and formats, and in what ways is it creative, using old resources in new ways? On the other hand, the analyst is concerned with the general, the overall structure of the order of discourse, and the way it is evolving in the context of social and cultural changes. The focus here is upon the configuration of genres and discourses which constitute the order of discourse, the shifting relationships between them, and between this order of discourse and other socially adjacent ones. These are not, let me stress, alternatives, but complementary perspectives on the same data which we can shift between during analysis. My presentation of a framework for critical analysis of media discourse will discuss the two perspectives in turn.

Analysis of communicative events

Critical discourse analysis of a communicative event is the analysis of relationships between three dimensions or facets of that event, which I call *text, discourse practice,* and *sociocultural practice.* 'Texts' may be written or oral, and oral texts may be just spoken (radio) or spoken and visual (television). By 'discourse practice' I mean the processes of text production and text consumption. And by 'sociocultural practice' I mean the social and cultural goings-on which the communicative event is a part of. The analytical framework is summarized in a diagram on page 59.

Let me briefly link this analytical framework to the discussion of communication in the mass media in the last chapter. The section on practices of media text production and consumption dealt with aspects of *discourse practice*. Most of the chapter was concerned with various aspects of *sociocultural practice*: mass communication as a particular type of situation, the economics of the media, the politics of the media, and the wider cultural context of communication in the mass media. These two features are addressed further below.

Texts

The analysis of texts, the properties of which were little mentioned in Chapter 3, covers traditional forms of linguistic analysis – analysis of vocabulary and semantics, the grammar of sentences and smaller units, and the sound system ('phonology') and writing system. But it also includes analysis of textual organization above the sentence, including the ways in which sentences are connected together ('cohesion'), and things like the organization of turn-taking in interviews or the overall structure of a newspaper article. I shall refer to all this as 'linguistic analysis', though this is using the term in an extended sense. For details on these types of analysis, see Chapters 6 and 7.

Analysis of texts is concerned with both their meanings and their forms. Although it may be useful analytically to contrast these two aspects of texts, it is in reality difficult to separate them. Meanings are necessarily realized in forms, and differences in meaning entail differences in form. Conversely, it is a sensible working assumption that where forms are different, there will be some difference in meaning.

As I have already indicated in Chapter 1, I work with a multifunctional view of text. This sees any text, and indeed even the individual clauses and sentences of a text, as simultaneously having three main categories of function, each of which has its own systems of choices: *ideational, interpersonal,* and *textual*. This view of text harmonizes with the constitutive view of discourse outlined above, providing a way of investigating the simultaneous constitution of systems of knowledge and belief (ideational function) and social relations and social identities (interpersonal function) in texts. Or, in the terminology of Chapter 1, with *representations, relations* and *identities*. So, for instance, in analysing a sentence in a written text, the analyst might focus upon how three aspects are articulated:

- particular representations and recontextualizations of social practice (ideational function) – perhaps carrying particular ideologies

- particular constructions of writer and reader identities (for example, in terms of what is highlighted – whether status and role aspects of identity, or individual and personality aspects of identity)

- a particular construction of the relationship between writer and reader (as, for instance, formal or informal, close or distant).

The analysis is sensitive to absences as well as presences in texts – to representations, categories of participant, constructions of participant identity or participant relations which are not found in a text.

Analysis of text needs to be multisemiotic analysis in the case of the press and television, including analysis of photographic images, layout and the overall visual organization of pages, and analysis of film and of sound effects. A key issue is how these other semiotic modalities interact with language in producing meanings, and how such interactions define different aesthetics for different media.

Discourse practice

The discourse practice dimension of the communicative event involves various aspects of the processes of text production and text consumption. Some of these have a more institutional character, whereas others are discourse processes in a narrower sense. This was shown in the discussion of mass media communication in Chapter 3: with respect to institutional processes, I referred to institutional routines such as editorial procedures involved in producing media texts, and how, for instance, watching television fits into the routines of the household; but I also referred to discourse processes in the narrower sense in discussing the transformations which texts undergo in production and consumption. I shall call these respectively 'institutional processes' and 'discourse processes'. (One could also include here more psychological and cognitivist concerns with how people arrive at interpretations for particular utterances – 'interpretative processes'. As I indicated in Chapter 2, van Dijk works with a more cognitively oriented framework which is otherwise rather similar in conception to mine.)

The analytical framework of critical discourse analysis is summarized in Figure 1.

The visual representation of the relationships between the three dimensions of communicative events in the diagram is significant: I see discourse practice as mediating between the textual and the social

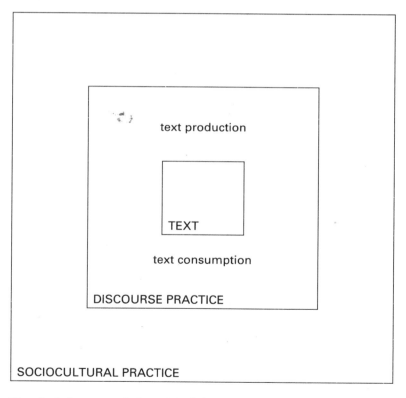

Fig. 1: A framework for critical discourse analysis of a communicative event

and cultural, between text and sociocultural practice, in the sense that the link between the sociocultural and the textual is an indirect one, made by way of discourse practice: properties of sociocultural practice shape texts, but by way of shaping the nature of the discourse practice, i.e. the ways in which texts are produced and consumed, which is realized in features of texts. Notice also that, as we have just seen with the distinction between 'institutional processes' and 'discourse processes', discourse practice straddles the division between society and culture on the one hand, and discourse, language and text on the other.

In referring to 'the nature of the discourse practice', I have in mind particularly the polarity alluded to earlier between broadly conventional and broadly creative discourse processes, involving either a normative use of discourse types (genres and discourses) or a creative mixture of them. This is where the two perspectives within critical discourse analysis – on the communicative event, and on the order of discourse – intersect. The question here is how the communicative event draws upon the order of discourse (normatively or creatively), and what effect it has upon the order of discourse – whether it helps reproduce its boundaries and relationships, or helps restructure them. Creative discourse practice can be expected to be relatively complex, in terms of the number of genres and discourses mixed together and the way they are mixed together. But complex discourse practice may also become conventionalized – for instance, there are now in documentary quite conventional combinations of genres of informing, persuading, and entertaining.

In very general terms, a conventional discourse practice is realized in a text which is relatively homogeneous in its forms and meanings, whereas a creative discourse practice is realized in a text which is relatively heterogeneous in its forms and meanings. Of course, it is the particular nature of the creativity of the discourse practice and of the heterogeneity of the text that is of interest in a specific analysis – and their relationship to the sociocultural practice that frames them. Also in general terms, one would expect a complex and creative discourse practice where the sociocultural practice is fluid, unstable and shifting, and a conventional discourse practice where the sociocultural practice is relatively fixed and stable. As I suggested in Chapter 3, media texts are sensitive barometers of cultural change which manifest in their heterogeneity and contradictoriness the often tentative, unfinished and messy nature of change. Textual heterogeneity can be seen as a materialization of social and cultural contradictions and as important evidence for investigating these contradictions and their evolution.

The focus on discursive creativity, hybridity, and heterogeneity in my analysis of media discourse in this book corresponds to the nature of the times. We are living through a period of rapid and continuous change in society and culture, the media play a significant role in reflecting and stimulating more general processes of change, and the practices of the media are correspondingly in constant flux. This includes the discursive practices of the media. The general point to emphasize is that creativity in discursive practices is tied to particular social conditions – conditions of change and instability. The term 'creativity' can be misleading in its individualistic connotations: discursive creativity is an effect of social conditions, not an achievement of individuals who have particular (creative) qualities.

I want to contrast the linguistic analysis of texts (in the extended sense I explained above) with the *intertextual* analysis of texts (see Bakhtin 1986, Fairclough 1992a, Kristeva 1986). Intertextual analysis focuses on the borderline between text and discourse practice in the analytical framework. Intertextual analysis is looking at text from the perspective of discourse practice, looking at the traces of the discourse practice in the text. Intertextual analysis aims to unravel the various genres and discourses – often, in creative discourse practice, a highly complex mixture – which are articulated together in the text. The question one is asking is, what genres and discourses were drawn upon in producing the text, and what traces of them are there in the text? To use a familiar example, the traces in a documentary text of a mixture of genres of information, persuasion and entertainment. Intertextual complexity in the mixing of genres and discourses is realized linguistically in the heterogeneity of meaning and form.

Linguistic analysis is descriptive in nature, whereas intertextual analysis is more interpretative. Linguistic features of texts provide evidence which can be used in intertextual analysis, and intertextual analysis is a particular sort of interpretation of that evidence – an interpretation which locates the text in relation to social repertoires of discourse practices, i.e. orders of discourse. It is a cultural interpretation in that it locates the particular text within that facet of the culture that is constituted by (networks of) orders of discourse. The linguistic analysis is, in an obvious sense, closer to what is 'there' on paper or on the audio- or video-tape, whereas the intertextual analysis is at one remove in abstraction from it. Consequently, in intertextual analysis the analyst is more dependent upon social and cultural understanding. This can seem problematic to those who expect more 'objective' forms of analysis, though it is easy to overstate the objectivity of linguistic analysis. Nevertheless, linking the linguistic analysis of texts to an intertextual analysis is crucial to bridging the gap between text and language on the one hand, and society and culture on the other. See Chapter 5 for further discussion.

Sociocultural practice

Analysis of the sociocultural practice dimension of a communicative event may be at different levels of abstraction from the particular event: it may involve its more immediate situational context, the wider context of institutional practices the event is embedded within, or the yet wider frame of the society and the culture. All of these layers may be relevant to understanding the particular event – and indeed particular events cumulatively constitute and reconstitute social and cultural practice at all levels. Many aspects of sociocultural practice may enter into critical discourse analysis – recall the various aspects discussed in Chapter 3 – but it may be useful to broadly differentiate three: economic, political (concerned with issues of power and ideology), and cultural (concerned with questions of value and identity).

The framework which I have sketched out here is compatible with various different emphases. One might, for instance, choose to focus on discourse practice, either on processes of text production, or on processes of text consumption. One might alternatively choose to focus on text, as I have done. It is, I believe, important to maintain the comprehensive orientation to communicative events which is built into the framework, even if one is concentrating upon only certain aspects of them in analysis. My emphasis will be upon linguistic analysis of texts, intertextual analysis of texts, and selective sociocultural analysis. Through intertextual analysis I link up with issues of discourse practice, but I am not concerned in this book with direct analysis of production or consumption of texts. The discussion of sociocultural practice is selective because I am not writing as a sociologist or cultural analyst, but as a discourse analyst with an interest in these other types of analysis.

Analysis of the order of discourse

I come now to the second of the twin perspectives within a critical discourse analysis of the media, the order of discourse – how it is structured in terms of configurations of genres and discourses, and shifts within the order of discourse and in its relationship to other socially adjacent orders of discourse.

I referred earlier to the positioning of the media between public orders of discourse and private orders of discourse, and to the way in which the media transform their source public discourse for consumption in domestic settings. This mediating position, and the *external* relations between the order of discourse of the media and socially adjacent public and private orders of discourse such as those of books and magazines, is the key to understanding the media order of discourse and the *internal* relations between its constituent genres and discourses. The order of discourse of the media has been shaped by the tension between its contradictory public sources and private targets, which act as contrary poles of attraction for media discourse; it is constantly being reshaped through redefining its relationship to – redrawing its boundaries with – these public and private orders of discourse. Moreover, the negotiation and renegotiation of the relationship between public and private discursive practices which takes place within the order of discourse of the media has a general influence on the relationship between these practices, and between the public and the private in an overall sense, in other domains of social life. Research on media orders of discourse is thus of more than parochial interest, because it impinges upon major changes in society and culture. Similar remarks apply, for instance, to the (re)negotiation within broadcast media discourse of the relationship between the more traditional order of discourse of public service broadcasting and the commercial order of discourse of the market and consumerism.

The general point here is that the relationship between institutions and discursive practices is not a neat or simple relationship. Different institutions come to share common discursive practices, and a particular discursive practice may have a complex distribution across many institutions. For instance, advertising may be rooted in the orders of discourse of commodity production, distribution and consumption, but it has come to be an element in the orders of discourse of diverse institutions – education, medicine, the arts, and so forth. It follows that discourse analysis should always attend to relationships, interactions and complicities between social institutions/domains and their orders of discourse, and be sensitive to similarities in social organization and discursive practices between different institutions. Although the media may be a particularly clear case of such fluid relationships between institutions, this property is widely shared.

It should also be emphasized that media discourse may shape socially adjacent orders of discourse as well as being shaped by them. For instance, television formats have considerable cultural salience, and one finds them as models in a variety of public domains. An example would be the way in which the celebrity-interview format is now quite widely used in higher education for introductory books on the thinking of prominent figures, as well as in magazines (such as the left-wing political magazine *Red Pepper*). Postman (1987: 91) refers to the influence of other television genres on education, including the television version of 'discussion' which he characterizes in these negative terms:

> . . . each of six men was given approximately five minutes to say something about the subject. There was however no agreement on exactly what the subject was, and no one felt obliged to respond to anything anyone else said. In fact, it would have been difficult to do so, since the participants were called upon *seriatim*, as if they were finalists in a beauty contest, each being given his share of minutes in front of the camera.

Media discourse also influences private domain discourse practices, providing models of conversational interaction in private life which are originally simulations of the latter but which can come to reshape it. A complex dialectic seems to exist between the media and the conversational discourse of everyday life.

External relations between orders of discourse, and internal relations between discourses and genres within the media order of discourse, may be difficult to disentangle, but the distinction between these two concerns in analysis of orders of discourse is a useful one. Both external and internal relations include *choice* relations, and *chain* relations. What I have said so far appertains to choice relations. (Let me remind readers of the point made towards the end of Chapter 1 that 'choice' does not here imply free choice on the part of participants – selection among alternatives is generally socially conditioned.) Externally, the issue is how the order of discourse of the media chooses within, and appropriates, the potential available in adjacent orders of discourse. Internally, the issue is to describe the paradigms of alternative discursive practices available within the order of discourse of the media, and the conditions governing selection amongst them. Discursive practices are functionally differentiated, providing contrasting formats for the main types of output in the media. Thus there are different discursive practices for news, documentary, drama, quiz and 'soap' programmes on television, and there are different discursive practices for hard news, soft news, comment and feature articles in newspapers. (As these two examples show, the classification of functionally different discursive practices may be at various levels of generality.) But there are also alternatives for any given type of output whose selection is governed by different conditions, which I come to shortly.

I have already referred to chain relations in suggesting that a communicative event in the mass media can be regarded as in fact a chain of communicative events. Such chains are partly internal – the process of text production within a media institution is a chain of communicative events – and partly external – the source communicative events at one end of the chain lie outside the media, as do the communicative events (conversations, debates, reports) which media texts may themselves be sources for. A description of the media order of discourse is concerned to specify what communicative events, internal and external, are chained together in this way; and the sorts of transformations that texts undergo in moving along such chains, and how earlier texts in the chain are embedded in later ones. Choice relations and chain relations intersect in an account of the order of discourse: one needs to specify the choice relations that apply at each link in the chain.

The distinction between choice and chain relations suggests a refinement of the intertextual analysis of texts discussed in the section on discourse practice above. Part of the intertextual analysis of a text is concerned with unravelling mixtures of genres and discourses which are in a choice relationship in the order of discourse. But the intertextual analysis of a text is also concerned with embedding – with how the transformations which texts undergo in shifting along chains leave traces in embedding relations within texts. See Chapter 5 for further discussion.

In trying to arrive at a characterization of the media order of discourse, the analyst constantly has in mind two important questions, which may receive different answers for different parts of this complex order of discourse: (a) how unitary, or how variable, are media discursive practices? and (b) how stable, or how changeable, are they?

The questions are linked: typical of a settled and conservative society are unitary and stable discursive practices, typical of an unsettled society are variable and changeable discursive practices. There are also more local institutional pressures towards unitary practice – standardized formats reduce production costs, and conform to audience expectations. In describing the order of discourse, one is trying to capture the particular balance that exists between what Bakhtin called 'centripetal' (unitary and stable) and 'centrifugal' (variable and changeable) pressures, and in which direction that balance is tending (Bakhtin 1981). The variability question links back to my mention above of alternatives for a particular type of output, such as television documentary. Where there is variability, selection between alternatives may, for instance, involve political and ideological differences and struggles, attempts to cater for different 'niche' audiences, as well as differences of professional or artistic judgement. Variability is also an issue in text consumption: what orders of discourse do audiences draw upon to appropriate media texts? Do they, for instance, talk or write about them in the genres and discourses of private life, or in those of public (e.g. academic) domains they are familiar with? And what social factors are relevant to that choice?

Changing media discursive practices, and their relation to wider social and cultural changes, are, as I have indicated, a particular concern of this book. Change can be conceptualized in terms of shifting external or internal, chain or choice relations. An account of the media order of discourse should particularly highlight major points of tension affecting internal or external boundaries. I have already identified some as central themes of the book: the public/private boundary and the privately oriented communicative ethos of broadcasting, with extending use of a conversational, public-colloquial discourse style; the boundary between public service and information on one side and the market on the other, with the construction of audiences as consumers and the colonization of even the news media by entertainment; and, related to this, the boundary between fiction and non-fiction, with non-fictional programmes such as documentary often drawing upon fictional, dramatic, formats.

I want to use the term *discourse type* for relatively stabilized configurations of genres and discourses within the order of discourse. One issue here is that genres occur in particular combinations with discourses – particular genres are predictably articulated with particular discourses. For instance, party political broadcast is a genre which predictably draws upon economic discourse, discourse of law and order and educational discourse, but not, for instance, on the discourses of science, cookery, or craft (e.g. knitting). But discourse types also standardly involve configurations of genres rather than a single genre. So, for instance, a party political broadcast may combine political oratory, interview, and simulated fireside conversation. Or again, 'chat' has emerged as an important studio-based discourse type in television, involving an articulation of elements of conversation with elements of entertainment. A major concern here is capturing the distinctive discourse types which have emerged in the order of the discourse of the media, such as chat, or what passes for discussion on television (recall the above quote from Postman), and properties which cut across types, such as the 'communicative ethos' identified by Scannell (1992). Another concern is a historical focus on the stabilization and destabilization of the configurations which constitute discourse types.

One might see the mass media as an interrelated set of orders of discourse, in that the orders of discourse of television, radio, and the press are distinct in important ways which relate to differences of technology and medium while also having significant similarities (recall the discussion of differences between media on pages 38–9). There are also sufficient differences between different outlets to distinguish at a more detailed level separate orders of discourse for different newspapers, radio stations, or television channels.

The media order of discourse can, I think, usefully be examined as a domain of cultural power and hegemony. The media have in the past often been described as if they were dominated by stable unitary practices imposed from above. This is certainly not an adequate characterization of the contemporary media, though it may have some truth for certain aspects of media practice, and was markedly less inadequate thirty years ago than it is now. It implies a *code* model of the media order of discourse: that it is made up of a number of well-defined, unitary and stable codes which dictate practice.

It does not, however, follow that because the code model is inadequate, questions of power and domination do not arise. One common picture of contemporary media stresses cultural diversity – a view of the media as highly pluralistic in practices, with no single web of power running through the whole system. This would perhaps compromise entirely the notion of a media order of discourse, or at least lead to a very different model of it as a *mosaic* of practices. Another possible approach, however, is to ask how the relative diversity and pluralism of the media might itself operate within a system of domination. Gramsci's concept of *hegemony* (Forgacs 1988, Gramsci 1971) is helpful here as a theory of power and domination which emphasizes power through achieving consent rather than through coercion, and the importance of cultural aspects of domination which depend upon a particular articulation of a plurality of practices. The issue with respect to a hegemony model becomes one of whether and how diverse discursive practices are articulated together within the order of discourse in ways which *overall* sustain relations of domination. See Fairclough (1992a) for a discussion of code, mosaic and hegemony models.

Various aspects of the critical discourse analysis framework are elaborated in the following three chapters. Chapter 5 focuses upon discourse practice, specifically discourse processes, intertextual analysis of texts, and the order of discourse. Chapters 6 and 7 are concerned with the linguistic analysis of texts, the former dealing with representation and the ideational function as well as the textual function, the latter dealing with relations, identities and the interpersonal function.

A sample critical discourse analysis

I conclude this chapter with a sample analysis to make the critical discourse analysis framework a little more concrete. My example is a report which appeared in 1985 in the British newspaper, the *Sun*, about a government document on hard-drug abuse. It is reproduced in Figure 2.

My objective is to give readers a quick overview of how the framework applies in a particular case, so I shall be very selective in my comments (for instance, not referring to consumption at all), and certainly will not attempt a full analysis (the example is more fully analysed in Fairclough 1988).

I shall shift slightly from the order in which I presented the framework, first analysing this as a communicative event in terms of *discourse practice* and *text*, but deferring discussion of *sociocultural practice* until after I comment on what the example indicates about the media order of discourse.

The communicative event

The *discourse practice* here involves transformations of source texts – most obviously the Committee report, but also presumably a press conference or interview alluded to in the penultimate paragraph – into an article. The text is likely to have gone through a number of versions, as it was transformed across a chain of linked communicative events. For a reconstruction of such a transformational history in detail, see Bell (1991). The discourse practice is complex, in the sense that it articulates together features of the source discourse (the report)

Britain faces a war to stop pedlars, warn MPs

CALL UP FORCES IN DRUG BATTLE!

By DAVID KEMP

THE armed forces should be called up to fight off a massive invasion by drug pushers, MPs demanded yesterday.

Cocaine pedlars are the greatest threat ever faced by Britain in peacetime — and could destroy the country's way of life, they said.

The MPs want Ministers to consider ordering the Navy and the RAF to track suspected drug-running ships approaching our coasts.

On shore there should be intensified law enforcement by Customs, police and security services.

Profits

The all-party Home Affairs Committee visited America and were deeply shocked by what they saw.

In one of the hardest-hitting Commons reports for years, the committee—chaired by Tory lawyer MP Sir Edward Gardner—warned gravely:

❝ Western society is faced by a warlike threat from the hard-drugs industry.

The traffickers amass princely incomes from the exploitation of human weakness, boredom and misery.

They must be made to lose everything — their homes, their money and all they possess which can be attributed to their profits from selling drugs. ❞

Sir Edward said yesterday: "We believe that trafficking in drugs is tantamount to murder and punishment ought to reflect this."

The Government is expected to bring in clampdown laws in the autumn.

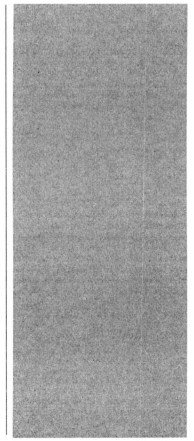

Fig. 2: Extract from the *Sun*, 24 May 1985

and features of the target discourse, the discourse of consumption, the informal, colloquial language of private life.

This is shown in an *intertextual analysis* of the text, an analysis which looks at the text from the perspective of discourse practice, aiming to unravel the genres and discourses which are articulated together in it. I shall focus on discourses, in particular how official discourses of drug trafficking and law enforcement are articulated with colloquial discourses of drug trafficking and law enforcement, within a genre of hard news (described below). Compare the article with a short extract from the source report:

> The Government should consider the use of the Royal Navy and the Royal Air Force for radar, airborne or ship surveillance duties. We recommend, therefore, that there should be intensified law enforcement against drug traffickers by H.M. Customs, the police, the security services and possibly the armed forces.

In part, the *Sun* article draws upon the official discourses which are illustrated in this extract. This is most obvious where the report and the Committee chairman are directly quoted, but it is also evident elsewhere.

What is striking about the text is that these contrasting official and colloquial discourses are both used within what is traditionally called 'reported speech' – or more precisely, the reporting of the source written document. Although the direct quotation is marked as coming directly from the report, the borderline between what the report actually said and the *Sun*'s transformation of it into colloquial discourse is not always clear. For instance, the main headline is in the form of a direct quotation, though it is not in quotation marks. The newspaper itself seems to be taking on the prerogative of the Committee to call for action, though its call is translated into a colloquial discourse, becomes a demand rather than a recommendation, and loses the nuances and caution of the original (*the Government should consider the use of* becomes *call up!*).

To show some of this in detail, I now move to *linguistic analysis* of the text, though in this case I shall focus upon certain relatively superficial linguistic features of vocabulary and metaphor. In accordance with the complex discourse practice and intertextual relations, this is a relatively heterogeneous text linguistically. For instance, in the directly quoted sections the article uses the same term (*traffickers*) as the report to refer to those dealing in drugs, whereas elsewhere it uses colloquial terms not found at all in the report – *pushers* and *pedlars*. But even in the parts of the article where the report is summarized rather than quoted, official discourse is sometimes used – for instance *armed forces, law enforcement*, and *security services*. Compare *forces* in the headline with *armed forces* in the first (lead) paragraph; the former is an expression from colloquial discourse, whereas the latter belongs to official discourse.

Why does the article use such pairs of terms? Perhaps because it is translating official discourse into colloquial discourse and thereby giving a populist force to official voices, but at the same time preserving the legitimacy of official discourse. The position and point of view of the newspaper is contradictory, and that contradiction is registered here in the heterogeneity of the language. Hall *et al.* (1978: 61) refer to a trend in media towards 'the translation of official viewpoints into a public idiom' which not only 'makes the former more "available" to the uninitiated' but also 'invests them with popular force and resonance, naturalizing them within the horizon of understanding of the various publics'. Notice that use of colloquial vocabulary in the *Sun* article has both ideational and interpersonal functions: it draws upon a particular representation of the social reality in question, but at the same time the newspaper, by using it, implicitly claims co-membership, with the audience, of the world of ordinary life and experience from which it is drawn, and a relationship of solidarity between newspaper and audience. (These implicit claims are modulated, however, by the use of the vocabulary of official discourse as well.) Thus this vocabulary is simultaneously functional with respect to representations, identities, and relations. It is also worth noting how a visual semiotic works together with language: it is colloquial and not official discourse that dominates the visually salient headlines.

Notice also the metaphor of dealing with drug traffickers as fighting a war. Although the metaphor does occur at one point in the report, it is elaborated in the *Sun* article in ways which are wholly absent from the report – the mobilization (again using a colloquial term, *call up*) of armed forces in the headline, and the representation of drug trafficking as an invasion in the lead paragraph. The metaphor is also significant in terms of the newspaper's implicit claim to a relationship of solidarity and common identity with the audience. It draws upon war as an evocative theme of popular memory and popular culture, claiming to share that memory and culture. The metaphor also links this text *intertextually* to popular media coverage of the drugs issue over a long period, where the representation of the issue as a war against traffickers is a standard feature of the discourse. It is an ideologically potent metaphor, construing drugs in a way which helps to marginalize other constructions from the perspective of oppositional groups – drugs as a symptom of massive alienation associated with the effects of capitalist reconstruction, unemployment, inadequate housing, and so forth.

The order of discourse

Turning to the second of the twin perspectives within critical discourse analysis, what does this example indicate about the order of discourse? The discourse type is a 'hard-news' story from the popular press. As a hard-news story, it is different in genre from other types of article which are in a choice relation within the order of discourse – soft-news stories, comments and features. It has the typical generic structure of a hard-news story: a 'nucleus' consisting of a headline (in fact both a major and a minor one) and a lead paragraph which gives the gist of the story; a series of 'satellite' paragraphs which elaborate the story in various directions; and a final 'wrap-up' paragraph which gives a sense of resolution to the story (Media Literacy Report 1993). In this discourse type within the order of discourse of the *Sun* (and other similar tabloid newspapers, though not the broadsheet newspapers), this genre is standardly articulated with the combination of official and colloquial discourses I have discussed above. So the discourse type here is a relatively stabilized, and recognizable, one.

An obvious external aspect of *choice* relations is the 'public-colloquial' nature of the style – indicative of a redrawing of boundaries between (external) public and private orders of discourse within the media order of discourse to produce this hybrid style. One feature of *chain* relations which is striking in this case is the way in which the source text is transformed into, and embedded in, the article. I have already commented in this regard on the ambivalence of voice, an ambivalence at times about whether the article is giving the words of the report or the newspaper's (radically transformed) reformulation of them. I suspect this ambivalence is common in this discourse type. It is linked in this case, and more generally, to a mixing of genre – the combination of the informative hard-news genre with elements of persuasive genre. Notice in particular that the main headline is an imperative sentence which, as I have already indicated, functions as a demand. In addition to reporting, the *Sun* article is characteristically also campaigning for particular policies and actions. Another feature of chain relations is the way the article is intertextually linked into another chain which consists of previous coverage of the drugs issue in the popular media. This sort of chaining is a quite general feature of media texts.

Let me finally comment, briefly and partially, on the sociocultural practice which has framed the stabilization of this sort of discourse type, summarizing points which I made in the last chapter. The newspaper is mediating source events in the public domain to a readership in a private (domestic), domain under intensely competitive economic conditions. The maximization of circulation is a constant preoccupation, in a wider economic context in which the accent is upon consumption and consumers and leisure, and a wider cultural context of detraditionalization and informalization which are problematizing traditional authority relations and profoundly changing traditional constructions and conceptions of self-identity. These features of sociocultural context have shaped, and are constituted in, the complex discourse practice that I have described, and the shift towards that discourse practice which has taken place over a period of time. The discourse practice mediates between this unstable sociocultural practice and heterogeneous texts.

Turning to the politics of this type of article, one important likely effect of the translation of official sources and official positions into colloquial discourse is to help legitimize these official sources and positions with the audience, which in this case means within sections of the British working class. (Notice, though, that one would need to investigate consumption, how people read such articles, to see what the effects actually are in detail.) In the terms I used earlier, this would seem to be a powerful strategy for sustaining the hegemony of dominant social forces, based upon a hybridization of practices which gives some legitimacy to both official and colloquial discourses (though the preservation of the former alongside the latter perhaps covertly signals their continuing greater legitimacy, while using the latter as a channel for official 'messages'). At the same time, the newspaper, as I have pointed out, not only takes on a persuasive role in campaigning for (its version of) the report's recommendations, but also, through the war metaphor, helps to sustain and reproduce dominant ideological representations of the drugs issue.

I have suggested that this example is representative of a relatively stable discourse type, but the restructuring within media discourse of boundaries between public and private orders of discourse, and the emergence of various forms of public-colloquial discourse, are striking features of the modern media which invite historical analysis. What we have here is a creative articulation of public and private orders of discourse which has become conventionalized. But the picture is rather more complex, in the sense that in the context of constant renegotiation of the public/private boundary, the heterogeneity of texts such as this might under certain circumstances be perceived as contradictions, and the relatively stable discourse type might come to be destabilized.

5

INTERTEXTUALITY AND THE NEWS

In this chapter I shall elaborate upon what I said in Chapter 4 about intertextual analysis of media texts, and in particular apply such analysis to some sample texts. Recall that intertextual analysis is a bridge between the 'text' and 'discourse practice' dimensions in the critical discourse analysis framework. It is an analysis of texts from the perspective of discourse practice, and more specifically from the perspective of 'discourse process' – in terms of the ways in which genres and discourses available within the repertoires of orders of discourse are drawn upon and combined in producing and consuming texts, and the ways in which texts transform and embed other texts which are in chain relationships with them.

This chapter will be centred around analyses of sample media texts which focus upon three aspects of intertextual analysis: the analysis of 'discourse representation', of how the speech and writing of others is embedded within media texts; generic analysis of discourse types, alternative theories of genre, and analysis of narrative; analysis of (configurations of) discourses in texts. First, however, I shall develop what I said in Chapter 4 about 'discourse types'.

Discourse types

I introduced the concept of 'discourse type' for the configurations of genres and discourses which actually occur, and which may become more or less stable and conventionalized within orders of discourse. In accordance with the twin perspectives discussed in Chapter 4, the focus in analysing discourse types may be either on orders of discourse and the stabilization – and destabilization – of discourse types within them; or upon communicative events, and particular configurations of genres and discourses articulated together in particular communicative events. Discourse types may involve complex configurations of several genres and several discourses, or may be closely modelled on single genres and discourses. In addition to genre and discourse, it is helpful to have other categories available for the intertextual analysis of discourse types. I find the following useful: *activity type, style, mode*, and *voice* (see Fairclough 1992a for a somewhat different account). Discourse types also differ in how they handle intertextual chain relations.

These categories are not, however, all of equal status. A genre is a way of using language which corresponds to the nature of the social practice that is being engaged in; a job interview, for instance, is associated with the special way of using language we call 'interview genre'. Discourse types are generally most easily characterized in generic terms. In fact, many analysts would use the term 'genre' in the way in which I am using 'discourse type' (e.g. Kress and Threadgold 1988). I am reluctant to do so, because discourse types often draw upon two or more genres – some types of job interview, for instance, have developed a discourse type which mixes interview genre with informal conversation. However, genre is the overarching category for analysing discourse types, and some discourse types are closely modelled on single genres.

I have defined a discourse as a particular way of constructing a particular (domain of) social practice (compare Foucault 1972, Gee 1990). Discourses are relatively independent of genres, in the sense that, for instance, a technocratic medical discourse might show up in interviews, lectures, news items or textbooks. There are, nevertheless, compatibilities and incompatibilities between genres (or genre mixes) and discourses, and one aspect of analysing a discourse type is to uncover these. It is necessary to specify both which fields (topics, subject-matters) are associated with a genre (see Chapter 6), and which discourses are drawn upon to construct these.

Styles, modes and voices (Bakhtin 1986) are ways of using language associated with particular relationships between producer and audience (writer and reader, speaker and listener). Modes are associated with particular media (spoken or conversational versus written modes). Voices are the identities of particular individual or collective agents. One feature of genres or combinations of genres is the styles, modes and voices associated with them. Finally, the compositional structure of a discourse type, its organization as a structured sequence of parts (activities), I shall refer to as its 'activity type' (Levinson 1979). Many accounts of genre emphasize activity type, and the term genre is often used in effect to mean activity type. This is, I think, a mistake, because it easily leads to the other categories I have introduced being ignored.

So far I have been referring to the axis of *choice* in the intertextual analysis of discourse types – to (combinations of) genres, discourses, styles, modes and voices selected from those socially available within orders of discourse. Discourse types also differ in terms of the types of intertextual *chain* relation they enter into with other discourse types, and ways in which texts are transformed along chains and embedded within subsequent texts in the chain (Foucault 1972). As I shall suggest in detail below, for instance, one striking feature of news discourse is the way in which it weaves together representations of the speech and writing of complex ranges of voices into a web which imposes order and interpretation upon them. The treatment of discourse representation (in the terms of traditional grammar, 'reported speech') is quite different in news and, for instance, the law, or ordinary conversation.

There are no definitive lists of genres, discourses, or any of the other categories I have distinguished for analysts to refer to, and no automatic procedures for deciding what genres etc. are operative in a given text. Intertextual analysis is an interpretative art which depends upon the analyst's judgement and experience. Of course, the analyst does have the evidence of language, and the most satisfactory intertextual analyses are those where the identification of genres, discourses and other categories in a text is supported by features of and distinctions within the language of the text. The labelling of intertextual categories may, moreover, be at varying levels of specificity. Different analysts might, for instance, depending upon their purpose and focus, identify the same text generically as interview, media interview, news interview, aggressive type of news interview, and so forth.

I see texts as drawing upon these intertextual categories, rather than, say, 'containing' or 'instantiating' them. They are models, ideal types, which are part of people's productive and interpretative resources. In identifying a category as operative in a text, the analyst is suggesting that it will be oriented to by those who produce and consume the text. One consequence is that a category may be marked or evoked by even the most minimal textual cue – a single word, a detail of oral delivery, a detail of visual appearance in the case of a written or televisual text. Moreover, particular textual features may be ambivalent, or polysemous, with respect to intertextual categories – it may be unclear, for instance, which genre a word evokes, or it may evoke more than one. The categories can be thought of as models which are summations of people's textual experience, and in drawing upon them people are making intertextual and historical links with prior texts or text types within their experience.

In the terms of the critical discourse analysis framework introduced in Chapter 4, the analysis of discourse types cuts across textual analysis, analysis of discourse practice (processes of text production and processes of text consumption), and sociocultural analysis. In addition to my concern here with intertextual analysis, discourse types require linguistic analysis and analysis of productive and consumptional situations and routines. And sociocultural analysis needs to address such issues as the relations of power that underlie the emergence and continuity of particular discourse types, ideological effects that might be associated with them, ways in which they construct social identities, cultural values that they project, and so forth.

From the perspective of discourse practice, the possibilities for creative reconfiguration of genres and discourses seem unlimited, but these creative processes are in fact substantially constrained by the sociocultural practice the discourse is embedded within, and in particular by relations of power. It is therefore important to combine a theory of discourse practice which highlights the productivity of discourse types with a theory of power – as I indicated in Chapter 4, I find the Gramscian theory of hegemony a particularly useful one. Part of the (cultural) hegemony of a dominant class or group is hegemony within the order of discourse – control over the internal and external economies of discourse types, i.e. over how genres and discourses are articulated together to constitute discourse types, and the boundaries and relationships between discourse types within orders of discourse. In this regard, analysis is needed of the relationships – of complementarity, opposition, resistance, etc. – between discourse types within and across orders of discourse. My objectives in this chapter, however, will be more modest. I shall use particular samples of media discourse to develop what I have said so far about particularities of intertextual chaining associated with discourse types, analysis of generic aspects of discourse types, and analysis of discourses and combinations of discourses in discourse types.

Discourse representation in media texts

A very high proportion of media output in news, current affairs and documentary consists of the mediation of the speech or writing of, mainly, prominent people in various domains of public life – politicians, police and lawyers, many categories of experts, and so forth. Sometimes such people speak for themselves – they may write articles in newspapers, they may be interviewed on radio, or they may be filmed and interviewed on television. Sometimes their discourse is represented by newsreaders or reporters. Here is an extract from a radio news slot that constitutes part of the BBC Radio 4 *Today* programme, broadcast every weekday morning between 6.30 a.m. and 8.40 a.m. It illustrates how a single news item commonly weaves together representations of the discourse of a number of people. Another way of putting it is in terms of 'voices': a complex web of voices is woven. (Stressed words are italicized.)

NEWSREADER: Libya has told the United Nations that it's willing to let the two men accused of the Lockerbie bombing come to Scotland to stand trial. The position was spelt out in New York last night by the Foreign Minister, Omar Al-Muntasir, when he emerged from a meeting with the Secretary-General, Dr Boutros-Ghali.

OMAR AL-MUNTASIR: The answers we have received from the UK and the US through the Secretary-General are very acceptable to us and we see them as a positive e: answer and enough guarantees to secure a fair . trial for these two suspects once they submit themselves to e: such jurisdiction.

NEWSREADER: Libyan officials at the UN, faced by the threat of more sanctions, said they wanted more time to sort out the details of the handover. Relatives of the 270 people who died on Flight 103 in December 1988 are treating the statement with caution. From the UN, our correspondent John Nian.

CORRESPONDENT: Western diplomats still believe Libya is playing for time. However on the face of it Libya does appear to be inching closer to handing over the two suspects. If this initiative *is* only a delaying tactic, its aim would be to persuade the waverers on the Security Council not to vote for the new sanctions, in what *is* likely to be a close vote. However the UN Secretary-General is reported to have been taking a tough line with Libya, demanding that it specify exactly when the two suspects would be handed over. The Libyan Foreign Minister has promised a reply on that point later today, but he's asked for more time to arrange the handover. Meanwhile the West has maintained the pressure on Libya. The Foreign Secretary Douglas Hurd, and the American Secretary of State Warren Christopher, have both reiterated the threat of sanctions. Western diplomats say that unless the two suspects *are* handed over immediately, a new resolution will be tabled tomorrow.

(*Today*, BBC Radio 4, 30 September 1993).

It is also worth noting how this story appears in the news 'headlines' at the beginning of the programme – rather a misnomer, because they are more like lead paragraphs in newspapers than headlines: *Libya has now told the United Nations that it is willing to see the two men accused of the Lockerbie bombing stand trial in Scotland, but it cannot meet the deadline to hand them over.*

The voices here – those speaking or whose speech is represented – are: the BBC (differentiated into the newsreader and the BBC UN correspondent), the Libyans (differentiated into 'Libya', Libyan officials at the UN, and the Libyan Foreign Minister), 'the West' (differentiated into western diplomats, the British Foreign Secretary and the US Secretary of State), the UN Secretary-General, and an unspecified reporter (*the UN Secretary-General is reported to have been taking a tough line*). Those who actually speak are the newsreader, the correspondent, and the Libyan Foreign Minister. In addition, speech (*answers* and *guarantees*) is attributed to 'the UK' and 'the US' by the Libyan Foreign Minister, though there is no representation of what was said beyond identification of the types of speech act. *Threat* in *faced by the threat of more sanctions* is similar, though in this case the voice is not identified – nearer the end of the report the (reiteration of the) threat is attributed, to the British Foreign Secretary and the US Secretary of State, though here again only the speech act is identified. There are also two cases where representations can rationally only be based upon what has been said, yet they are not formulated as representations of discourse: *Relatives of the 270 people who died on Flight 103 in December 1988 are treating the statement with caution*, and *Western diplomats still believe Libya is playing for time*. The first is formulated as a representation of action (*treating . . . with caution*), the second as a representation of thought (*believe*) – what they are doing and thinking, rather than saying. This gives us another voice, that of the relatives. (See discussion of the analysis of the 'population' of a text in Talbot 1990.)

An important variable in the representation of discourse is the degree to which boundaries are maintained between the representing discourse and the represented discourse – between the voices of the reporter and the person reported. One way of maintaining boundaries is to allow people to speak for themselves, as the Libyan Foreign Minister does. Even if this does not happen, it is possible to quote what was said directly. In writing, direct quotation is marked off by quotation marks, and even in speech reporters can use intonation to put a quote in vocal 'quotation marks'. Direct quotations also preserve the original wording, not, for instance, changing the tense of verbs, the person of pronouns, or 'deictic' words such as *this* and *here*. Compare the direct quotation *She said: 'I want you here now'* with the summary *She said she wanted them there then*. In traditional grammar, the former is called 'direct speech' and the *quotation* direct speech'.

In this example, apart from where the BBC correspondent and the Libyan Foreign Minister speak for themselves, boundaries between reporting and reported voices are not strongly maintained. The represented discourse is integrated into the representing discourse, summarized rather than quoted, using indirect speech in many cases. One feature of indirect speech is that although it is expected to be accurate about the propositional content of what was said, it is ambivalent about the actual words that were used – it may simply reproduce them, or it may transform and translate them into discourses which fit more easily with the reporter's voice. An interesting example is: *Libyan officials at the UN, faced by the threat of more sanctions, said they wanted more time to sort out the details of the handover*. Is *the handover* the Libyan formulation, or a translation of what the Libyans actually said into another discourse? We can compare this formulation with the one used by the Libyan Foreign Minister: *once they submit themselves to such jurisdiction*. Other reports suggest that there is in fact a clash of perspectives and discourses in this political confrontation, that 'the West' talks in terms of Libya handing over the suspects, whereas Libya talks in terms of giving them the option of standing trial in Scotland.

Reports are rarely even-handed with all the various voices represented. Some are given prominence, and some marginalized. Some are used to frame others. Some are legitimized by being taken up in the newsreader's or reporter's voice, others are not. Equity and balance cannot be assessed by merely noting which voices are represented, and, for instance, how much space is given to each; the web of voices is an often subtle ordering and hierarchization of voices. For instance, *hand over* is used six times, as a noun or a verb. It is used in representations of the discourse of the Libyan officials, the Libyan Foreign Minister, the UN Secretary-General, western diplomats, and it is also given the legitimacy of being used in the voices of the *Today* anchor person (who reads the opening headlines), the newsreader, and the BBC UN correspondent. It is located in two informationally prominent positions in the story, in the headline which gives a prominent and authoritative summary of the whole story, and at the end of the story. By contrast, the other formulation occurs only once, in a backgrounded position (in a subordinate clause) within the statement by the Libyan Foreign Minister, which is itself in an unprominent position in the middle of the report. The formulation in the newsreader's first sentence (*let the two men . . . stand trial*) is ambivalent between these two alternatives.

Another more general point about positioning in the report is that Libyan voices are more prominent in the earlier part of the report, whereas in the second half of the report, from the BBC UN correspondent, the voices of 'the West' and the UN – both portrayed as critical of the Libyan position – are dominant. The last three sentences, from *Meanwhile*, wrap up the report with western voices, with the last sentence summarizing what is implicitly a western dismissal of the Libyan overture, and containing a threat. Despite appearances of 'balance' which are important to creating an impression of objectivity, it is often easy to divide voices into *protaganists* and *antagonists* (Martin 1986) – in this case, 'the West' and Libya respectively.

Sentence connectors (*however, meanwhile*) and a conjunction (*but*) are markers of the ordering of voices in the BBC UN correspondent's report (on these and other cohesive devices, see Halliday and Hasan 1976). The first and second sentences are linked with *however*. This sets up a contrast between what western diplomats believe Libya is doing and what Libya appears to be doing. The second and third sentences are interesting. The second sentence is the correspondent's voice, not a representation of another voice. Reporters' statements are generally authoritative, but this one is doubly hedged (*on the face of it, appear to be*), so there is little conviction expressed that Libya is actually moving towards a 'handover'. ('Hedges' are devices for toning down what you say to reduce its riskiness, e.g. to make it sound less assertive or more polite. See Brown and Levinson 1978.) Sentences 2 and 3 are also in a contrastive relationship though there is no marker of it, in that there is an implicit shift in sentence 3 back to the voice of the western diplomats in the formulation of Libya's 'aim' (*to persuade the waverers on the Security Council not to vote for new sanctions*).

However in sentence 4 sets the 'tough' voice of the UN Secretary-General against the hypothetical manipulative 'aim' of Libya. Sentence 5 is the only one in the correspondent's report that represents a Libyan voice, though the *but* in the sentence implicitly contrasts positive and negative sides of the Libyan Foreign Minister's response to the UN Secretary-General – his 'promise' and his request for more time. Finally, *meanwhile* draws a line between these diplomatic moves and what 'the West' is doing, using the latter to frame and to minimize the former.

Analysis of 'framing' draws attention to how surrounding features of the reporting discourse can influence the way in which represented discourse is interpreted. Framing can be blatantly manipulative. For instance, instead of *said* in *Libyan officials . . . said they wanted more time . . .*, we might have had (in certain newspapers, for instance) *claimed* or even *made out* – reporting verbs which question the truthfulness of what the officials said. This report is not blatant, however; it is more subtle in its framing. On the face of it, the Libyan voices are treated equitably, being given the headline and the lead (opening sentences) in the report as well as the recorded statement by the Libyan Foreign Minister. In accordance with the ethos of public service broadcasting, the report is *designed* as 'objective' and 'balanced'. Nevertheless, framing and the subtle management of audience interpretation are there.

Consider, for instance, how the Libyan Foreign Minister's statement is framed within the newsreader's discourse. Characteristically, it is preceded by a sentence which both gives the time, place and situational context of the statement, and formulates what it says (*the position was spelt out* – where 'the position' is that Libya is willing to let the two men go to Scotland to stand trial). But the gist of what the Foreign Minister actually says is that the UK and US have given Libya acceptable guarantees that the men would receive a fair trial, and their going to Scotland is referred to only hypothetically and non-factively in a backgrounded subordinate clause (with the conjunction *once*). The newsreader's framing thus points the audience towards a misleading interpretation of what was said.

There is further interpretative framing of Libyan voices after the Libyan Foreign Minister's statement. The statement that Libyan officials wanted more time is framed by *faced by the threat of more sanctions*, which might imply a ploy to deflect more sanctions (compare the correspondent's statement *western diplomats still believe Libya is playing for time*). And the following non-attributed formulation of the position of the relatives of those who died (*relatives*

. . . are treating the statement with caution) frames the newsreader's whole representation of the Libyan initiative, and casts doubt upon it. Yet no evidence is given to justify this authoritative statement about the views of a large number of people. It is significant that this unsubstantiated piece of interpretation is positioned after the carefully substantiated account of the Libyan position: the aura of objectivity has been established, and interpretation now perhaps stands a good chance of passing as fact.

Let me mention just one more instance of framing and interpretation management, the correspondent's sentence about the UN Secretary-General. The first part of the sentence (before the comma) is a partly attributed interpretation of what the Secretary-General is claimed to have said (partly attributed in the sense that source is not identified), which frames the following 'demand' that Libya specify exactly when the two suspects would be 'handed over'. The choice of reporting verb, *demanding*, of course further frames and reinterprets what the Secretary-General is reported to have said. Readers are firmly guided towards an interpretation of Boutros-Ghali's words which is negative for Libya.

The report from the *Sun* newspaper discussed in Chapter 4 makes quite an interesting contrast with the Radio 4 news report. The former is much more populist than the latter, and there is a much clearer sense of the source document being translated into a simulated conversational discourse – recall the use of (drug) *pushers* alongside the document's *traffickers*, and the elaborated metaphor of a 'battle' to 'fight off' the 'invasion' of the drug pushers. Another contrast is that the *Sun* shifts overtly from report to campaign – notably in the headline *Call Up Forces in Drug Battle!*, which the radio news does not do. The style of the radio news is much closer to its official sources – in contrast to the other more magazine-type elements of the *Today* programme, which are populist though in a rather different way from the *Sun*.

My main point above has been to suggest that news reports (and the same is true for instance, in documentaries) include mechanisms for ordering voices, subjecting them to social control. The mere fact that a plethora of voices is included in media treatments of social and political issues does not entail an absence of control, merely that the question of how voices are woven together, how they are ordered with respect to each other, becomes decisive. Television adds an important extra dimension in that the voices are often given bodily forms, movement and action through film, which means that relationships within a programme as a visual experience, and questions of how a variety of voices may be given a visual closure, need to be addressed. But attention to the weave of the web is a common concern across press, radio and television.

Generic analysis of discourse types

My objective in this section is to compare three different conceptions of genre in terms of their value in analysing discourse types in the media. Rather than opting entirely for one of these and rejecting the others, I want to argue that the analysis of discourse types should incorporate the insights of all three, but that it needs to do so in a way which avoids the overly rigid view of genre which characterizes the first of them. The final part of this section is a discussion of narrative.

Genre: schematic view

The first view of genre I shall call the schematic view, in which a genre is seen as what I am calling an activity type: a schematic structure made up of stages, either all obligatory or some obligatory and some optional, which occur in a fixed or partially fixed order. This view of genre is common amongst linguists, and perhaps the best-known example is in a paper on analysis of conversational narratives by Labov and Waletzky (1967). It has also been widely used by systemic linguists especially in Australia, and has been at the centre of an intense debate about the teaching of genre (see Cope and Kalantzis 1993, Threadgold 1989).

I have already illustrated the schematic view of genre in discussing the article on drugs from the *Sun* (Figure 2, page 69) at the end of Chapter 4. On page 72 I referred to the 'generic structure' of the article as consisting of: Headline + Lead + Satellites + Wrap-up. The order of these four stages is fixed – the Lead cannot, for instance, precede the Headline. As the example showed, the Headline can be complex – the article actually had a major and a minor Headline. It also had a two-paragraph Lead – the first two paragraphs summarize the gist of the whole story. There are then eight Satellite paragraphs which elaborate various aspects of the story. It is characteristic of satellite paragraphs that there is little progression within them – they could be quite extensively reordered without disrupting the story. They all link back to the Lead, but they are relatively independent of one another. There is, however, some embedding in this case: three of the paragraphs are direct quotations and obviously group together.

Another detail is that the schema allows for the Satellite paragraphs to be divided by sub-headlines – *Profits* in this example. The Wrap-up (which is the one optional stage in this generic schema) consists of the final paragraph of the story, which offers some sort of resolution in the form of future government action. (See Media Literacy Report 1993 for extensive analysis of this sort, and van Dijk 1988a.)

This sort of schematic analysis is good at showing the routine and formulaic nature of much media output, and alerting us, for instance, to the way in which the immense diversity of events in the world is reduced to the often rigid formats of news. But there is a suggestion of its limitations in the main headline of this article. As I pointed out in Chapter 4, it is an imperative sentence with the force of demand. There is, I suggested, a multiplicity of purpose here, with the newspaper campaigning and trying to persuade people as well as give them information about the Committee's findings. Yet simply labelling this as the headline stage of the news report genre fails to capture this.

Generic heterogeneity: sequential and embedded

Van Leeuwen (1987) proposed the second of the three conceptions of genre I want to discuss, precisely to deal with problems of this sort. He suggests that the social purposes of journalism, part overt and part covert, are complex and contradictory – the production of descriptions which can be seen as impartial and objective, but also entertainment, social control, and legitimation. These are social constraints on journalistic practice which are negotiated through selecting options within a network of generic strategies, depending upon the relative salience of these different social purposes on particular occasions. Accordingly, journalists' stories vary extensively in their activity-type structures according to van Leeuwen, and rigid generic schemata cannot account for the actual diversity of output.

This is one of his examples, taken from the Australian (Sydney) newspaper *Daily Mirror*. I have followed van Leeuwen in numbering the separate clauses (simple sentences) of the article:

1   'When Mum first took me to school
2   I started to cry
3   because I thought I would never see her again.'
4   'But after a few days I really loved school' – Mark, aged six.
5   Mark, now 10, quickly discovered starting school wasn't as scary as he thought.

6   Mark was one of the many children teacher-turned-author Valerie Martin spoke to when writing *From Home to School*, a book dealing with the first day.

7   'The first day at school can be a happy and a memorable one', Valerie said.

8   'But the secret is getting ready and preparing now.'

9   Valerie said the main problems for new pupils were separation from families, meeting large numbers of children they didn't know and conforming to a classroom situation.

10 Here are some of Valerie's suggestions to help take the hassle out of the big day.

11 Over the next few days try to get your child used to:
    – putting on and taking off clothes
    – tying shoe laces
    – eating and drinking without help
    – using a handkerchief

12 Valerie says it is important your child knows how to:
    – use and flush a toilet
    – ask for things clearly
    – say his or her name and address
    – cross a road safely

13 On the first day it is important not to rush children.

14 Valerie says give them plenty of time to get ready, eat breakfast, and wash and clean their teeth.

15 If possible, get everything ready the night before

16 because children become unsettled if they have to rush.

17 'And finally don't worry if you or your child cries', Valerie says.

18 'It won't last long.'

Van Leeuwen describes the staging of the article as follows. The article begins (clauses 1–5) with Narration, a story about an individual child, but then after a transitional sentence (6) shifts into Exposition as Valerie – the expert – explains aspects of starting school (7–9), but then after another transitional sentence (10) shifts again into 'Adhortation', urging parents to do certain things (11–18). Actually the picture is rather more complex, because the Exposition and Adhortation stages have, according to van Leeuwen, a 'double structure': as representations of Valerie's discourse they can be called Report or Description – the Exposition and Adhortation comes from Valerie not the reporter, though van Leeuwen suggests that these are purposes of journalism even if they are usually made covert through being mediated via 'experts'.

One important feature of the analysis is that the stages are differentiated on the basis of linguistic features. Each stage can be characterized in terms of a bundle of linguistic features, and the bundles change as we move from stage to stage. For instance, in the Narration clauses (1–5) the conjunctions are mainly temporal (*when, after*), the tense is past, the processes are actional (*took, started to cry*) or mental (*thought, loved*), the characters in the story are the themes (initial elements, most often subjects) of the clauses (*Mum, I*), and reference is to specific individuals. By contrast, in the Exposition clauses (7–9), the conjunction *but* is non-temporal, the tense in the represented discourse clauses in 7 and 8 is present, the main processes are relational (processes of being), and the themes of the clauses are topics rather than people (*the first day at school, the secret*), and reference is generic rather than specific (e.g. *the first day at school* refers to any and all first days at school). The analysis is quite complex – see van Leeuwen's article for more detail, and Chapters 6 and 7 for some of the terminology.

A key point about this analysis is that the stages are predictable parts of a generic schema, but are actually themselves what are usually thought of as *different* genres (e.g. Narrative, Exposition). Van Leeuwen is suggesting that the complex social constraints on journalism and its multiple purposes commonly manifest themselves in generically heterogeneous texts – and indeed that heterogeneity is the norm rather than exceptional. This is, I think, an important insight, and the sort of generic complexity van Leeuwen's method shows up is something to look out for in analysing media texts. But I don't think it tells the whole story about generic heterogeneity. Its limitation is that it deals only with what I have called elsewhere (Fairclough 1992a: 118) *sequential* and *embedded* forms of intertextuality – where different generic types alternate within a text, or where one is embedded within the other (as Exposition and Adhortation are embedded within Report in the example above). What it does not account for is *mixed* intertextuality, where genres are merged in a more complex and less easily separable way, *within* stages of an activity type.

Generic heterogeneity: polyphonic

One example of mixed intertextuality was the extract I discussed in Chapter 1 from the BBC Television education programme 'Slippery When Wet', from a series on engineering called *The Works* (page 8). I suggested that the extract was an instance of conversationalization of public (scientific) discourse, and involved the mixing of scientific exposition with features of conversation – a sort of conversational modulation of the genre of scientific exposition. It is not possible to isolate distinct parts of the extract as either exposition or conversation. I pointed out, for instance, that even where the words as they appear in the transcription seem to be straightforwardly scientific exposition, the voice which speaks them, in terms both of accent and delivery, conversationally modulates the exposition. There are also instances of conversational vocabulary (e.g. *booze*) in expositional clauses. In contrast with the sequential intertextuality described by van Leeuwen where stages are realized in configurations of congruent linguistic features, in mixed intertextuality we find configurations of non-congruent, contradictory linguistic features. In addition to this mixture, however, when we bring the visual images and sound effects into the picture it seems that the genre of scientific exposition is simultaneously modulated in another direction. Images and sounds are articulated together in a complex and fast-moving way which is reminiscent of pop video, and which in broad terms adds the modulation of entertainment to the mix of scientific exposition and conversation.

This may seem to be a rather exceptional example, and it may give the impression that mixed genre texts are rather unusual in the media. I don't think that is so at all. I referred in Chapters 1 and 3 to conversationalization, the colonization of the discursive practices of the media by private domain practices, as a pervasive feature of the contemporary media. Conversationalization is precisely the sort of modulation I have referred to in this example, productive of mixed forms of intertextuality where the text is, as it were, generically polyphonic (Bakhtin 1986). For example, various forms of media interview, including political interviews and chat show interviews with, for instance, show-business celebrities, are now standardly conversationally modulated, to varying degrees. Indeed, the three-way mix which we have in a rather unusual form in the extract from 'Slippery When Wet' between more traditional discourse practices in the public service tradition, elements of conversation, and elements of entertainment, is generally evident in a great deal of media output, as I suggested in Chapter 1 when identifying two major simultaneous tendencies in discourse change affecting media: conversationalization, and marketization.

This third view of genre focuses less upon activity-type structures associated with genres than the other views, bringing also questions of genre-associated styles, modes and voices more into the picture. For instance, conversational modulation of scientific exposition is a matter of both style and of mode – a mixing of the language of private-domain relationships with the language of public-domain relationships, and a mixing of the language of face-to-face interaction with the language of mass communication. Also, one aspect of conversational modulation, the reporter's accent, projects a particular identity and voice.

It is not my intention to choose between these three views of genre. All of them contain insights about media discourse. In part this is because of the diversity of media output: it is possible to find cases which have the formulaic properties predicted by the schematic view of genre, cases where diversity of purpose is mapped on to the staging of the activity-type structure of genre as in van Leeuwen's account, and cases where there is a more radical deconstruction of genre boundaries, and emergent new genres such as the radical-television-science genre of 'Slippery When Wet'. In part it is because the three views of genre to some extent complement one another. For instance, van Leeuwen's position does not entail that the formulaic structure which has been attributed to hard-news stories, Headline + Lead + Satellites (+ Wrap-up) is wrong. The same story can have this formulaic structure and the sort of sequentially intertextual generic structure van Leeuwen discusses, they are not mutually exclusive. Van Leeuwen's position is better seen as a claim that such a terribly abstract formula or schema does not tell us enough about staging in activity-type structure – though it does tell us something. Similarly, the second and third views focus on different aspects of generic heterogeneity – van Leeuwen's view on heterogeneity in activity-type staging, the third view on heterogeneity in the styles, modes and voices associated with genres. Again, the same text can have both sequential and mixed intertextuality. What I am suggesting, then, is that it is helpful to keep all three views of genre in mind in doing analysis, and consider their relevance and usefulness for each piece of analysis.

Narrative

A substantial proportion of media output consists of narratives. According to Swales (1990), narrative is a 'pre-genre': it is broadly genre-like in being a way of using language associated with a particular category of purposeful social activity, but it is so pervasive a way of using language and there are so many distinct types of narrative (each of which can be seen as a genre in its own right) that it would be misleading to treat it as an ordinary genre.

Journalists themselves talk about 'stories', not only in connection with news programmes but also, for instance, in documentaries

(Silverstone 1985), even applying the term to items which are not really narratives at all. One obvious reason why narratives are so prominent in the media is that the very notion of reporting centrally involves recounting past events, i.e. telling the story of what happened, and much of media output consists of or includes reports. But the social purposes of journalism are, as we saw above, complex; journalists don't only recount events, they also interpret and explain them, try to get people to see things and to act in certain ways, and aim to entertain. The concept of a 'story' suggests this multiplicity of purpose, in that we normally think of stories as forms of entertainment and diversion, and often fictional rather than factual. In fact, not all news stories have this character. There may be important variations linked to class. The 'stories' of news are far more story-like in this sense in outlets for predominantly working-class audiences: 'stories are for those who, because of their social status and education, are denied the power of exposition, while exposition is for those who have been given the right to participate in the debates that may change society' (van Leeuwen 1987: 199).

Theories of narrative standardly distinguish two facets of a narrative: (a) the actual *story*, a basic, chronologically ordered series of events including the participants (or 'actants') involved in them; and (b) the *presentation*, the way is which the story is realized and organized as a particular text (Toolan 1988). Presentation is often called *discourse*, but adding another meaning to that term is confusing. The story element of a narrative raises issues of representation and issues relating to the ideational function of the language, whereas the presentation element raises issues of identity and of relations relating to the interpersonal function.

Montgomery (1991) makes use of this distinction in his analysis of 'Our Tune', referred to in Chapter 2 (page 91). The ideological focus of the stories is the family: a story typically involves a problem arising out of family life, which is resolved within and through the family. This gives stories a Complication + Resolution structure, where the Complication involves some destabilization of family harmony and the Resolution is restoration of harmony, which may be cyclically repeated within a story.

One aspect of presentation in narrative is the issue of generic structure or staging discussed in the previous section. Montgomery uses and develops the influential work of Labov (1972) on conversational narrative. This approach stresses that the staging of a narrative involves not only 'event-line' (story) elements concerned with recounting events, but also non-event-line elements which relate to presentation, 'the management of the discursive event as a bounded whole', or to its reception by the audience. The salience of non-event-line elements in media narratives is a measure of the degree to which stories are mediated by presenters. They include Framing elements which manage the transition between the rest of the programme and 'Our Tune', Focusing elements which give a preliminary indication of what a narrative is about, and Situating elements which define the temporal and spatial parameters of the events narrated. Let me illustrate another element, Orientation. Orientations function on the one hand to orient the audience behind the experience of a character, to generate empathy towards the character. For example:

> so you can imagine
> not only has she tried to top herself and got herself taken to hospital
> but now as she's recovering from that she's had the biggest blow or one
> of the biggest blows you can have

Or, on the other hand, they function to anticipate audience reaction:

> and one night
> you guessed it
> she took half a bottle of pills

Other elements include Evaluations, which take the form of general maxims on the model of 'these things do happen'; and Codas, which make the transition from (the time frame of) the narrative to the present. Some of these elements are positionally rigid (e.g. Framing comes at the beginning and the end of a narrative), others (e.g. Orientation or Evaluation) are positionally quite flexible.

Other aspects of narrative presentation discussed by Montgomery are to do with the relationship between Simon Bates and the writer of the letter (the Broadcast Narrator and the Epistolary Narrator), and Simon Bates and the audience. There is a contradiction and a tension between the genres of confessional personal letter that is the material for 'Our Tune' and public narrative within the programme, which manifests itself, for instance, in the handling of judgements of the Epistolary Narrator's behaviour. Self-assessments in a confessional mode (e.g. *I went haywire*) cannot be directly transformed into public narrative without acquiring a strong condemnatory force. Hence the frequency of hedges which tone down reported self-assessments (e.g. *I guess* and *a little* in *so I guess Marianne went a little haywire*). The relationship between Simon Bates and the audience makes sense of one interesting linguistic feature of 'Our Tune', the frequency of interpolations which reformulate an immediately preceding formulation, such as *the elder sister* in *er the sister the elder sister became the person who looked after everybody.* Such interpolations show an ongoing orientation by Bates to possible interpretative problems or misunderstandings by the audience. Along with the extensive non-event-line elements in the generic staging, they are indicative of the extent to which the Epistolary Narrator's tale is mediated by Bates. The interpolations also have an identity function, providing 'a repetitive signalling of the DJ's role as "honest broker" of the story materials' (Montgomery 1991: 164).

A further feature of narrative presentation is the extent to which the material dealt with is presented as scandalous or risky and needing to be negotiated with delicacy. Montgomery suggests that this tendency is indicative of the influence upon 'Our Tune' of fictional narrative models, creating a tension between pressure to fictionalize and sensationalize the narratives, and pressure to establish their authenticity and truth. A tension, in broader terms, between entertainment and information. Recall in this connection the extract from the *This Week* programme 'Vigilante!' discussed in Chapter 1. I suggested that in that case the tension manifested itself in a contradiction between the dramatic and sensational representation of events in the film, and the more cautious, explanatory and expositional representation of events in the linguistic commentary.

If the analysis of narrative presentation draws attention to how narratives are fictionalized in response to pressures to entertain, it also draws attention to factuality as a property of narratives which is discursively achieved. There is a range of devices within the rhetoric of factuality which are standardly drawn upon in the production of, for instance, news stories, involving visual and aural semiotics as well as language, including the layout of the newsroom, the opening sequence and theme music of the news programme, the appearance of the newsreader. One objective here has to be the creating of a sense of authority, though even in news that may come into conflict with the pressure to entertain. (For example, at the time of writing, there is some discussion in the British press about whether changes to the format of the prestigious ITN *News at Ten*, which includes a dramatic opening sequence and a 'space-age' newsroom, have undermined the authority of the well-known newsreader Trevor Macdonald.) Within the language, the attribution of news statements to authoritative sources is a key part of the rhetoric of factuality, profoundly affecting the structuring of news texts with respect to the construction of complex embedding relationships between voices (interviews, reports, film sequences, and, of course, discourse representation). The section on discourse representation above provided some illustration.

Another important area here is modality, and in particular the prevalence of various linguistic realizations of categorical modalities which make strong truth claims. Recall the discussion of the *Panorama* extract in Chapter 1. Also important is presupposition: as I show in Chapter 6, presupposition helps to authenticate the new by locating it within a matrix of purportedly given (presupposed) information.

Analysis of discourses in texts

Discourses are, as I have indicated, constructions or significations of some domain of social practice from a particular perspective. It is useful to identify discourses with names which specify both domain and perspective – for instance, one might contrast a Marxist political discourse with a liberal political discourse, or a progressive educational discourse with a conservative educational discourse. I shall illustrate the analysis of texts in terms of discourses using press coverage of an air attack on Iraq by the USA, Britain and France on 13 January 1993 (two years after the Gulf War), referring to 14 January editions of five British newspapers: the *Daily Mirror*, the *Sun*, the *Daily Mail*, the *Daily Telegraph* and the *Guardian*, and the *Guardian Weekly* for the week ending 24 January 1993. I focus upon two issues: the 'congruent' as opposed to 'metaphorical' selection of discourses for formulating who did what to whom and why within the attack; and the role of *configurations* of discourses in the construction of these events.

The distinction between congruent and metaphorical discourses is the extension of a terminology used by Halliday (1985). A congruent application is the use of a discourse to signify those sorts of experience it most usually signifies; a metaphorical application is the extension of a discourse to signify a sort of experience other than that which it most usually signifies. The distinction is a rough one, but a useful one. Metaphorical applications of discourses are socially motivated, different metaphors may correspond to different interests and perspectives, and may have different ideological loadings. The following examples (headlines and lead paragraphs) illustrate how congruent and metaphorical discourses combine in the coverage of the attack.

> *Spank You And Goodnight*
> *Bombers Humble Saddam in 30 Minutes*
> More than 100 Allied jets yesterday gave tyrant Saddam Hussein a spanking – blasting missile sites in a raid that took just 30 minutes. (*Sun*)

Saddam's UN Envoy Promises Good Behaviour After Raid by US, British and French Aircraft
Gulf Allies Attack Iraqi Missiles
More than 100 aircraft blasted Iraqi missile sites last night after the allies' patience with Saddam Hussein's defiance finally snapped. (*Daily Telegraph*)

In the examples I looked at, it is a discourse of military attack that is congruently applied (e.g. *jets* or *aircraft blasting missile sites* and *Gulf Allies Attack Iraqi Missiles* in the examples above). Not surprisingly, we find such formulations in all the reports, along with expressions like 'retaliate' and 'hit back' (e.g. *Iraq To Hit Back*, in the *Sun*) which represent these events as a contest between two military powers. But there are distinctions to be drawn. Whereas the *Guardian*, the *Daily Mail* and the *Daily Telegraph* use what one might call an 'official' discourse of military attack – that is, they use the sort of language that might be used in official and military accounts – the *Sun* and the *Daily Mirror* (and exceptionally the *Daily Telegraph* in the example above: *more than 100 aircraft blasted Iraqi missile sites*) use a fictional discourse of military attack, the discourse of stories about war (whether purely fictional, or fictionalized versions of fact), which highlights physical violence. The *Daily Mirror* is particularly rich in expressions for processes of attack which link to this discourse: *blitz, blast, hammer, pound, blaze into action*, (warplanes) *scream in*. While the attacks are mainly formulated as action by aircraft or 'the allies' against 'Iraq' or specific targets (e.g. 'missile sites' or 'control centres'), both the *Daily Mirror* and the *Sun* also formulate them in a personalized way as directed at Saddam Hussein (*The Gulf allies struck hard at Saddam Hussein, 'Spot Raids Give Saddam Pasting', allied warplanes have bombed the hell out of Saddam Hussein*).

The main headline and lead paragraph from the *Sun* above show that formulations of the attack do not by any means draw only upon military discourse: *Spank You And Goodnight* (notice the play on 'Thank you and goodnight' which makes a joke even of this serious event) and *More than 100 Allied jets . . . gave tyrant Saddam Hussein a spanking*. This is a metaphorical application of an authoritarian discourse of family discipline which is a prominent element in representations of the attack – Saddam as the naughty child punished by his exasperated parents. The *Guardian* editorial sums it up as *an act of punishment against a very bad boy who thumbed his nose several times too often* – also notice *the allies' patience . . . finally snapped* and *good behaviour* in the *Daily Telegraph* example, both consistent with this disciplinary discourse. (One might also be tempted to read 'spanking' in terms of a discourse of sexual 'correction'.) The attack is formulated several times in the reports as 'teaching Saddam a lesson' (for instance, *The allies launched 114 war planes to teach defiant Saddam a lesson* in the *Daily Mirror*, and *Let's hope he's learnt his lesson*, attributed to a US official in the *Sun*). This is again consistent with the discourse of family discipline, or disciplinary discourses more generally. So too with *Toe The Line Or . . . We'll Be Back!*, the main page-one headline in the *Daily Mirror*. Such conditional threats ('do x or we'll do y', 'if you do x – or don't do x – we'll do y') occur several times in the report.

A related but rather more specific metaphorical discourse that is evoked is that of the disciplining of young offenders, juveniles found guilty of crimes (with the focus on crimes of particular sorts, such as 'joy-riding'). A British government official is quoted in most reports as saying that the attack was *a short, sharp and telling lesson* for Saddam. This evokes the expression used by the British Conservative government in the 1980s, when it tried to develop the policy of delivering a 'short, sharp shock' (in the form of incarceration in highly disciplined quasi-military institutions) to juvenile offenders. The same group of discourses is indicated in reasons given for the attack. The headline for a report on pages 2–3 of the *Sun* is *He Had It Coming*, and the lead paragraph refers to the *pasting* that Saddam Hussein *has been asking for*. According to the *Daily Mirror*, Saddam had *pushed his luck too far*. These formulations evoke a conversational or 'lifeworld' version of an authority-based discourse of discipline, referring to what is elsewhere frequently formulated in the reports as the 'provocations' of the subordinate party in this disciplinary relationship, i.e. Saddam (note also formulations such as Saddam 'goading' or 'taunting the West'). Disciplinary formulations such as 'provocations' alternate with legalistic formulations such as 'breaches' and 'infringements' (of the UN ceasefire conditions).

The metaphorical application of such discourses is a very prominent feature of these reports, and in assessing that application one might wonder whether such a disciplinary relationship applies or ought to apply in relations between nations, or indeed whether the relations between nations ought to be personalized as they consistently are here: the target of discipline is Saddam, not Iraq or the Iraqi government – whereas its source is mainly 'the (Gulf) allies' or 'the West', and rarely George Bush (the American president at the time).

Other discourses are metaphorically applied, though they are less prominent in the reports. One is evident in the *Sun* headline *Bombers Humble Saddam in 30 Minutes* as well as the *Daily Mail* headlines *Allies*

Humble Saddam and *Retribution in the Gulf*. I think these can be read in terms of a (Christian) religious discourse, though 'retribution' also evokes a legal discourse. Another discourse which features only once here – attributed to a Whitehall official by the *Daily Mirror* – but was quite common in coverage of hostilities in the Gulf at the time, is a discourse of communication exchange, of 'signals' sent through military actions. (In the words of the Whitehall official, *If Saddam does not get this message . . . he knows there will be more to come.*) Again, both the *Sun* and the *Daily Mirror* draw upon a discourse of dangerous-animal control in their editorials: the air strikes are intended to 'curb' Saddam, and if *he doesn't learn this time, he will have to be put down for good like the mad dog he is* (*Daily Mirror*), *the tragedy is that we did not finish him off last time* (the *Sun*).

An important distinction within a report, which takes us back to the discussion of discourse representation earlier in this chapter, is between discourses which occur in represented discourse attributed to the 'voices' of others in quotations or summaries, as opposed to discourses which are unattributed and are drawn upon by the 'voice' of the report itself. However, a key question (which requires historical research and research on production processes) is where the discourses of reporters come from. By comparing attributed and unattributed formulations within and across reports, one can often see the same discourses being drawn upon by reporters and official sources. For example, the discourse of correction (in *Spank You And Goodnight*, also in the *Daily Mirror* inside-page headline *A Spanking Not A Beating* and in the headline of the *Guardian* editorial *More A Smack Than A Strike*) may have originated in a statement by a US official: *It's just a spanking for Saddam, not a real beating.* Similarly the *Sun* headline *He Had It Coming* and more generally 'teach-Saddam-a-lesson' formulations apparently echo official sources – the *Sun* quotes a White House statement: *Saddam had this coming. Let's hope he has learnt his lesson.*

Official influence upon media formulations is built up over the longer term rather than just on a day-by-day basis; 'teach-Saddam-a-lesson' formulations had been widely used officially and by the press for a period before the attack, and similarly official sources including President Bush had spoken of 'patience running out' in the weeks before the attack. (Also, this relatively minor Iraq crisis was intertextually linked to earlier ones including the Gulf War, and fed discoursally from them. See the discussion of 'discourse-historical' method of analysis in Wodak 1990.) The *Guardian*, the *Daily Telegraph* and the *Daily Mail* are more likely generally to use such formulations only as attributions. There is a constant flow between official sources and the media: the latter may take up the discourses of the former, but the former also design their statements and press releases to harmonize with discourses favoured by the media. Bruck (1989) points out that the influence of official discourses on media discourse depends upon the discourse type – it is, for instance, likely to be greater in news reports than in editorials or features.

While the discourses and specific formulations of certain favoured sources are massively present and foregrounded, those of other – and especially oppositional – sources are either omitted altogether from some reports, or backgrounded. For example, the Labour Party left-winger Tony Benn described the attack as the *last piece of gunboat diplomacy* of a *lame-duck US president* according to the *Guardian*, but that was the only report of Benn's comment, and it was backgrounded (positioned in a single paragraph in the middle of a report in the bottom left-hand corner of a centre page). Formulations of the attack attributed to the Kuwaiti government, which draw upon a discourse of disease and surgical intervention (*bursting the abscess of the Baghdad government* according to the Sun, *removing the Iraqi cancer* according to the *Daily Telegraph*), were quite widely reported though backgrounded. By contrast, only the *Guardian* reports formulations of Saddam's actions prior to the attack as 'acrobatics' and 'mere fireworks' (from the newspaper *al-Ahram*, Cairo), and 'clownish' behaviour (*al-Thaurah*, Damascus), constructing Saddam in the less threatening role of a clown/performer (clowns don't generally merit bombing). Significantly, the same reports highlight the 'double standards' applied by the West, in not reacting as vigorously to the plight of Muslims under attack by Serbians in Bosnia, or of the 400 Palestinians extradited by Israel and isolated in No Man's Land between Israel and Lebanon at that time, in defiance of a United Nations resolution. Why no air attacks on Israel?

If selection between alternative congruent and metaphorical discourses is one issue, another is configurations of discourses, how discourses are articulated together within discourse types. Bruck (1989), for instance, suggests that five main discourses were drawn upon by the Canadian media in the mid-1980s in their coverage of disarmament, peace and security issues, which he calls: the discourse of state leaders, bureaucratic-technical discourse, scientific-technical discourse, the discourse of victims, and the discourse of survival. The first three are dominant discourses, the last two oppositional discourses. The analysis of news output is concerned with both the selections made between these discourses, and the ways in which they are articulated together, which between them allow the analyst to describe the range of discursive practice in the coverage of these issues.

The following report was inset in a double-page spread in the *Daily Mirror* of 14 January, dealing with the attack in Iraq. (Major reports are often made up in this way of combinations of smaller reports, and the relationship between articles on a page in such cases is worth attending to.)

The Mother Of All Rantings

Evil dictator Saddam Hussein promised Iraq last night they were winning a new great victory – just like they had in the 'Mother of All Battles' in Kuwait. His pledge came three hours after allied aircraft pounded his missile sites.

In a ranting, confused speech, he told his nation on television that a new jihad – holy war – had begun. He urged the Iraqis to fight 'in the name of God' . . . and he promised them they would humiliate the allies.

Saddam called the allies 'the infidels' and said they were 'under the influence of Satan'. And he raged: 'Every aeroplane of the aggressors in the Iraq sky shall be a target for us and we shall fight in the name of God and down their aircraft. The aggressors will be defeated.'

Reading stiffly from hand-held notes, he said: 'The criminals have come back. But tonight they came back without any cover, not even a transparent one.

'They came back for the purpose they never spoke about the first time in their evil aggression, namely to impose colonialism.'

This report includes a new and clearly oppositional configuration of discourses for formulating the attack, attributed to Saddam himself: an Islamic religious discourse (*infidels, under the influence of Satan*), and political discourses of aggression and colonialism. The reference to the absence of any 'cover' obliquely cues also a legal discourse – the attacks were condemned as 'illegal' by those who opposed them. Notice also that the allies are referred to here as *criminals*.

However, this oppositional configuration of discourses is framed within a larger configuration by the dominant discourses I have discussed above. Saddam's speech is firstly formulated and summed up in the headline in an ironic play upon his own (in)famous description of the Gulf War as 'the mother of all battles', with *rantings* evoking discourses of madness and political fanaticism. In the lead paragraph, Saddam is referred to as an *evil dictator*, deploying the religious and political discourses I referred to earlier as part of the anti-Saddam armoury. The summary of Saddam's speech in the second paragraph is framed by the initial thematized phrase *In a ranting, confused speech*, and similar framing devices are used where Saddam is directly quoted – notice the choice of *raged* as a reporting verb, and *reading stiffly*. In the first two of these cases there is again an evocation of the discourse of madness. The net effect of the framing of Saddam's oppositional discourses with the dominant ones is to undermine and ridicule the former.

Diverse discourses are articulated together in the naming and identification of both the protaganists and the antagonists, though to quite different effects. The identification of the protaganists caused some difficulty in that the USA, Britain and France were claiming to act to enforce a United Nations resolution, but neither the 'no-fly' zone they had imposed on southern Iraq nor the attack had been endorsed by the UN. The attackers are referred to in the reports as 'the Gulf allies', 'the West', and most frequently 'the allies'. 'The Gulf allies' is problematic in that the alliance which fought Iraq in the Gulf War was actually divided on this later attack, and none of the Arab members of the alliance was involved. 'The West' is problematic because a number of members of 'the West' were also critical. 'The allies', with its reassuring evocation of the Second World War, seems to have been the least problematic label. The *Guardian* also refers 'correctly' to 'the United States, Britain and France'. A number of other identifications were used elsewhere: in the *Guardian Weekly* 'the coalition' and 'the US and its allies' were used, and President Clinton was quoted as supporting *the international community's actions*. The variety of these formulations, the range of discourses they draw upon, and the instability of naming practices here, are indicative of the difficulty in constructing an identity for the protaganists.

By contrast, the considerable range of expressions used to refer to Saddam Hussein shows a number of discourses working together to discredit him, as in the following editorial from the *Sun* on 14 January:

Wipe Out The Mad Menace

At long last, Allied warplanes have bombed the hell out of Saddam Hussein.

The Iraqi madman has pushed the West too far.

He has played a dangerous game and now he must pay the price.

Four times Saddam has sent raiding parties over the border into Kuwait.

Menace

His boast that Iraq planned to 'recover' Kuwait was the last straw.

The tinpot tyrant could not be allowed to cling onto power a moment longer.

He is an international terrorist, a constant menace to peace.
The tragedy is that we did not finish him off last time.
Go get him, boys!

This is discoursal overkill: a remarkable range of discourses are articulated together in the verbal annihilation of Saddam Hussein. The
density of the assembled discourses is no doubt attributable to the
fact that the genre is editorial rather than news report: this is an
apologia for the attack, based upon a thorough discrediting of
Saddam Hussein. He is referred to as a *madman*, a *menace to peace*, a
tyrant, a *terrorist*, a *blusterer* (cf. *his boast*), and a figure of ridicule (the
implication of *tinpot*), yet at the same time a calculating politician
(who has *pushed the West too far*, and *played a dangerous game*), and
actions against him are formulated in terms of discourses of legal
retribution (*he must pay the price*), war fiction (*bombed the hell out of*) and
even westerns (*wipe out, finish off, go get him, boys*). We find the range
of discourses extending further elsewhere – he is referred to, for
instance, in the terms of religious and ethical discourses as 'evil' and a
'coward'.

A configuration of discourses is put to different effect in the editorial in the *Guardian Weekly*, where evaluation of competing discourses
is itself a topic. The editorial is a critique of the attack, under the
deadline *What Signal Will He Read?* The editorial is a dialogue with
opposing positions represented by different discourses. Thus it
refers to – and distances itself from – *headmasterly talk of Teaching
Saddam a Lesson*, and attributes the discourse of *delivering a signal* to
Saddam to what it calls *the tough-minded* (this discourse generates the
expression 'coercive bombing' in another report in the same edition).
It does, however, in its own voice draw upon some of the dominant
discourses for formulating Saddam and his actions (he is *evilly brutal
Saddam*, with a *record of provocation* – though perhaps *deliberate*). The
editorial also formulates the attack, tentatively, in a different
discourse: *Mr Bush's likely desire to settle accounts before leaving office.*

Other terms which are roughly equivalent to 'discourses', but derive
from different theoretical frameworks and traditions, are quite
widely used, including schemata, frames, and scripts (from cognitive
psychology), metaphors, and vocabularies. I have discussed metaphorical applications of discourses, and for the most part the discourses I have referred to are realized in the vocabulary of texts.
Aspects of grammar may also be involved in the realization of
discourses. For instance, I noted earlier that conditional threats (e.g.

Toe The Line . . . Or We'll Be Back) are a feature of disciplinary discourse, and these are realized in particular syntactic constructions (in this example, imperative clause + *or* + declarative clause).

Analysis of *collocations* in texts (patterns of co-occurrence between words) is a way of linking analysis of discourses to the linguistic analysis of texts (Sinclair 1992). Configurations of discourses identified in the analysis of discourses may be realized in – condensed into – collocational relations in phrases or clauses (Fairclough 1991). Collocations are often a good place to look for contradictions in texts. For example, in the editorial from the *Sun* above, the following collocations occur: *mad menace, tinpot tyrant, the Iraqi madman has pushed the West too far. Mad* evokes the discourse of madness whereas *menace* evokes the discourse of political extremism, and the collocation bonds the two discourses together in a detail of the text. Similarly, *the Iraqi madman has pushed the West too far* compacts together the discourse of madness and the discourse of political calculation.

Both selections amongst available discourses and selection of particular ways of articulating them together are likely to be ideologically significant choices. There may, for instance, be various ways of rationalizing the decision to construct relations between 'the West' and a 'Third World' country like Iraq as relations between a teacher and a recalcitrant child, but such a construction implicitly evokes an imperialist and indeed racist ideology of relations between nations, which contributes to the continuity of imperialist and neo-colonialist relations in practice. Of course, in accordance with what I said about ideology in Chapter 3, one cannot assume ideological effects consequent upon selections of discourses, merely that the question of potential ideological effects is always worth raising.

6

REPRESENTATIONS IN DOCUMENTARY
AND NEWS

In terms of the framework for analysis of media discourse introduced
in Chapter 4, the focus now shifts from discourse practice and intertextual analysis of texts – the concern of Chapter 5 – to linguistic
analysis of texts. As I indicated in the section on texts in Chapter 4, I
am working with a broad and enhanced understanding of linguistic
analysis which includes, for instance, analysis of relationships
between sentences, or of relationships between speaking turns
within a dialogue. This chapter will deal with one of the three processes which I have argued are always simultaneously going on in a
text: representation. The other two, construction of relations, and
construction of identities, are discussed in Chapter 7. This chapter
will accordingly be mainly concerned with the ideational and textual
functions of language in texts, and Chapter 7 with the interpersonal
function.

The focus, then, is upon how events, situations, relationships,
people, and so forth are represented in texts. A basic assumption is
that media texts do not merely 'mirror realities' as is sometimes
naïvely assumed; they constitute versions of reality in ways which

depend on the social positions and interests and objectives of those who produce them. They do so through choices which are made at various levels in the process of producing texts. The analysis of representational processes in a text, therefore, comes down to an account of what choices are made – what is included and what is excluded, what is made explicit or left implicit, what is foregrounded and what is backgrounded, what is thematized and what is unthematized, what process types and categories are drawn upon to represent events, and so on. Questions about the social motivations for particular choices, and about ideologies and relations of domination, are a constant concern in the analyses of such choices in this chapter. A longer-term goal in analysis of representation is description of networks of available options from which such choices are made. See Halliday (1985) for an account of the systemic grammatical framework which I draw upon here.

There are two major aspects of representation in texts, discussed in turn in this chapter. In a logical terminology, the first has to do with the structuring of propositions, the second with the combination and sequencing of propositions. The first is concerned with how events and relationships and situations are represented. Actually, since the analysis here is linguistic rather than logical, we shall be looking at this question with respect to the *clause,* a term linguists use for a grammatically simple sentence. Clauses roughly correspond to propositions – in many cases, a clause will consist of a single proposition. So the question will be, how is this clause structured in terms of the process (typically realized in its verb), participant (typically realized in its nouns and nominal groups), and circumstantial (typically realized in adverbials) elements it contains? What choices have been made from among the possible types of process, participant and circumstance? For instance, what appears in one text as a relational process without an agent (*life gets harder*) might appear in another text as a causative process with an agent (*the profiteers are making life harder*). The question is, what motivates one set of choices over another?

Turning to the second aspect of representation in texts, concerned with the combination and sequencing of propositions, again, since the analysis is linguistic rather than logical, we shall be looking at this in terms of the combination and sequencing of clauses. We can broadly contrast two levels at which choices are available here (van Dijk 1988a):

1. Local coherence relations between clauses. The initial question is:
(a) how are clauses combined together into the complexes of clauses that are generally referred to as sentences? Actually, 'clause

complex' is a better term for spoken language, because it is often difficult to find units which correspond to the sentences of written language (Halliday 1989). Two further questions within local coherence relations are:

(b) what relations of cohesion are set up between such complexes of clauses (sentences – see Halliday and Hasan 1976)? and

(c) what forms of argumentation are used within different texts?

2. Global text structure. This involves the sort of analysis of genre and activity type that I introduced in Chapter 5. The question here is what choices are made between alternative available activity types or generic schemata in a given text.

At both levels, questions of sequencing – what precedes or follows what, and why – are a central concern, and for that reason I also include in this part of the treatment of representation the thematic (and more generally informational) structuring of clauses. A major concern here is what element of a clause is thematized, placed in initial position, and why.

This chapter links with Chapter 5 not only in the analyses of activity type and generic structure, but also, importantly, with the analysis of discourses. The analysis of discourses shares with the analyses of representation in this chapter a common concern with choices that are made in texts in the representation, signification and construction of reality, and social motivations for these choices. The much more detailed attention to language in this chapter provides a resource both for spelling out how properties of and differences between discourses are realized in the language of the text (in vocabulary, metaphor, grammar), and for specifying the representational options which are available within a particular discourse.

My concern is with the analysis of representation in particular texts, but for certain purposes within media research it will make sense to combine such 'microanalysis' with other forms of text-oriented analysis. If, for example, one wishes to analyse the media coverage of a particular issue such as a war, microanalysis alone will not give the necessary overview. What may also be needed is some form of content analysis which allows, for instance, a generalized comparison of how 'enemy' forces and 'our' forces are represented (see, e.g., Herman and Chomsky 1988, Kellner 1992 on the Vietnam War and the Gulf War). I would, however, argue that close textual analysis is a valuable complement to content analysis in such cases.

Before engaging in analysis of what is in the text, however, one needs to attend to the question of what is excluded from it.

Presences and absences in texts: presupposition

Unsurprisingly, analysis of representation is mainly analysis of what is 'there' in the text. But it is also important to be sensitive to absences from the text, to things which might have been 'there', but aren't – or, and this really comes down to the same thing, to things which are present in some texts appertaining to a given area of social practice, but not in others. For instance, one revealing comparison within the collection of reports about air attacks on Iraq by the USA and its allies discussed in Chapter 5 is between texts which include the topic of civilian casualties and texts which exclude it. Another more specific example of significant absence is from a speech by the British Prime Minister, John Major (Carlton Club, London, 3 February 1993), in which he said, 'I increasingly wonder whether paying unemployment benefit, without offering or requiring any activity in return, serves unemployed people or society well.' The absence here is the word 'Workfare' – the name of the American scheme which requires unemployed people to carry out usually menial work in return for social security benefits. At the time, Workfare was arousing impassioned responses and a great deal of hostility, and Major seems to have been 'testing the water' without wanting to clearly position himself as a target for that hostility. Much of the media coverage treated the absence as a matter of note, but the government was still left with room for manœuvre and the capacity to hedge over whether Workfare was *really* what Major had in mind. A more general absence which commentators have noted is an absence of historical context in most news stories; news is standardly constructed in terms of events which are treated as more or less isolated from prior or subsequent events – isolated from history (Herman and Chomsky 1988, Pilger 1992).

Actually, it makes sense to differentiate degrees of presence, as it were, rather than just contrasting what is present and what is absent. We might think in terms of a scale of presence, running from 'absent' to 'foregrounded': absent – presupposed – backgrounded – foregrounded. If something is presupposed, it is in a sense present in the text, but as part of its implicit meaning. If something is explicitly present in a text, it may be informationally backgrounded, or informationally foregrounded. The distinction between backgrounding and foregrounding will be discussed in the section dealing with combination and sequencing of clauses.

Any text is a combination of explicit meanings – what is actually 'said' – and implicit meanings – what is left 'unsaid' but taken as given, as presupposed. Presuppositions anchor the new in the old, the unknown in the known, the contentious in the commonsensical. A text's presuppositions are important in the way in which it positions its readers or viewers or listeners: how a text positions you is very much a matter of the common-sense assumptions it attributes to you. The presuppositions of a text are part of its intertextuality (and in that sense belong with the concerns of Chapter 5): presupposing something is tantamount to assuming that there are other texts (which may or may not actually exist) that are common ground for oneself and one's readers, in which what is now presupposed is explicitly present, part of the 'said' (Fairclough 1992a). Presuppositions are what French discourse analysts call 'preconstructed' elements in a text, elements which have been constructed elsewhere in other texts (Pêcheux 1982, Williams forthcoming).

In various types of reports and narratives, presuppositions help establish represented realities as convincing. For instance, the opening parts of a documentary need to establish for the audience a reality, a world, which carries conviction as authentic. The following extract occurs near the beginning of a documentary in the Channel 4 *Critical Eye* series, broadcast on 15 October 1992. Called 'Wind of Memory', the programme documents the genocide of the Indian population of Guatemala.

> REPORTER (voice-over): Santiago de Plan. The Sutowilas Indians call this place (Indian language term) the heart of the world. Perhaps that's because the ancient traditions are still so strong in this village. Maybe it's also because Santiago de Plan is the sanctuary of Machimon.

Part of the authenticity in this case is achieved through film, music and sound effect, and through the voice of the reporter (which sounds authentic as Guatemalan). But achieving authenticity is also partly a matter of positioning the viewer through presupposition as someone who is already familiar with the culture and community depicted. The effect of the definite article in *the Sutowilas Indians* is to presuppose the existence of this group of Indians, that is, take it as given knowledge for the audience. The propositions of the two *because*-clauses are also presupposed: it's taken for granted that the ancient traditions *are* still strong, and that Santiago de Plan *is* the sanctuary of Machimon. It is also presupposed that there *are* ancient traditions, and knowledge of the existence of Machimon, and of Machimon being a god, are presupposed.

Another example is the opening of the documentary 'A New Green Revolution?', a television documentary programme in the science documentary series *Horizon*, which was broadcast in January 1984 on BBC2. The programme is about the social and economic effects on the 'Third World' of breeding new high-yielding varieties of staple crops. See Silverstone (1985) for a detailed analysis. Here are the opening words, followed by an extract which occurs shortly afterwards.

> KEITH GRIFFIN (Sync): The difficulty is that if we persist with our current line, looking for technological solutions to socio-economic problems, then we will run out of time. These problems of impoverishment, inequality, social tension, of conflict, will explode.

> KEITH GRIFFIN (voice-over): Normally the crisis in the Third World, poverty, inequality, hunger, is a silent crisis. Only occasionally does the crisis of the peasantry erupt in the form of violence and civil discord.

There are many presuppositions here which again draw the viewer into the common-sense assumptions, the world-view, upon which the programme is founded. For instance, it is presupposed that there is a difficulty, that our current line is a bad one (implied by *persist with*), that this line is attributable to all of 'us', that we are trying to achieve something in a limited amount of time, that what we are trying to achieve is the avoidance of an explosion (we need this presupposition to make a coherent connection between the two sentences of the first extract), that there is a crisis in the Third World, that there is a crisis of the peasantry. In addition, there are presuppositions associated with the major categories drawn upon here, such as 'the Third World'. Actually, it is not simply presupposed that the Third World exists, it is presupposed that the expression *Third World* is *the* appropriate designator for – the name of – the countries concerned. Similar presuppositions hold for 'the peasantry', 'impoverishment', 'inequality', 'social discord': both the category and its relevance to the point at issue are presupposed, taken as common sense. (For some, a presupposition is a particular category of implicit proposition, upon which the truth or falsity of a presupposing sentence depends. Presupposition is contrasted with entailment and implicature, other categories of implicit meaning. See Levinson 1983.)

The unsaid, the already said, the presupposed, is of particular importance in ideological analysis, in that ideologies are generally embedded within the implicit meaning of a text rather than being explicit (Fairclough 1989, chapter 4). Consider, for example, the presupposition I have just suggested, that the 'current line' is attributable to all of 'us'. The fudging of the boundary between the generality of the population and its government or other powerful agents or élites, such that the actions or practices or values of the latter are generalized to the former, is commonplace in the media. In so far as it legitimizes and so helps to reproduce relations of domination through assuming a consensus that doesn't exist, it can be seen as having an ideological function. The discussion of local coherence relations at the end of this chapter is also relevant to the issue of presupposition.

Representations in clauses

I come now to the first of the two major aspects of representation distinguished above, representation in clauses. As I have already suggested, when people represent in language events, actions, relationships and states, the people and objects involved in them, the time and place and other circumstances of their occurrence, and so forth, there are always choices available. Partly these choices are a matter of vocabulary: the vocabulary one is familiar with provides sets of preconstructed categories, and representation always involves deciding how to 'place' what is being represented within these sets of categories – shall I call the violent death of people at the hands of others a 'killing', 'murder' or 'massacre'? It may also be a matter of metaphor: shall I call it a 'holocaust' or an 'extermination'? But these choices are also partly a matter of grammar. The grammar of a language differentiates a small number of 'process types' and associated 'participant types'. It may seem at first glance that the difference between an action (with a causal actor) and an event (without a causal actor) is a difference in reality, in the nature of things, but that is not so, at least in any simple sense. When people represent in language something that happens, they have to choose whether to represent it as an action or an event. Recall the example on page 25 from the *Today* programme, commenting about 'cheap' Russian fish being 'dumped' on the British market: 'the funny thing is, it's not transferring itself to the consumer at terribly low prices at all'. There is no actor, no one responsible for the prices, in this formulation – as if the fish distributed themselves and set their own prices.

There are two points to make about such relatively low-level choices in texts – low-level in the sense that they involve single clauses, and even single words within them. First, there are often systematic patterns and tendencies in particular types of text and particular discourse types. Work in critical linguistics, for instance (Fowler *et al.* 1979, Hodge and Kress 1979), has suggested that some newspapers systematically background the involvement of the police in violence and other forms of undesirable social behaviour. Cumulatively such representational practices may have significant ideological effects. Second, as I indicated above, such choices may realize contrasting discourses. For instance, the example at the end of the last paragraph is indicative of the sorts of linguistic realization associated with a major divide in the representation of economic and social problems and disasters (e.g. unemployment, violence, environmental disaster): between discourses which foreground (often hidden) causality, responsibility and even conspiracy, and discourses which represent such problems and disasters as a matter of fate, happenings beyond human control.

The grammar of English differentiates the following process types: Action, Event, State, Mental Process, Verbal Process (Fairclough 1992a, Halliday 1985). An Action involves both the participant-types Actor and Patient (person or thing affected by action): the Actor does something to the Patient. A typical Action clause has a transitive structure (Subject + Verb + Object) (e.g. *police kill 15, child breaks window*). An Event involves just one participant, which may either be affected by what happens and hence a Patient (e.g. *15 die, window breaks*), or be in an active, causal relationship to what happens, and hence an Actor (e.g. *victims screamed*). Events have an intransitive structure (Subject + Verb). A State is 'being' (e.g. *15 are dead*) or 'having' (*many have serious wounds*), and has an 'equative' structure (Subject + Verb + Complement). A Mental Process involves the participant-types Senser – the person who experiences or undergoes the mental process – and Phenomenon – what impinges on consciousness from outside. There are mental processes of cognition (e.g. *Thatcher realizes it's time to go*), perception (e.g. *Thatcher sees the writing on the wall*) and affect (e.g. *Thatcher wants to go*). Finally, a Verbal Process involves an Actor and a participant-type we might call Verbiage – what is said (*Thatcher says it's time to go*).

I want to illustrate the analysis of process and participant types – and try to show what insights it can yield – with three extracts from the opening few minutes of 'A New Green Revolution?'. The first, part of which I have already used above, occurs shortly after the programme begins:

KEITH GRIFFIN (voice-over): Normally the crisis in the Third World, poverty, inequality, hunger, is a silent crisis. Only occasionally does the crisis of the peasantry erupt in the form of violence and civil discord.

NARRATION: Millions of poor people in the Third World may not be silent much longer. They're caught up in an economic system which is steadily driving them towards red revolution. Agricultural technology is a crucial part of that economic system.

The second extract begins shortly afterwards:

KEITH GRIFFIN (Sync): Wherever one looks throughout the world one sees rising political tensions and violence and civil disturbance. The hope would be that if an appropriate technology could be found and introduced which increased the demand for labour, while at the same time increasing production of the things that the poor consume, that this would help to diminish the social tensions.

NARRATION: Several international agricultural research centres, funded by Western aid, are looking for new techniques to help solve the problems of hunger.

In the Philippines at Los Banos, the International Rice Research Institute was set up to help Asia increase rice production.

The scientists there are working against the odds and against the clock.

As individuals, most of them do genuinely want to help the poor – but is that what they achieve?

The third extract again follows shortly afterwards. (I have included a representation of visual images: CU is 'close-up', MS 'medium shot', WS 'wide shot', MCU 'medium close-up'.)

MIX to pipes in slum area of Manila, pan to WS slums	NARRATION: Everywhere in the Third World life in rural areas gets harder – and poor people flock to the city. The urban poor get poorer.
CU child standing in pipe Slum area, mother and child	When rice prices go up, hunger and unrest grows. In the city, the people can usually be kept in their place.
MS Filipino soldiers marching towards camera *WS remote mountain village (zoom in)*	But in remote rural areas, out of the eye of the regime, the New People's Army, dedicated to supporting poorer people and small farmers, plans violent revolt. GUERRILLA: 'Standing position!'
NPA guerrillas weapons training MCU they raise their machine guns WS Borlaug and Knapp by plots	NARRATION: Have the scientists' new techniques helped to increase or to decrease this violence and tension?

The people who are in focus here are the poor in countries like Bangladesh. The first thing to notice is that events and situations that involve the poor are often worded in a way that doesn't directly refer to them – the poor don't figure as a participant in the process. The first extract illustrates this: 'crisis', 'poverty', 'inequality', 'hunger', 'violence' and 'civil discord' are all situations affecting or involving the poor, but they are worded without direct reference to the poor. These are all 'nominalizations': that is, processes that have been turned into noun-like terms (nominals) which can themselves function as participants in other processes (e.g. 'the crisis of the peasantry' is Patient in the Event process, 'does the crisis of the peasantry erupt'). When a process is nominalized, some or all of its participants are omitted – that is why the poor don't figure explicitly in 'hunger', 'violence', and so forth, in this example. A lot of nominalizations in a text, as there are in this case, make it very abstract and distant from concrete events and situations (Hodge and Kress 1979).

The second point is that where the poor are explicitly referred to, it is not as Actors – as people who are doing something – but more as Patients – as people who are affected by the actions of others – or as participants in States. Again, the first extract illustrates this, twice in the penultimate sentence. In *they're caught up in an economic system, they*, the poor, is Patient in a passive clause which lacks an explicit Actor (and so doesn't specify who or what is responsible for their being so caught up); in *which is steadily driving them towards red revolution*, *them* is Patient, with an abstract nominalization ('economic system' – substituted by *which*) as Actor. Both of these are Action processes. Notice here the nominalization *red revolution* within a directional Adjunct *towards red revolution*: a revolution implies the poor actually doing something on their own behalf, but wording it as a nominalization backgrounds the active role of the poor, and wording them as Patient of the clause foregrounds their passivity. There are other examples of the poor as Patients in the other extracts: *most of them do genuinely want to help the poor, the urban poor get poorer, the people can usually be kept in their place.*

If the poor are not the active agents, the Actors, who are? There are three main types of Actor. First, nominalizations, such as *economic system* in the example just referred to, or in the second extract: *an appropriate technology . . . which increased the demand for labour*, and presumably: 'finding an appropriate technology' (*this* in the text) *would help diminish the social tensions.* Second, the scientists, and the scientists collectively as 'centres', in the second extract, for example: *several international agricultural research centres . . . are looking for new techniques, As individuals, most of them* (i.e. scientists) *do genuinely want to help the poor.* And third, the New People's Army, which is *(dedicated to) supporting poorer people* and *plans violent revolution.* Notice how the activity of the poor is again backgrounded in the former by *poorer people* figuring as Patient while *the New People's Army* (which presumably in fact consists of poorer people) is Actor.

In fact there are only two Actors in the third extract, the New People's Army and, exceptionally, the poor, in *the poor people flock to the city.* Interestingly, the Action here is one more usually associated with sheep – notoriously passive – than people, so the exception does not really contradict what I have said so far. What is striking in this extract, though, is how processes which might have been worded as Actions, in ways that foregrounded agency, causality and responsibility, are worded in ways that background them: *life . . . gets harder, the urban poor get poorer, rice prices go up, hunger and unrest grows.* The first two are State processes and the second pair Event processes with Patients. They all background and mystify who or what caused the processes referred to – one might, for instance, have had, instead of *rice prices go up,* an Action process, *when rice producers* (or shops, or governments – it is precisely not clear who) *raise rice prices.* What such choices have in common – choices of process type, the choice of a nominalized rather than a clausal process, and the choice of a passive clause with a deleted Actor rather than an active clause (there are quite a few examples here) – is the capacity to background and in some cases to mystify agency and responsibility. ✱

Let me turn now to choice of categories (Hodge and Kress 1979), and questions of vocabulary. Notice that the poor are categorized in various ways in these extracts: as poor (*the poor, the urban poor, poor people, poorer people*), as peasants (*the peasantry*), and as *the people.* They are not, for instance, categorized as 'the oppressed' (as in the title of Paolo Freire's celebrated book on literacy, *Pedagogy of the oppressed* (1972). The main categorization is in terms of poverty – in other words, in terms of their condition, rather than in terms of the relationships of exploitation implied by 'the oppressed'. One wonders whether this – along with the positioning of the poor I noted above, as passive rather than active participants in events – is how these people see themselves, or whose way of seeing them it is – their own government's? that of overseas governments or agencies? The general point is that one should also ask where the media get their categorizations from, both those that are explicit in the vocabulary, and those that are implicit in how people or things figure in process types. Recall the discussion of the sources of formulations and discourses used in the media in Chapters 4 and 5.

Generalizing from this example, we may say that there are always alternative ways of wording any (aspect of a) social practice, that alternative wordings may correspond to different categorizations, and that such alternative wordings and categorizations often realize different discourses. In this case, for instance, a discourse of poverty is drawn upon and realized in the wording which constrasts with a discourse of oppression, which might have been drawn upon, but significantly was not. Recall also, however, my comments in Chapter 5 on collocation: by focusing upon patterns of co-occurrence in the vocabulary of a text, the analyst can show how different discourses can be condensed together in short phrases within a text which easily pass unnoticed (e.g. referring to Saddam Hussein as a *mad menace*).

A further sphere of choice is metaphor (Lakoff and Johnson 1980). Contrary to common assumptions, metaphor is not just a literary device. Choice of metaphor may be a key factor in differentiating representations in any domain, literary or non-literary, including even scientific and technological. Notice, for example, the metaphors in the first extract from 'A New Green Revolution?'. A contrast is set up between the usual *silence* of the poor in the 'Third World' and their occasional, and likely future, *eruptions*. Actually, as I have already pointed out, the poor are partly implicit rather than explicit here; the Narration does say *millions of poor people in the Third World may not be silent much longer*, but Griffin refers to a silent *crisis*, and the *crisis of the peasantry* as erupting, *in the form of violence and civil discord*. Metaphorizing the usual inaudibility of the poor as *silence* begs the question of whether they are inaudible because they have nothing to say (implausible, I would suggest) or inaudible because the media of communication do not represent what they have to say. Except when there is an *eruption*: political activism on a scale which cannot be ignored is metaphorized in terms of that other eminently newsworthy category, the large-scale natural disaster. The poor are attributed with two political options: inert passivity and silence, or irrational and uncontrollable explosion (also implicit in the other wording of this option, *red revolution*). See Montgomery *et al.* (1989) for an interesting discussion of the metaphorization of elections as war, and how the metaphor shapes an electoral campaign and its media coverage.

Van Leeuwen (1993) suggests that representation can be seen as the recontextualization of social practices. For any text, the analyst can explore how represented social practices are recontextualized within the social practice which the text is part of. Recontextualization entails transformation – represented social practices are transformed in ways which are determined by the concerns and values and purposes of the text in its own social practice. The same social practice (e.g. coping with poverty in the 'Third World', or the induction of children into the school system) will be differently recontextualized, and differently transformed, in different texts.

Texts can be compared in terms of their relationship to the sort of account of a social practice which an ethnographer might produce. Van Leeuwen suggests eight primary elements of a social practice: its *participants*, their *activities*, the *circumstances* (time and place) of activities, the *tools* and *dress* prescribed, the *eligibility criteria* for participation, *performance indicators* for activities (e.g. should they be performed quietly and slowly, or quickly and efficiently), and *reactions* of participants to each other. I have referred above to participants and activities (i.e. 'processes') and in passing to circumstances. Texts recontextualizing a given social practice can be compared initially in terms of which elements they include or exclude and what relative weight they give them. Then, for each element, there are alternative ways in which it may figure in a text, and the analyst can show what choices have been made. We have seen above some of the sorts of choices available for the participant and activity elements.

Let me give an example of other choices for the participant element, and make some points about the circumstance element, drawing upon news reports of an important speech by prominent Conservative right-winger and ex-Cabinet Minister Lord Tebbit at the Conservative Party Conference in 1992, in which he galvanized Conservative opposition to the further economic and political integration of the European Union envisaged in the Maastricht Treaty. I shall use these reports to make a link between this and the next section. Here is the front-page report from the *Daily Mirror*, and the headline and first two paragraphs of the *Guardian* front-page report, both for 7 October 1992:

HE HASN'T GOT A PRAYER
Major in Crisis as Tebbit twists knife
By Alistair Campbell, Political Editor

John Major was facing a leadership crisis last night after being savaged by ex-Tory Party chairman Norman Tebbit.

Lord Tebbit warned the Prime Minister that he hadn't a prayer of staying in power unless he changed his policies. His vicious attack at the Tory Conference in Brighton was cheered by delegates and he was given a standing ovation.

Mr Major could only look on in dismay as his stance on the Maastricht Treaty and the economy was crucified.

Lord Tebbit piled on the agony by later claiming he was simply offering a 'hand of friendship'.

But in the same breath he warned the Premier that if he didn't get the economy right – he could kiss goodbye to his job.

Daily Mirror

MAJOR TOUGHS OUT EURO-MUTINY

The Conservative leadership last night began cracking the whip over Euro-sceptical MPs after successfully gambling that it could crush Lord Tebbit's head-on challenge to the Maastricht treaty on the Brighton conference floor.

The Chancellor, Norman Lamont, will face the conference over the economic crisis and the Exchange Rate Mechanism controversy tomorrow, but John Major's leadership is far from out of the woods.

Guardian

Participants are, of course, prominent in both reports, but whereas participants in the *Daily Mirror* report are referred to only individually and by name (*Major* etc.), participants in the *Guardian* are also frequently referred to collectively, either in terms of their function (*the leadership, ministers*) or impersonally in terms of location at or within the conference (*the conference*, and later in the report *the assembly, the platform* – in the sense of the leaders *on* the platform). These locational designations blur the distinction between participants and circumstances in van Leeuwen's framework, and are part of a greater concern with circumstances in the *Guardian* report. Notice also the temporal circumstances in paragraphs 1 and 2 of the Guardian report (*last night, tomorrow*), as well as the locational circumstance in paragraph 1 (*on the Brighton conference floor*). The *Daily Mirror* report has only one reference to location, in the second sentence of paragraph 2, and two temporal circumstances (*last night* and *later*, in sentences 1 and 5). These differences of linguistic detail are, I think, significant in helping to project profoundly different constructions of politics. The *Daily Mirror* projects a simple, relatively static and decontextualized confrontation between individuals (indeed personalities), the *Guardian* projects a more complex game played out over time and largely involving collective agents amongst whom distinctions of function and status (partly represented in spatial terms, e.g. 'platform' versus 'floor') are important.

Combination and sequencing of clauses

I shift now to the second major aspect of representation, combination and sequencing of clauses (propositions). As a way into some of the issues here, I shall discuss the most prominent parts of the coverage of the Tebbit speech in two media outlets: the beginning of the report on the main evening news bulletin on BBC1 on 6 October 1992, preceded by the section of the opening headlines which dealt with the issue; and the front-page report in the *Daily Mirror* on 7 October (reproduced above).

> At the Conservative Party Conference, Lord Tebbit urged the government to abandon the Maastricht treaty and put Britain first, second and third. The Foreign Secretary admitted the party could break itself over Europe and urged it to give that madness a miss.

> The former Cabinet Minister Lord Tebbit drew noisy cheers from a sizeable minority of representatives at the Conservative Party conference today when he urged the government to abandon the Maastricht treaty and negotiate a new one with no mention of economic, monetary or political union. He mockingly talked of the terrible wounds inflicted on industry and home owners as we established our credentials as good Europeans. And he said that politics, like charity, should begin at home. But the Foreign Secretary, Mr Douglas Hurd, said it was not in Britain's interests to be on the sidelines when the security and prosperity of Europe was being decided. And he said that the European summit in Birmingham would focus on how the community could learn to do fewer things better. The conference passed a motion calling for the government to continue to build an open and outward-looking community.

> *BBC1 Nine o'clock News*

Van Leeuwen's view of representation as recontextualization can be applied, as I have already suggested, to the analysis of clauses, but it is also useful in comparing combinations of clauses in texts. One aspect of social practices which may or may not be prominent in recontextualizations is Reactions – ways in which participants react to other participants. For present purposes, I shall distinguish as topics in the reports the Speech itself (and other speeches in the debate) and Reactions to it. Also, as van Leeuwen points out, recontextualization of a social practice is likely to involve to a greater or lesser degree Evaluations of it, in this case especially evaluations of the wider political effects and consequences of the Tebbit speech. With respect to reporting of the Speech itself, I shall also differentiate: direct Quotations from it, Summaries of it, and Formulations of it. Whereas

Summaries give the gist of what was said, Formulations give interpretations (recall the discussion of discourse representation in Chapter 5).

In terms of these distinctions, the BBC1 report can be represented as follows (S stands for 'sentence'):

HEADLINES: S1: SPEECH (Summary)
            S2: SPEECH (Summary + Quotation)
REPORT: S1: REACTION + SPEECH (Summary)
            S2: SPEECH (Summary + Quotation)
            S3: SPEECH (Summary)
            S4: SPEECH (Summary)
            S5: SPEECH (Summary)
            S6: SPEECH (Formulation)

and the *Daily Mirror* report as follows:

HEADLINES: S1: EVALUATION *or* SPEECH (Formulation)
            S2: EVALUATION + SPEECH (Formulation)
REPORT: S1: EVALUATION + SPEECH (Formulation)
            S2: SPEECH (Formulation)
            S3: REACTION [SPEECH (Formulation)] + REACTION
            S4: REACTION + SPEECH (Formulation)
            S5: SPEECH (Formulation + Quotation)
            S6: SPEECH (Formulation)

As the coding indicates, the main headline of the *Daily Mirror* is ambiguous. Since the same wording appears in a formulation of Tebbit's speech in the second paragraph of the report (*Lord Tebbit warned the Prime Minister that he hadn't a prayer of staying in power . . .*), we could analyse the headline as a formulation of what Tebbit said. But there is no indication in the headline that these words *are* reported, so it could also be analysed as the reporter's Evaluation of the effect of Tebbit's attack on Major's political position. Another point to notice is that although we have what appear to be two Summaries of Tebbit's speech in sentences 2 and 6 introduced by the reporting verb *warned*, they are so distant from what Tebbit actually said in his speech that they need to be taken as Formulations. In sentence 3 we have two Reactions, with a Formulation of Tebbit's speech embedded in the first of them (*His vicious attack at the Tory conference in Brighton*). The embedding is shown with square brackets in the analysis. The *Daily Mirror* text is accompanied by a photograph of Major in what appears to be an attitude of prayer, with the caption: *OH LORD: John Major can only pray his luck will change as he listens to Norman Tebbit tearing his policies apart.* This consists of a Reaction (*OH LORD*) followed by an Evaluation with a Formulation of Tebbit's speech embedded in it. There is an obvious play on words in the headline, where *he hasn't got a prayer* is used in the sense 'he hasn't got a chance'; notice too that *OH LORD* is not only the conventional way of beginning a prayer, but also a way of expressing a reaction of dismay, and a play on Tebbit's title. There is also a much smaller photograph of Tebbit, confidently smiling, with the caption: *VICIOUS: Tebbit*.

The two reports are strikingly different. The BBC1 report predominantly consists of Summaries of the speeches in the debate, with no Evaluations and only one instance of Reaction. The *Daily Mirror* report, by contrast, focuses very much on Evaluations of the political effects of the speech and Reactions to it, and reports of Tebbit's speech are mainly interpretative Formulations rather than Summaries. Its main emphasis – not surprisingly given its general critical stance towards the government – is on the damaging political effects of the speech rather than the speech itself.

But there is more to the comparison of the reports than the relative frequency of the different Evaluations or Reactions or the other topics. There are various ways, in addition to sheer frequency, in which topics can be relatively foregrounded or backgrounded. It is always worth first of all looking at the relative positioning of different topics within the generic structure of the text. Topics which appear in the informationally prominent headline position in television or press reports, or in the lead (i.e. the first) paragraph in a press report, are informationally foregrounded (recall the discussion in Chapter 5). In this case, the overall emphasis in the *Daily Mirror* report on political effects is sharply focused in the positioning of Evaluations in the headline and lead paragraph.

Positioning in headlines and leads is a matter of what I called 'global text structure' in the introduction to this chapter. Foregrounding is also partly due to 'local coherence relations'. In sentences (clause complexes), main clauses generally foreground information, whereas subordinate clauses generally background it. This is especially so when the main clause precedes a subordinate clause. So in the second *Daily Mirror* headline (*Major in crisis as Tebbit twists knife*), the reported political effect is both in the main clause and at the beginning of the sentence, whereas the formulation of the speech is in the subordinate clause at the end. Exactly the same is true of the lead paragraph (*John Major was facing a leadership crisis last night after being savaged by ex-Tory Party chairman Norman Tebbit*). Evaluation of effect is foregrounded in both cases, in accordance with the tendency I have already noted in the *Mirror* report.

Local coherence relations *between* sentences may also contribute to the relative salience of propositions. In the case of the BBC1 report, intersentential relations subtly contain and defuse Tebbit's potentially explosive intervention. Notice firstly that the first of the sentences reporting Hurd's speech is linked with the report of Tebbit's speech with the conjunction *but (But the Foreign Secretary, Mr Douglas Hurd . . .). But* is often used in a reassuring way linking some risk or threat with the means of avoiding it (e.g. *we had a gas leak last night but the Gas Board were round in less than half an hour*). The BBC1 report strikes me as similar: Hurd's speech is portrayed as effectively rebutting Tebbit's attack. Notice also the last sentence of the newsreader's introduction. In this case there is no explicit linking word, but there is nevertheless a coherent meaning relation between the sentence and those preceding it, which might have been explicitly worded as something like *after the debate* or *in the end* or *finally*. This sentence imposes a closure, a conclusion, on the report, in a form which supports the report of Hurd's speech in defusing Tebbit's attack: since the motion is calling upon the government to *continue* to build an open and outward-looking community, that implies – in contrast to Tebbit's speech – support for what the government has been doing. The BBC report appears on the face of it to treat Tebbit and Hurd equally, but they are subtly differentiated into antagonist and protagonist respectively (Martin 1986), with the latter's position being given more weight.

The informational structuring of clauses is another significant factor in foregrounding. The element at the beginning of a clause is called its 'theme' (Fairclough 1992a, Halliday 1985); the theme is the topic of the clause, what it is 'about', so theme is in a prominent position informationally. It is often the subject of the clause, but not always (for example, the theme is *in the same breath*, a 'circumstantial' element [Halliday 1985] in the first clause of the last paragraph of the *Daily Mirror* report). A significant contrast between the BBC1 and *Daily Mirror* reports is that whereas the theme in the former mainly alternates between Tebbit and Hurd, the two main speakers in the debate, in the latter the theme alternates between Major and Tebbit. The BBC1 report represents the debate as a division about policies, the *Daily Mirror* report represents it as about the misfortunes, and survival, of John Major.

The final position in a clause, or what is sometimes called the 'information focus' position, is also prominent, especially if it comes at the end of a sentence. In spoken language – and so in radio and television reports – this position is usually prominent in terms of intonation

– it is where the intonational 'nucleus', the main movement in pitch, tends to occur (Halliday 1985). In the lead paragraph of the *Daily Mirror* report both Major (theme) and Tebbit (information focus) are informationally prominent: *John Major* is in the initial theme position (and also subject of the clause, as is often the case), while when one reads the sentence out loud the nucleus most naturally falls on the final word *Tebbit*. Another position which is worth watching out for is initial position in a paragraph, which is again prominent, though this is not particularly interesting in the *Daily Mirror*, where paragraphs tend to correspond to sentences.

The example of the coverage of Tebbit's speech shows that the relative foregrounding or backgrounding of aspects of represented social practices is an important part of their representation. The analyst does not only need to know what is represented, but what relative weight or importance is attached to different elements within a representation.

Local coherence relations and ideology

I would like to develop what I have said about local coherence. Local coherence relations between clauses, clause complexes or sentences are of three main types: *elaboration, extension,* and *enhancement* (Halliday 1985: 202–27). In elaboration, one clause elaborates on another by describing it or making it more specific – by rewording it, exemplifying it, or clarifying it. In extension, one clause 'extends the meaning of another by adding something new to it'. This may be straight addition (marked with *and, moreover,* etc.), adversative or contrastive (marked with *but, yet, however,* etc.), or variation (marked with *or, alternatively,* etc.). In enhancement, 'one clause enhances the meaning of another by qualifying it', in terms of time (e.g. A then B, A after B, A while B – where A and B are clauses or sentences), place (e.g. A where B), cause (e.g. A because B, A so B) or condition (e.g. if A then B).

Local coherence relations between clauses or sentences (clause complexes) may be explicit or implicit; they may be, but are not necessarily, signalled by markers of cohesion such as conjunctions or sentence-linking adverbials (*but, accordingly, nevertheless, afterwards,* for example). Halliday and Hasan (1976) distinguish four main types of cohesion: *conjunction, lexical cohesion, reference,* and *ellipsis.* The markers of cohesion I have referred to so far are cases of conjunction, including both what traditional grammar calls conjunctions (e.g. *and, but, because*) and 'sentence adverbials' like *however* and *nevertheless.*

Lexical cohesion is cohesion through vocabulary – through repetition of words, and words that are linked in meaning occurring across clause and sentence boundaries. Reference includes referring back or forward in a text with pronouns, the definite article or demonstratives (*this, that*). Ellipsis is missing out repeated material or replacing it with a substitute word (e.g. *Tebbit failed to mention Thatcher. Hurd on the other hand did.* i.e., did mention Thatcher).

Relations of coherence between clauses and sentences of a text are not objective properties of the text, they are relations that have to be established by people interpreting it. This is clear in the case of implicit relations, where there is nothing in the text to show how one sentence links to its predecessor. Even where there are markers of cohesion, these may have to be interpreted. Interpreters need to decide what a pronoun refers back to, or which items of vocabulary are cohesively linked together. In doing so, interpreters need more than the propositions which are explicit in the text. They draw upon other propositions which allow them to make inferential leaps between the clauses and sentences of the text. But texts are structured in ways which predispose interpreters to leap one way rather than another – which is no guarantee that they will do so, because interpreters may read texts in different ways. However, there will be certain predominant readings, and we can say that the non-explicit propositions which they depend on are part of the implicit meaning of the text. What that means is that a text addresses a sort of 'ideal interpreter' who will bring to bear just the propositions (the implicit meanings) needed to give the text what has been called its 'preferred reading' (Hall *et al.* 1978).

The upshot of all this is that local coherence relations are very significant indeed in the ways in which texts position people as subjects and cumulatively shape identities (see also Chapter 7), and how texts work ideologically. Let us take as an example the last of the three extracts from 'A New Green Revolution?' on page 111.

Cohesion relations are largely implicit in this sequence. For example, I interpret the clauses of the first three sentences as in relations of enhancement, and more specifically cause–effect relations, but they lack markers of causal cohesion. In sentence 1, the two clauses are linked by the all-purpose conjunction *and*, which leaves implicit the cause–effect relation (poor people flock to the city *because* life in rural areas gets harder). I also see an unmarked cause–effect relation between the second clause of sentence 1 and sentence 2 (the urban poor get poorer *because* so many people flock to the city). Again, although the first clause of sentence 3 is marked with a temporal conjunction (*when*), there is an implicit causal relation between the two clauses (hunger and unrest grow *because* rice prices go up). It takes quite an inferential leap on the interpreter's part to establish a coherent meaning relation between sentences 3 and 4. I interpret this as an extension-type relation of an adversative type (unrest grows, *but* the people can usually be kept in their place; or, *although* unrest grows, the people can usually be kept in their place). The connection between these sentences rests upon a 'bridging assumption' (Brown and Yule 1983, Fairclough 1992a): that popular unrest gives rise to a problem of order, and the need for official action to try to contain it.

Overall, this part of the extract addresses an ideal interpreter who is familiar with a particular preconstructed 'script' (Montgomery *et al.* 1989) that is being evoked here: a predictable sequence of events leading from rural poverty to urban squalor and unrest and consequential problems of order. The ideal interpreter is relied upon to fill in the gaps, make explicit what is left implicit, and construct a coherent, preferred, meaning for the text.

But this is not just a matter of textual economy, not bothering to spell out what can be taken for granted. It is a moot point how many real audience members might, if asked, actually agree with the stereotypical narrative of Third World urban problems which constitutes the script. But the text takes the script as universally given for its audience, and so positions audience members that they are induced to draw upon it to arrive at a coherent interpretation. Recall also my earlier observation that processes affecting the poor are represented as processes without agents: life getting harder, or poverty increasing, are things that happen (like thunderstorms) rather than effects created by people. The script represents social processes on a natural scientific model, as a sequence of causally linked events devoid of human agency and outside human control. This is a representation which (depending on context) has a potential ideological function, in the sense that eliding responsibility for social processes and the possibility of intervention to change them is conducive to a fatalism which can help sustain existing relations of domination. Local coherence relations in cases of this sort can therefore contribute significantly to textual processes of ideological interpolation (Althusser 1971): audience members are, so to speak, called upon to acknowledge the framework of ideological common sense (in this case, the Third World script) within which they are positioned. Such texts can cumulatively shape the knowledge, beliefs and values of audience members.

The interpretative activity of the audience member in arriving at coherent meanings is even clearer in the case of the visual images of television, represented on the left of the transcription of the extract. Documentary producers depend upon audiences drawing upon visual scripts in interpreting sequences of images coherently. For example, not only are we assumed to recognize images of a child and a mother and child as images of poverty, we are also assumed to know what follows – in terms of 'keeping people in their place' – upon soldiers marching through city streets. As with the language, such inferential work on the viewer's part can contribute to the ideological work of texts.

The connection between the question which closes this sequence (*Have the scientists' new techniques helped to increase or to decrease this violence and tension?*) and the sentences which precede it is worth commenting on. There is a cohesive link of the reference type (*this* in the phrase *this violence and tension* refers back to earlier sentences), and there is also lexical cohesion (*violence* echoes *violent*, and *tension* is semantically close to *unrest*). But notice that the phrase presupposes the existence of violence and tension, even though no actual violence had been referred to or visually depicted. As so often, the way in which the text formulates or paraphrases earlier parts of the text turns out to be significant (Heritage and Watson 1979): the New People's Army's planning for 'violent revolt' is transformed into 'violence'. This can again been seen in terms of ideological interpolation, in that it calls upon audience members to draw upon, in interpreting a text, a stereotype which associates especially left-wing oppositional groups with violence, rather than governments. It is also noteworthy that the information focus and the intonational nucleus fall on *decrease* rather than *this violence and tension*, in accordance with the presupposed, taken-for-granted status of the latter. Notice also that the impact of this contentious presupposition is increased by its positioning in the activity-type structure associated with the genre here. This is an investigative reporting genre where the activity type – the argumentation – is quite standardly structured as a sequence of: authoritative orientation for the report + question for investigation + evidence bearing on the question. The question element, which the presupposition is built into, is an informationally salient hinge between the orientation and evidential stages of the report. This shows how local coherence relations, global text structure, and the information structure of the clause can work together in texts.

7

IDENTITY AND SOCIAL RELATIONS IN
MEDIA TEXTS

Chapter 6 was concerned with representation in texts, and this chapter deals with the other two processes which are always simultaneously going on in texts: the construction of identities, and the construction of relations. I suggested in Chapter 3 (page 39) that media discourse can usefully be seen in terms of the interaction between three major categories of participants, and this can provide a starting point here. The categories are: reporters (a term I use for all categories of media personnel, including announcers, presenters, anchorpersons); audiences; and various categories of 'other participants', mainly from the public domain (politicians, trade unionists, religious leaders, scientists and other experts, etc.).

Notice that the concern here is not with how 'others' are referred to and represented (part of the business of Chapter 6), but with others as direct participants in media output, for instance as interviewees in broadcasting. We need to include amongst 'other participants' people who participate as in some sense representatives of the audience – 'members of the public' who are asked for their views on a shift in government policy, for example, or participants in audience discussion programmes (discussed in Chapter 9). One important concern is with relationships between categories of 'others': which are most salient, which are similarly constructed and which are contrastively constructed. Another issue is absences: for instance, whereas politicians are a well-defined and salient category, capitalists – those who dominate the economy – significantly are not. There are interesting slippages between these three main categories: for instance, the right to directly address audiences on television, usually the prerogative of broadcasters, is extended in certain cases to categories of 'others' – such as politicians in election broadcasts and, in open access types of programme, to people seen as representative of audiences.

The chapter will be constructed around these three broad categories of participant. I shall be concerned on the one hand with questions of identity: the sorts of social and personal identity that are set up in media output for reporters, for audiences, and for the various categories of 'other' participant. On the other hand, I shall be concerned with relations: between reporters and audiences, between various categories of 'others' and audiences, and between reporters and politicians, experts, and other categories of 'others'. Although it is analytically useful to distinguish questions of identity from questions of relations, the two are, in practice, inseparable: how a reporter's identity is constructed is in part a question of how a reporter relates to an audience.

Analysis of the construction of relations and identities in media texts is, I suggest, a significant constituent in addressing a range of important sociocultural questions. This is so because of the uniquely influential and formative position of the media in contemporary societies. Understanding how relations are constructed in the media between audiences and those who dominate the economy, politics and culture, is an important part of a general understanding of relations of power and domination in contemporary societies. And there is a key question about contemporary changes in the media construction of relations between reporters and audiences and between politicians and audiences: do they constitute a substantive democratization, or do they primarily have a legitimizing role in respect of existing power relations? There are also questions about whether and to what extent the media, in the ways in which they construct audience and reporter identities, operate as an agency for projecting cultural values – individualism, entrepreneurialism, consumerism – and whose values these might be.

It is important to ensure that a critical perspective is applied in the analysis of relational and identity dimensions of texts, as well as in the analysis of representations. Given the questions I have just raised about how relations of domination in the wider society underlie the media construction of relations and identities, how these processes take place in texts is a major concern in ideological analysis. Indeed, perhaps a shift has taken place over the past two or three decades in the relative importance, ideologically, of representational aspects of texts and interpersonal (identity and relational) aspects of texts. Most accounts of ideology in the media stress representational issues. Yet perhaps relatively stable constructions of social and personal identity and relations which have become naturalized as facets of familiar media genres and formats (the news, magazine programmes, soaps) are now more ideologically significant in the implicit messages they convey about people and relationships than the variable representational contents that these programmes may accommodate.

I want to emphasize the diversity, multiplicity, and variability of identities and relations in the media. I am referring here not to the obvious variation between different types of programme (current affairs versus soaps versus television drama, for example), but to diversity within a programme type such as news. This is partly because sub-categories of a particular category of participant may be involved in different sorts of activity within the one programme. There is, for instance, a division of labour between newsreaders, reporters, and correspondents in news programmes, which may well involve different constructions of identity and different relationships with the audience or other participants. Also, a single participant may have a complex identity in the sense that s/he may individually be having to negotiate a number of activities successively or simultaneously within a programme, involving perhaps the sort of changes in 'footing' described by Goffman (1981). But even a particular single activity may involve a multiplicity of simultaneous social purposes (van Leeuwen 1987 – see Chapter 5) that entail complex and potentially contradictory identities and relations. A presenter may, for instance, be trying to simultaneously manage the roles of purveyor of authoritative information and entertainer, while also trying to project herself or himself as an 'ordinary person', like the audience (see below for examples). Furthermore, the practices of a particular type of output such as news or documentary may be variable, so that a presenter, for instance, has a range of models to choose between.

An added complication is that this complex picture is changing through time. The diversity of available models at a particular point in time may be seen as the synchronic effect of a longer-term process of change. I referred for instance in Chapter 3 (page 46) to Kumar's work (1977) on changes in the institutional voice of the BBC, which shows how presenters have shifted in a more populist direction, claiming common identity with audiences. There has been a shift in the relative weighting of broadly collective and institutional and broadly personal aspects of identity in favour of the latter, with adherence to defined role on the part of presenters becoming relatively less important, and projection of an attractive personality becoming relatively more important.

The focus on the construction of relations and identities in this chapter, as opposed to the focus on representation in the last chapter, entails a concern with a different set of linguistic features of texts, namely those which are associated with the interpersonal function in texts. These include the linguistic systems of mood and modality, which are concerned respectively with clause and sentence types (choice between declarative, interrogative, and imperative clauses and sentences), and the stance of speaker or writer to 'message' – the degree of affinity with or commitment to a proposition expressed by a speaker or writer, for instance. They also include what I broadly refer to as 'interactional control features', including turn-taking (the way in which talking turns are distributed in, say, an interview), exchange system (organization of, for instance, interviews in terms of question–answer sequences), control of topics and topic change, and formulation (ways in which earlier parts of a text or interaction are paraphrased). And they include features of texts which are relevant to 'politeness' in the sense in which that term is used within pragmatics (Brown and Levinson 1978, Leech 1983) – features, for instance, that may mitigate a particularly challenging question in an interview.

In this chapter I shall explore some of these issues through analysis of extracts from four broadcast programmes: the regular BBC Radio 4 medical programme *Medicine Now*; *High Resolution*, a six-part series broadcast on BBC Radio 4 in 1992, described by *Radio Times* as 'exploring the popular side of science'; a popular television programme produced in the USA, the *Oprah Winfrey Show*, broadcast in the UK originally on Channel 4 and now on BBC2; and the *Today* programme which is broadcast every weekday morning on BBC Radio 4.

Medicine Now

The edition of *Medicine Now* which I refer to here was broadcast on 12 August 1992. I shall focus on one item in the programme which deals

with the influence of patients' mental states on the incidence of epileptic fits, and possibilities for controlling mental state to avoid fits. The
item is structured as follows: (1) an opening account of these new
developments in the treatment of epilepsy by the programme's
presenter, (2) an interview between the presenter and an expert in this
form of treatment, identified as Dr Peter Fennick, (3) an interview
between the presenter and one of Dr Fennick's patients, identified as
Kathleen Baker, on her particular case and treatment, (4) further interview between the producer and Dr Fennick, (5) a wind-up of the issue
from the presenter. There is actually some slippage between stages (3)
and (4), in that there is for a short period a three-way interaction with
the presenter questioning Dr Fennick and Kathleen Baker in turn. The
item is quite a long one, lasting approximately seven minutes, so I shall
use a number of short extracts from different stages.

The first extract is the opening of the item. I have transcribed the
extract as normal orthographic sentences because the presenter is evi-
dently reading from a written script, with sentence boundaries clearly
marked. In the first three sentences I have italicized all the words
which are made prosodically prominent in the delivery, either because
they are heavily or contrastively stressed, or because they carry an
intonational nucleus (main pitch movement). I have also marked with
a slash the boundaries of tone units except where they come before a
full stop, question mark, or colon – these punctuation marks also correspond to tone unit boundaries. (A tone unit is a stretch of talk containing a locus of pitch prominence – generally movement upwards or
downwards or a combination of the two – also called a 'nucleus'.)

Extract 1

PRESENTER: *Most* illness/ is affected to *some* degree/ by the sufferer's
state of *mind*. In the case of certain attacks of *epilepsy*/ it may even be
what's *in* the patient's mind/ that sets them *off*/ and this *raises*/ an intriguing *question*: might conscious attempts to *avoid*/ certain states of *mind*/
help to *prevent*/ epileptic *seizures*? Sometimes dramatic *symptoms* of
epilepsy/ are caused by a *wave*/ of *ab*normal electrical *activity*/ *sweeping*
through/ the *brain*. Exactly what then happens, loss of consciousness,
loss of sensations, convulsions or whatever, depends on which parts
of the brain are affected. There's more than one kind of epilepsy, but in
some patients it's possible to detect abnormal brain activity between
seizures as well as during them. This often takes the form of small electrical discharges referred to as 'spikes'. If patients could learn to
suppress these discharges, or at least reduce their frequency, they
might prevent a full-blown seizure from beginning.

The first issue I want to take up is how the identity of the presenter is constructed. My summary of the structuring of the item into five stages indicates that the presenter is engaged in different activities within the programme. In particular, he is engaged in exposition (in the extract above from stage 1), interviewing, and the managerial role implied by the term 'wind-up' in stage 5 (which consists solely of: *Dr Peter Fennick and a more thoughtful way of fending off epilepsy*). In fact, managerial work is also being done in stage 1, as well as in the interviewing: the first sentence of the extract above, apart from prefacing the account of new approaches to epilepsy, manages the transition between this and the previous item, which dealt in more general terms with the influence of mind on body. The picture is actually rather more complex, because (as I show below) the interviewing involves not just asking questions but also comment and evaluation. The range of these activities in itself entails a multiple and complex presenter identity, and there are further complicating factors I deal with below.

Having grossly identified the range of activities, the next question is how each activity is actually handled. As my discussion of the *High Resolution* programme will show, there are options available to presenters in respect of the construction of identity and the construction of relations. In the extract above, representing stage 1, the presenter adopts the position of announcer, delivering an orienting account of the new research on epilepsy which he does not claim as his own. Comparison with the *High Resolution* extract shows that the option exists for a presenter to take more personal responsibility for such an account, but in this case the option was not taken up. The comparison also shows that the presenter can address and engage with the audience as an entertainer, even a comic, and can in various ways claim solidarity and co-membership with the audience, but again these options are not taken up here. The audience is constructed as seeking information rather than entertainment, and the presenter does not go beyond the conventional announcer's role of facilitating the informational and educative process. A fundamental contrast between the *Medicine Now* and *High Resolution* programmes is that the presenter's institutional identity (role) is foregrounded in the former, whereas the presenter's personal identity is foregrounded in the latter.

Let us look in more detail at the first extract. The words on the page, as they appear in the transcription, could have come from a lecture, but when the delivery is taken into account it becomes clear that the presenter is not straightforwardly lecturing. Apart from one question which is there for expositional purposes (the text goes on to answer it), the extract consists of clauses which are declarative in mood (on mood, see Halliday 1985, Quirk *et al.* 1972) and make assertions, though the last sentence differs from the others in being conditional (conditional clause + declarative clause). These assertions are authoritative. They are not attributed to others, they are made on the author's authority. The modality is not always categorical, i.e. these are not just black-or-white assertions of truth or falsity (though one or two are, e.g. *there's more than one kind of epilepsy*). Some are quite extensively modalized – these are assertions about degrees of probability and usuality, as is indicated by the number of modal verbs (*may, might*), temporal adverbs (*sometimes, often*), quantifiers (*most, some*), and the modal adjective *possible*. These modalizations do not diminish the text's authoritativeness, for they evoke the cautious (and authoritative) discourse of science and other academic disciplines in their careful specification of probabilities (on modality, see Halliday 1985). The vocabulary is not severely technical, and ordinary language expressions are used in preference to professional ones in some cases (e.g. *what's in the patient's mind, sets them off*); notice also the acceptable vagueness of ordinary language in *convulsions or whatever*. But quite a number of semi-technical expressions are used (e.g. *epileptic seizures, electrical discharges*) which also contribute to authoritativeness, as indeed does the evaluation *and this raises an intriguing question*: such an evaluation implies the author's expertise. Taking together these features of mood (declarative clauses as assertions), modality, and vocabulary, the audience addressed is a well-informed but not specialist one (though sufficiently in tune with scientific curiosity to be 'intrigued' by the question), and audience members are positioned as learners.

However, the extract is read out with an announcer's delivery rather than a lecturer's delivery. There are a number of markers of this delivery style. First, the text is divided into a large number of tone units. This has the effect of dividing the information here into a large number of small information units, a typical feature of announcer talk. Second, an unusually large number of words are stressed – all the underlined words in the transcription. Third, quite a few of these have exceptionally heavy stress or contrastive stress. Fourth, the presenter uses a greater pitch range than one would expect in conversation or lecturing. On these and other features of announcers' deliveries, see van Leeuwen (1984).

The contrast between the announcer's delivery and the authoritative lecturing style of the language points to an ambivalence in the presenter's identity. As a reporter with specialized interests in medical journalism, the presenter is in a marginal position between medicine and the media: he is in possession of a certain amount of what normally counts as expert knowledge, but at the same time he lacks the credentials of expertise and is in the business of mediating experts to radio audiences. We can see this in terms of an ambivalence of ownership of these assertions. From the transcript, it might appear that the presenter is claiming to be author (the person whose words these are) and principal (the person(s) whose position is represented in the account) and not merely animator (the person who says the words on this occasion), yet the delivery belies this appearance – see Goffman (1981) for these distinctions.

In stages 1 and 5, the presenter is addressing the audience directly, whereas in stages 2–4 he is addressing the other participants directly. The next extract follows immediately upon extract 1, completing stage 1 and initiating stage 2 (the interview with Dr Fennick).

Extract 2

PRESENTER: Dr Peter Fennick of London's the Institute of Psychiatry identifies various strategies by means of which patients may be able to control their brain activity one he says is bio-feedback

DR FENNICK: that involves taking these abnormal . electrical discharges . converting them into a form that the patient can see . and then asking them to suppress them . for example you can put a couple of electrodes on the head that's just how you measure the electrical activity . amplified . in an amplifier and then turn it into . a pulse . which triggers a counter . so every time a spike occurs . then the counter advances itself by one and you say . stop it counting . and they have to find some way of stopping it counting

PRESENTER: you say they have to find some way of stopping it counting you can't really give any instructions about how they set about controlling the electrical discharges inside their own heads

DR FENNICK: well the interesting thing is that if you do this many people have strategies of their own anyway . and they finally . sometimes say . well I've been doing this for many years . in other words there's something that they know they do to stop these di– discharges . but they didn't know they were doing it

PRESENTER: how effective is it I mean in in people in whom you can see these kinds of e abnormal e: patterns of electrical activity between fits . how many are actually able to control them in this way

Dr Fennick's first speaking turn is the only one in the programme that is not a response to a question from the presenter. In that sense, the contribution of the medical expert to the programme is heavily mediated (managed, framed and controlled) by the presenter, and there is a strong managerial element in the interviewing stages generally. Notice, however, that the presenter's two questions do not have the same character. The first is not strictly a question at all, though it shares with ordinary questions the property of requiring a reply. It is a comment on what the expert has said, and might be taken as a negative evaluation. It shows that the presenter is not entirely limited to being a facilitator. So too does a later contribution:

PRESENTER: the the conditioning you talked about just now sounds rather like Pavlov's dogs except instead of the dogs salivating when they hear the bell ring in this case e: the stimulus whatever it happens to be that was originally paired with the the fit causes a seizure
DR FENNICK: that's absolutely right

Correspondingly, the doctor's response here counts as agreement with the presenter's comment rather than answer to a question.

By contrast, the second question is a proper question, which asks the expert to develop the account he has given so far of his approach to treatment. In the third stage, where the presenter interviews the patient, the presenter uses only such information-eliciting questions. Their role in the development of the patient's account of her own particular case is interesting. The next extract is an abbreviated version of part of this stage. (P stands for Presenter, KB for Kathleen Baker, the patient, and a string of dots indicate where I have omitted material, for reasons of space):

Extract 3

P: what Kathleen . ar– is the situation on the circumstances or the thoughts which tend to bring on a seizure in your case
KB: in my case guilt
P: . when did it start
KB: e: when I was quite young . . . . . attacks started occurring
    ⌈ epil–
P: ⌊epileptic attacks
KB: yes . . . . .

P: and did this pattern ⌈continue . for for ⌈years
KB: ⌊yes   ⌊yes
P: after
KB: there are certain attacks that I know were induced by guilt
P: what about e more recent times
KB: on two very important occasions . . .

A feature of this sequence is the way in which the patient's narrative has been divided up into topical chunks for presentational purposes, with the presenter's questions controlling the topical development, moving from what causes her attacks, to when they started, to how long they went on, to what's happening now. The mediating and managerial work of the presenter as interviewer is particularly clear.

These differences in the exchange systems and in the turn-taking between stages 2 and 3 mark a contrast between the presenter's relationship to the doctor and his relationship to the patient. (An exchange system is the system operative within a particular discourse type for distributing turns at talking between participants. Exchange systems and turn-taking have been extensively documented by conversation analysts. See Sacks *et al.* 1974.) Given the ambivalence in the identity of the presenter as a specialist medical journalist, the former relationship approximates a relationship between equals. The presenter, as we have seen, comments on and evaluates what the doctor says on the basis of his own knowledge of the field, and his questions (e.g. the second question in extract 2) also display a knowledge and understanding of the subject-matter. It is noteworthy that the doctor seems to make (as I show below) more accommodations towards the lay audience than the presenter does: the latter's questions are rather complex and sometimes difficult to understand. By contrast, the relationship between presenter and patient is an unequal one. The marked degree of presenter control over the presentation of the patient's story might be seen as motivated by the need to make it digestible for the audience. If so, why is there no such accommodation to the audience when the presenter interviews the doctor? It may, on the other hand, show that the presenter sees the patient as needing more guidance. Notice also that whereas the doctor is not addressed, the patient is – by her first name. All this points again to the complexity of presenter identity.

What about the identity of the doctor? As with the presenter, there are alternative models available. In fact the doctor adopts a voice which is quite conventional amongst professionals of this sort. It is a markedly pedagogical voice, which combines an authoritative account of the research with considerable accommodation to the lay audience. The delivery is slow and measured, showing considerable and indeed exaggerated care to ensure clarity and comprehensibility. It is also, at times, an expressive delivery. For example, one accommodative feature of the pedagogical style in extract 2 is direct quotation (recall the discussion of discourse representation in Chapter 5), not of authoritative sources, but of patients or the doctor himself (*you say stop it counting, they finally sometimes say well I've been doing this for many years*), and where this occurs the doctor dramatizes it by simulating the way it was actually said. Or again, he turns the conclusion of his second turn (*but they didn't know they were doing it*) into a sort of punchline by a marked reduction in loudness, a very slow tempo, and a rhythmical delivery which divides it into three feet each with a stressed syllable (in capitals): *but they DIDn't/KNOW they were/ DOing it*. Similarly, later in the interview, when the doctor declares *seizures can be learnt*, again as a punchline at the end of the turn, he delivers it in a slow, quiet and breathy voice. The cumulative effect of these features is a heavily marked teacher–learner relationship between expert and audience which in the context of other contemporary constructions of expertise (see the discussion of *High Resolution* below) sounds patronizing. Part of the pedagogical accommodation is an accommodation towards certain features of informal conversational language – notice the use of the indefinite pronoun *you* and the non-specific quantifier *a couple* (Quirk *et al.* 1972).

Both presenter and doctor are constructed in this programme in conventional ways, as traditional professionals. The presenter is constructed as a professional broadcaster whose primary concerns are facilitation and mediation, though he is in a somewhat ambivalent position with respect to medical knowledge as a specialist in this area of broadcasting. The doctor is constructed in conventional terms as an expert with pedagogical skills. Notice that the accommodation to audience in the doctor's style is not specifically an accommodation to the media: one can imagine something very like this as a first-year university lecture. This is an accommodation made from within the profession on the professional's terms.

High Resolution

High Resolution is a popular science radio programme. The topic of the particular edition I am using, broadcast on 8 September 1992, is bones: what different fields of science can tell us about the way people lived in the past through analysis of bones found in archaeological excavations. The extract begins quite early in the programme with the presenter working on an archaeological site, and in the process of uncovering a skeleton.

PRESENTER (sounds of scraping of trowel on soil): I just want to have a look in the soil . surrounding the skeleton . to see if I can find out if he was buried in a coffin . . . what I'm looking for is a line of iron nails or a . thin dark line in the soil that might be left by the side of the coffin (song: 'Dig dig dig from early morn to night') now this is interesting . . I've found a small brass pin . in the rib cage . (sounds of seagulls) it's about the size of those tailor's pins you get in men's shirts when they're new . but this one's a shroud pin . so there we are . this was a shroud burial . no coffin . just laid in the grave in his shroud . now as an archaeologist I can work out details like these . but I can't say much more about the skeleton itself . in fact I can't even say what sex it is . and when we take the bones to anatomists like Margaret Bruce . that's one of the first questions we ask

MARGARET BRUCE: what we do is to look for the bits where you would expect the best difference it's in the pelvis . what we've got in a female pelvis . is a big and roomy one for a baby . the male doesn't need that so his pelvis is much narrower

PRESENTER: well that's alright for the skeletons of people who actually grew up to be adults . but how do anatomists sex the more junior members of the cemetery

MARGARET BRUCE: we can't really with any reliability tell . boys . from girls . it's only at puberty . that the real differences in the sexes emerge

PRESENTER: now believe it or not . although it's easier to sex an adult than a child . it's the other way round when it comes to answering another common question . how old were people when they died

MARGARET BRUCE: it's much easier for us to tell how old a child was . at death . because we've got perhaps fifteen years of development with nice clearly demarcated stages along dental and . skeletal development . once we get older . we're really looking at the process of degeneration . and as we all know just looking at people sometimes the grey hair comes in quickly . sometimes the . aches and pains come in quickly . so we age at different . rates . and it's very difficult to put a precise age . on an adult skeleton . easier . on an immature one

(bone song)

The extract is in two stages which are roughly comparable to stages 1 and 2 in the *Medicine Now* item – direct address of the audience by the presenter, followed by interview with an expert. But there are major differences. In the first stage, the presenter is actually engaged in research rather than just giving an account of it. And in the second stage, the presenter is framing and commenting on the expert's contributions but not directly addressing the expert, not asking questions.

In the first stage, the division between presenter and expert breaks down, for the presenter is a working archaeologist. Correspondingly, in Goffman's terms (see page 132) he is constructed as author and principal of what he says, not just as animator, i.e. it is he whose words these are and whose position this is, not just he who says the words. Also, this programme differs from *Medicine Now* in combining information with entertainment, the most obvious marker of which is the periodic insertion of songs about bones, digging, and so forth. The presenter is also constructed as an entertainer, an actor, engaged in a simulation of archaeological work – this is obviously a dramatic reconstruction of a dig, not a recording of a real dig. But he is also constructed as an ordinary person, a co-member of the world of common experience, the 'lifeworld' (Habermas 1984) which audience members are positioned within. We thus have a configuration of purposes, informing and educating, and an associated configuration of identities in the person of the presenter – giver of information, entertainer, and fellow member of the lifeworld, which is characteristic of the contemporary media, and which is widely displacing the more traditional model of *Medicine Now*. A further consequential aspect of presenter identity is that the presenter's personal identity and personality are foregrounded, in contrast to the foregrounding of institutional role in *Medicine Now*.

How are these properties of presenter identity realized in the language? Delivery is again at least as important as the words on the page. One significant difference between *High Resolution* and *Medicine Now* is that whereas both presenter and expert in the latter are men with middle-class 'received pronunciation' accents (Trudgill 1986), the presenter in the former has a Mancunian accent, and several of the experts are women with regional accents. This in itself indicates the bond with ordinary life implicitly claimed by the *High Resolution* programme. More generally, both the words on the page and the delivery are reminiscent of an operational form of ordinary conversation – the sort of language you might use face-to-face to talk someone through a job you were doing. This is relevant to both the entertainer and the 'ordinary bloke' elements of the presenter's identity – it is an entertaining simulation of an ordinary-life scenario.

As an example, take the beginning of the extract, *I just want to have a look in the soil . surrounding the skeleton . to see if I can find out if he was buried in a coffin*, and the sequence that follows the song, *now this is interesting . . I've found a small brass pin . in the rib cage . it's about the size of those tailor's pins you get in men's shirts when they're new*. Here, *I just want to* and *now this is interesting* are conversational formulae, the former recognizable as operational language; *have a look* and *find out* are conversational-style verbs; referring to a skeleton by gender (*he*), the use of the demonstrative determiner (*those*) to refer to an item of common experience, use of *about* for approximation, and use of *you* as an indefinite pronoun (equivalent to the middle-class pronoun *one*) are all features of informal conversation. The delivery is effective not only in making this plausible as a simulation, but also in projecting a particular, attractive, personality for the presenter. Personality is expressed through a configuration of linguistic choices, including vocabulary, accent, pace of talk (slow and measured in this case), expressiveness (for instance, *I just want to have a look* is delivered in a breathy voice, and in *now this is interesting*, pitch range is used to express interestingness), and so forth. At the same time, the presenter is giving archaeological information in stage 1, though in an experiential way rather than through abstract theoretical discourse, by way of the presuppositions which are drawn upon in the account of the particular find. For example, instead of asserting *corpses were either buried in coffins or in shrouds*, or *a line of nails or a thin dark line in the soil provide evidence of coffin burials*, these propositions are implicitly present as presuppositions.

As I have already indicated, in the second stage the presenter does not directly address or question Margaret Bruce, but his interventions in her account do frame and control what she says in the sense of orchestrating change of topic, commenting on what she says (*well that's all right for skeletons of people who actually grew up to be adults*), and formulating (Heritage and Watson 1979) what she says (his last contribution summarizes hers in advance). In terms of presenter–audience relations, the mediating role of the presenter is accentuated through maintaining the audience as addressee throughout; the presenter is talking to 'us' about 'them', extending his implicitly claimed co-membership of the audience lifeworld to a claim to represent the audience point of view in commenting on the experts. This could be seen as moving towards the more thorough-going demystification of experts which we find in audience discussion programmes like *Kilroy* (see the discussion of the *Oprah Winfrey Show* below, and Chapter 9). At the same time, the presenter continues to entertain and inform – the comment containing the joke about the 'more junior members of the cemetery' is also informative in indicating a problem with sexing skeletons of children.

The identity of the expert in *High Resolution* differs from that of the doctor in the *Medicine Now* extract in that while the latter is overtly constructed as a pedagogue, the pedagogic function of the former's talk is implicit; and whereas the latter comes across as patronizing, the former does not. The expert here seems to be a knowledgeable person talking in a conversational way, rather than a professional making obvious efforts to talk to lay people. Both, of course, are professionals, but the difference is between more traditional and more current models of professional behaviour. Currently, professionals are widely induced to regard talking in an ordinary conversational way in public contexts (commonly referred to in advertisements for professional posts as an ability to 'communicate') as a part of their repertoire. This is a matter of accommodating professional practices to the demands of external agencies, and most notably the media. The differences between the two experts are again partly matters of delivery and accent (the *High Resolution* expert has a Scottish accent), but notice also the use of pronouns. The expert in *High Resolution* makes extensive use of *we*. This personalizes the anatomists, in contrast with the impersonal construction of scientific procedures in some of the doctor's formulations in *Medicine Now* (e.g. *that involves taking these abnormal electrical discharges . converting them into a form the patient can see*). But there is also a slippage between 'exclusive *we*' ('we the anatomists' – e.g. *easier for us to tell how old a child was*) and 'inclusive *we*' ('we human beings' or 'we members of this society' – including the audience – e.g. *once we get older*), marking a certain ambivalence in Margaret Bruce's identity between the expert and the ordinary person.

To sum up the contrasts in presenter and expert identities and relations with audiences between *Medicine Now* and *High Resolution*: the emphasis in *Medicine Now* is upon institutional roles and relations, with the presenter as facilitator and mediator and the doctor as professional expert and pedagogue; the emphasis in *High Resolution* is upon personal identity and personality and a simulation of lifeworld, conversational relations with the audience, as well as (in the case of the presenter) entertainment of the audience.

The *Oprah Winfrey Show*

The *Oprah Winfrey Show* is a popular television show produced in the USA but widely distributed in other countries including the UK. Each show addresses a topic of concern to people in their social or personal lives, with a panel of invited guests including ordinary people talking about their own experiences, and contributions from experts and a studio audience. Oprah Winfrey orchestrates the various contributions, positioning herself with a hand-held microphone in front of or within the studio audience. I shall refer to a programme broadcast in the UK on 9 September 1992 which dealt with women who were 'dumped' by boyfriends when they were young (but not, incidentally, with men dumped by girlfriends). For legal reasons, I am unable to quote directly from the transcript.

One striking feature is the diversity of the voices that are given space in the programme. These include expert voices, but are predominantly the voices of ordinary people. And in contrast to some media output which gives access to ordinary people, these people sometimes give opinions and even speak authoritatively on the issues, as well as recounting their experiences. The diversity of voices arises partly from the selection of guests to represent a range of opposing perspectives, partly from the relationship between lay and expert voices, and partly from the variety of perspectives voiced from the audience. One interesting feature of these programmes with respect to relationships between participants is the management of diversity: how an *Oprah Winfrey Show* orders these various voices in relation to each other, how certain voices frame others, how voices are hierarchized, and in particular how the voices of ordinary people are given space yet at the same time contained and managed.

The relationship between the voice of the expert and other voices in the panel and the audience is particularly noteworthy. The expert is introduced as a 'therapist' and author of two books on love and the breakdown of relationships. In one part of the programme an opinion is expressed, and forcefully and eloquently expressed, by an audience member. But that opinion is, interestingly, referred by Oprah Winfrey to the expert, who in this case endorses it. The same thing happens at the end of the programme – in fact the programme actually closes with the therapist still speaking, which underscores the way in which other voices are framed by the therapist's. Audience and panel members may be allowed opinions as well as experiences, but their opinions are given value through being endorsed by the expert.

The way in which the therapist is constructed as expert is in contrast with both *Medicine Now* and *High Resolution*. The expert here is herself an accomplished *media* professional, a good 'communicator' in a common contemporary sense of that term, in contrast with the medical professional of *Medicine Now*, and the anatomist expert of *High Resolution* (who accommodates to media requirements for a conversational mode of expert talk, but is still far from the therapist's media-designed performance). One aspect of this is the fluency and flow of her talk. This comes across in the relative absence of pauses, and of hesitations and other disfluencies, but also in the high degree of structuring and verbal planning evident in her contributions. The fluency and the flow depend, however, upon the freedom that Oprah Winfrey gives to the therapist to hold the floor and develop her arguments at some considerable length, in contrast with the more heavily mediated and controlled presence of experts in the *Medicine Now* and *High Resolution* programmes. Fluency and flow are also part of a contrast in purpose: the therapist here aims to persuade the panel and audience to see their own experience in relationships in particular ways, whereas there is no such persuasive objective in the other programmes.

The difference in medium (television versus radio) is, not surprisingly, important. Therapist identity and therapist–audience relations are constructed visually as well as in language. The audience reactions shown on camera while the therapist is talking construct the therapist as an authority whose pronouncements the audience is prepared to accept. Audience members are shown listening more carefully and concentrating more seriously and intently than during other contributions. The authoritative role of the therapist within the configuration of voices is also symbolized in her physical positioning, on the panel facing the audience (and Oprah Winfrey), with four other panel members – two sets of former partners on each side of her. A significant part of the performance is the expert's non-verbal communication. Her talk is accompanied by almost continuous expressive hand movements (a great deal more than any other contributor's), and she also uses her body more than others in alternating address – addressing the couple on the left, the couple on the right, particular sections of the audience, or Oprah Winfrey. Linguistically, her authoritativeness comes across in the modality, in the categorical assertions she makes not only about relationships in general, but also about the particular experiences of the ex-partners on the panel. The therapist is making the extremely powerful implicit claim of a capacity to interpret people's experiences for them. Significantly, the only hint of a challenge to this claim to power comes not from the panel or the audience, but from Oprah Winfrey, in the form of interruptions. Oprah, as presenter, claims precedence even over the professional mystique of the therapist. It is Oprah herself who orchestrates the hierarchization of voices in the final analysis. Also, the therapist is faded out in full flow at the end of the programme, which we must read as a little covert undermining of her. There is perhaps a hint of ambivalence about the authority of the expert here which points to the more explicit challenging of experts in other audience discussion programmes (Livingstone and Lunt 1994; see also Chapter 9).

Most of the voices are, as I have indicated, voices of ordinary people, but the fact that the programme is called a 'show' is not, I think, irrelevant in assessing the import of what appears to be a substantive elevation of audience to the status of participant. Ordinary people, and especially those on the panel, are partly there for their entertainment value. In so far as the programme generates controversy, as it standardly does, it is partly because *controlled* controversy makes for good television. But there is often a tension between the serious social or emotional aspects of the issues and experiences dealt with and the search for entertainment.

The identity of Oprah Winfrey herself is very complex. In her capacity as manager of the hierarchization of voices in the show, the one who holds and controls the microphone, she sometimes evaluates contributions as well as controlling their length and order, and sometimes also seeks to reconcile conflicting voices. Oprah's identity includes also her roles as a serious social investigator questioning the panel, and as a chat-show hostess. In the latter capacity she is an accomplished performer, witty, humorous, with a winning smile, a contagious laugh and a generally attractive personality. In addition, she is also at times a moralist and educator, directly addressing viewers on the themes of the programme. So, like the presenter of *High Resolution*, she is simultaneously educator and entertainer, though the particular realization and configuration of these elements is quite different – these are different types of programme, emanating from different cultures, and we have the contrast between a black American woman and a white British man. Also, like the presenter in *High Resolution*, Oprah Winfrey is constructed as an ordinary person sharing the lifeworld of people in the studio and home audiences, though again the realizations of this ordinariness in her talk are quite different.

Today

The *Today* programme is broadcast every weekday morning on BBC Radio 4. It is particularly noteworthy for the populist, common-sense style of its presenters, which is all I shall discuss here. The following extracts are from an edition of the programme broadcast on 8 April 1992 during the UK general election, involving two presenters, John Humphrys (JH) and Brian Redhead (BH). The first extract is from an interview with an expert on elections about the possibility of a coalition government. Because my focus is on presenters, I have omitted most of the expert's contributions.

Extract 1

JH: twenty to nine so what are the odds on a hung Parliament I shall be asking the man from Ladbroke's in a moment but first someone who's seen it all before many times before Dr David Butler . of Nuffield College Oxford who was studying elections when Messrs Kinnock, Major and Ashdown were still in their prams I suspect . perhaps I'm dating you too much there David am I

DB: I was first election was well forty-five I was in the army fifty I was it was the first one I watched

JH: well there you are they were in their prams at that
(DB: yes absolutely) so are we seeing anything different this time

DB: oh yes (part of answer omitted) and it's the first election in which a hung Parliament has seemed the likeliest outcome

JH: and you believe that is the case this time
(answer from DB omitted)

JH: so because we haven't seen this before in quite this way in recent history what's going to happen
(answer from DB omitted)

JH: coz a lot of people have been saying oh well an October election you don't think that's likely or at least
(answer from DB omitted)

JH: an awful lot of people when you ask them say oh I don't much care for any of em why don't we have coalition that would be the best thing what's your view of that
(answer from DB omitted)

JH: but if you ask the politicians of course they will say as you say absolutely terr– at least some of them will say absolutely terrible idea e– it's simply unworkable . e: is is that . purely self-interest
(answer from DB omitted)

The second extract is from a panel interview with representatives of the three main political parties (Conservative, Labour, and Liberal Democrat) about how they would answer questions from an imaginary floating voter. I have included only Brian Redhead's questions and omitted the politicians' answers. (Recall that I used part of this extract as an example in Chapter 1.)

Extract 2

BR: right now thank you all three first of all for being positive and not being negative and knocking the others now imagine this floating voter is very thoughtful and serious and he comes back to you he comes back to you Chris Patten and he says well that's all very well but you know you've been in power so long we're not a one-party country we do need changes occasionally maybe you lot are looking tired and perplexed don't you need a spell in opposition just to rethink
(answer from Chris Patten omitted)

BR: well now Chris Patten thank you now our floating voter turns to you Brian Gould and he says look (BG: yeah) I don't really fancy another Conservative government I think we've had enough of that but I can't really bring myself to vote for you because you've been out of office for so long you haven't got the experience if you get in the City might say do this lot know enough to run the country I'm nervous that a vote for you would mean a vote for some kind of flight from the pound
(answer from Brian Gould, question from BR to Des Wilson, and answer from Des Wilson omitted)
BR: Des Wilson thank you now . imagine this floating voter actually is a mate of all three of you . knows you personally . and has sat up he's a different bloke altogether this one's been here through the whole election he's listened to every blooming broadcast (one of panel: lucky chap) he's fed up to the back teeth (one of panel: haven't we all) . and he rings you up and he says the same question to each of you and I just want a quick answer from each if you would . he says . hey Chris . e:m . your campaign has been dreadful . I mean you've just underestimated the intelligence of the electorate and particularly of me . what would you why did you get it wrong

As in earlier examples in this chapter, delivery is an important element in the construction of presenter identity and presenter–audience relations. But I shall focus for this final example just on the language of the transcriptions.

The populism of the style manifests itself in a high degree of conversationalization. One aspect of this is the direct representation of the discourse of others, including an attempt to simulate the voice of the (real or imaginary) original. Recall that the expert in *Medicine Now* did the same, but the two cases differ considerably, not only in the sorts of voices that are simulated (roughly, they are middle-class voices in *Medicine Now* but working-class voices here), but also in how these simulations are framed. Whereas the doctor's own voice in *Medicine Now* is that of a traditional professional, the presenters' own voices here are very similar to the voices that are simulated – both are the voices of ordinary experience. In other words, even when the presenters do not signal the representation of the discourse of others, they are still in a sense speaking in the voices of others, those of what are taken to be typical audience members, and there is nothing in the represented discourse within these extracts that could not be the presenters' own words. In the second extract, with Brian Redhead, the whole item is built around the simulated voice of the floating voter, but there are also simulations in the latter part of the first extract (e.g. *oh I don't much care for any of em why don't we have coalition that would be the best thing*).

The conversationalization of the presenters' talk is realized in a variety of linguistic features. Most obvious are items of colloquial vocabulary such as *knocking, fancy, mate, bloke,* and so forth. Notice also the colloquial way of quantifying in *an awful lot of people.* There are also cases of vocabulary items which are not *per se* colloquial but which are used in colloquial senses, such as *dating* (meaning showing how old someone is, as in expressions like *that dates you*) and *negative* (meaning critical). Certain expressions evoke the specific know-ledges, wisdom or preoccupations of the culture of the lifeworld: *the man from Ladbroke's, who's seen it all before, when (they) were still in their prams,* and so forth. Pronouns (as always) are worth noting, especi-ally the use of inclusive *we* (e.g. *are we seeing anything different, we're not a one-party country*) and the colloquial use of *you* as an indefinite pronoun (e.g. *an awful lot of people when you ask them say*). Notice also in the second extract the colloquial use of the demonstrative pronoun *this* to refer to someone (e.g. *imagine this floating voter actually is a mate of all three of you*). The presenters also use discourse markers (words like *oh, well,* and *right*) in ways that are typical of conversation, and conversational ways of using conjunctions (such as *so* and *coz* in *so because we haven't seen this before* . . . and *coz a lot of people have been say-ing* . . . in extract 1). There are also features of conversational nar-rative and argumentation, such as the use of present tense in narrative in extract 2 (e.g. *he comes back to you Chris Patten and he says*), and the formula for prefacing a disagreement *that's all very well but.* . . . Finally, we get something of the compression and high level of implicitness that is common in ordinary conversation in *(a lot of people have been saying) oh well an October election* in extract 1, which might be more explicitly formulated as something like 'it seems from what's happening that there is likely to be an October election'.

On the *Today* programme, as with the other programmes I have discussed, presenter identity is more complex than I have indicated so far. Part of this complexity derives from the duality of address: the presenter is for much of the programme addressing an interviewee or another reporter as well as (indirectly) the audience. In extract 1, for example, the formulation *and you believe that is the case this time* would pass perfectly well within academic discourse, and indicates an accommodation to the expert which is generally lacking here. As with the presenter in *Medicine Now*, there is a certain ambivalence – if a less clearly expressed one – in the presenter's relationship to the domain of specialist knowledge, academic analysis of politics in this case, so that on occasion the presenter displays his credentials as a part-specialist.

This chapter demonstrates some of the diversity in the construction of identities and relations that I referred to on page 127. *Medicine Now* is the most conservative of the four programmes I have discussed and contrasts with the others in several ways: informing is not mixed with entertaining, institutional distance is maintained, and institutional roles are foregrounded over personalities. The other programmes, in differing degrees and ways, shift towards entertainment, claimed co-membership of the audience lifeworld, and the foregrounding of personality, though entertainment is not as salient in the *Today* programme as in the other two. I have shown how these developments variously affect the construction of presenters in the three programmes, and the experts in *High Resolution* and the *Oprah Winfrey Show*.

These developments also entail important differences in how audiences are constructed: the audience of *Medicine Now* is constructed as a group of citizens, people who have an intelligent interest in keeping up with the advancement of knowledge. The audiences of the other programmes (particularly *High Resolution* and the *Oprah Winfrey Show*) are in addition constructed as consumers, as people for whom listening to radio or watching television are leisure activities, involving the expectation of entertainment. There are also, as I have indicated, differences in terms of the ways in which ordinary people make the transition from audience to participant. In *Medicine Now*, the patient is present as a tightly managed witness who is limited to recounting a relevant experience, as an illustration. In the *Oprah Winfrey Show* by contrast, ordinary people are the main participants, giving opinions as well as recounting experiences, though they are partly there as spectacles for audience entertainment, and so positioned within the presenter's orchestration and hierarchization of voices that their opinions and experiences are subordinated to the legitimated opinion (counting as knowledge) of the expert.

I have referred at times to the options or choices available in the construction of presenters or experts. The notion of choice, as I indicated in Chapter 1, is a helpful one on one level but can be misleading, especially since market values and ideologies which centre around choice are very much at issue in these constructions. When I refer to choices or options, I mean that practices are variable, that the order of discourse includes alternative sets of practices. This variability, as it appears at a particular point in time, can be seen from a historical perspective as change in progress. In this case, *Medicine Now* is representative of older media practices whereas the other programmes are more representative of newer practices which have come to be dominant. Within the newer practices there are various degrees to which the shifts towards entertainment, personality, and commonsensicalness can be taken. There are also various ways in which, for instance, being 'conversational' can be realized linguistically. These are choices, but that does not necessarily imply freedom of choice for individuals, since many of them are determined by factors such as the type of programme, the target audience, pressures for audience maximization, and so forth.

The concept of 'personality' is salient in contemporary media (Tolson 1990, 1991), but it is important to clarify what is meant by the suggestion of a shift away from institutional roles towards a foregrounding of personality. This is often perceived and portrayed in a way which harmonizes with the core contemporary cultural value of individualism, in terms of a foregrounding of the unique and individual personalities of, especially, different presenters. The shift in the way identities are constructed can indeed be seen as significant in projecting and spreading ideas and values of individualism within contemporary society. Yet how individual are these various presenter identities? Of course, there are clear differences between individuals such as Brian Redhead and John Humphrys on the *Today* programme, but then there were clear differences between different announcers in the earlier history of broadcasting when institutional role was more in focus. Even fairly rigid roles allow considerable space for individual style, in addition to the individualizing effects of differences in voice quality and accent. On the other hand, contemporary presenter personalities fall into fairly clear types. The *Today* programme is interesting in this regard, because it was built around the personality of the late Brian Redhead over a number of years, but John Humphrys, having taken over as the main presenter, projects the same type of personality as Redhead through a similar style of talk. This shows how personality can become transformed into product image, and in that sense become depersonalized, on the leisure market. Or again, there is the aggressive school of interviewers, including Sir Robin Day, more recently Jeremy Paxman, and various others. The shift that has taken place has a personalizing nature in the sense that aspects of identity traditionally associated with the private domain (e.g. aggression) are being appropriated by the media, but that does not necessarily entail a substantive increase in individuality. This strikes me as an ideological representation of the shift in the sense that it reads it in terms of individualist ideologies which obfuscate ways in which the media reflect and help shape changes of a social and cultural order.

Changes in construction of presenter–audience relations, also, may have ideological import. Consider the following sequence from extract 2 of the *Today* programme:

> you haven't got the experience if you get in the City might say do this lot know enough to run the country I'm nervous that a vote for you would mean a vote for some kind of flight from the pound

One question to ask is how particular constructions of relations (and identities) relate to particular representations, the concerns of Chapter 6. In this case, notice the presupposition that a flight from the pound is a City judgement on the competence of a government. This particular piece of preconstructed knowledge may work ideologically in representing the City in terms of a preoccupation with competence which may obfuscate its preoccupation with profits. The construction of presenter–audience relations in terms of shared membership of a common-sense lifeworld, the 'communicative ethos' (Scannell 1992) that is realized in a conversationalized, public-colloquial style, can be seen as instrumental in legitimizing such ideological aspects of representations (see also the discussion of Fowler 1991 in Chapter 1, page 13). It is significant, too, that the City is attributed with the same conversationalized communicative style as the presenter and the floating voter (notice *this lot*). But the communicative style also has a potential ideological import in itself, in the implicit claims it makes about the validity of social relations (Habermas 1984): when reporters address audiences in such a communicative style, they implicitly claim, as I have suggested, shared membership of the same lifeworld, and in so doing implicitly negate the differences of position, perspective and interest that are implied by practices in which contrasts of institutional role are explicit. The same is true when politicians or senior managers or archbishops or (as we have seen) various categories of expert address the public in a conversationalized communicative style. What I am suggesting is that the style can help in an imaginary ideological construction of social relations whose real nature is less symmetrical and benign (Bernstein 1990).

But the communicative ethos of broadcasting is more ambivalent politically than this suggests. It can be read at the same time as forming part of a substantive democratization of cultural life and cultural relations which has given value to popular culture and ordinary practices within the wider culture. I see relational and identity aspects of media texts as a complex field of negotiation and contestation where complex, overlapping and contradictory cultural tendencies meet and are enacted, are given texture. Cultural democratization takes place in a society which is built upon relations of domination and exploitation which must be reproduced and legitimized, and where the market and market–consumer relations are colonizing new domains of social life including 'leisure' and the media. The communicative style of broadcasting lies at the intersection of these democratizing, legitimizing and marketizing pressures, and its ambivalence follows from that.

8

CRIMEWATCH UK

In this chapter and Chapter 9, I shall be applying the analytical framework, presented in previous chapters, in two case-studies. My focus in this chapter is upon a programme which has been appearing regularly on BBC1 television for a number of years, *Crimewatch UK*. The programme enlists public help for the police in the solving of crimes. It includes re-enactments of crimes, interviews with the police, and public appeals for information which could help solve crimes. I shall also refer for comparison, and more briefly, to a somewhat similar programme also regularly shown on BBC1 over the same period, *999*, which is described in the weekly TV and radio programme guide *Radio Times* as 'dramatic stories of real-life rescues, reconstructed by the emergency services, actors and those people involved in the actual rescues'.

My main concern will be with how television in these instances contributes to a particular construction of the relationship between the public and the state – more precisely, between the public and the police in the case of *Crimewatch UK*, and between the public and the emergency services (fire brigade, police, ambulance service) in the case of *999*. I shall suggest that we can use discourse analysis to throw some light on this general issue by focusing upon the nature of the discourse practice in these programmes – upon how genres, voices, and discourses are articulated together. I shall look at the mix of public information and entertainment, and of official discourse and the discourse of ordinary experience; and how relationships between the voices of the police, emergency services, ordinary people, and media journalists are structured. What I think is going on in both programmes is intervention to shore up the crumbling public legitimacy of the state.

The *Crimewatch* format

Crimewatch UK programmes are put together according to a relatively fixed formula involving combinations of a small number of regular types of feature: 'Photocall', 'Incident desk' and 'Aladdin's cave' (unclaimed and stolen property) are regular slots which are interspersed with a number of re-enactments of crimes. Reports and updates on cases treated in previous programmes or earlier in the programme – information about responses from the audience and what the police have done on the basis of them – are another element. Here, for example, is how one edition of *Crimewatch* (broadcast on 18 February 1993) was structured:

Opening sequence
James Bulger case: latest information
Re-enactment: Claire Tiltman murder
Report: previous Photocall
Photocall
Re-enactment: Muriel Harvey rape
Update: James Bulger feature
Incident desk
Re-enactment: Doncaster robbery
Aladdin's cave: unclaimed and stolen property
Update: James Bulger and Claire Tiltman features
Closing

There is, additionally, a separately scheduled *Crimewatch Update* one-and-a-half hours after the end of the programme.

Let us look more closely at the elements in this structure. The opening sequence is a series of shots showing members of the public witnessing criminal activity (mainly getaways) – one watches from an upstairs window, another from a passing car, another is a pedestrian with a good view of a number plate. The last shot in the sequence shows a disembodied hand lifting a telephone receiver and dialling – presumably – the police. The shots highlight the potentially danger-ous consequences of crime for ordinary people not directly involved: they show some near misses – a pedestrian with a pram narrowly missed by a speeding vehicle, a passing motorist almost in collision with a getaway car. The programme's assumptions about relation-ships between criminals, the public and the police are clearly signalled at the outset. The dramatic percussion music is reminiscent of the theme tunes of police drama series.

The featured re-enactments have a regular and predictable struc-ture: an on-camera introduction by the presenter, a filmed re-enactment of the crime, an interview by the presenter with a police officer, an on-camera closing by the presenter. Appeals for help from the audience sometimes occur within the filmed re-enactment and in the interview, but they are particularly the focus of the presenter's closing which always includes a telephone number for people to call. Appeals for information are directed at possible witnesses of the crime, but suspects and the families and friends of possible suspects are also urged to come forward. Constantly repeated motifs are that there is someone out there who knows who committed the crime, and that the criminal may strike again.

The first feature, on the James Bulger case, has the substance and some of the structure of a re-enactment, but is actually not a typical feature. James Bulger was a small child who later proved to have been murdered by two older boys. The case attracted a great deal of public attention. The item here is a summary of the latest information on the case. There is no filmed re-enactment, but instead an extended presenter account of new security video pictures of the two boys, the exact route they took with James (with precise timings), what James was wearing, and a forensic psychologist's report about the likely identity and behaviour of the two boys. This is followed by the usual sequel to a re-enactment: an interview with a police officer, plus a closing appeal for help, on-camera, from the presenter.

In both the 'Photocall' and 'Incident desk' features, police officers themselves take over the job of presenting. The police presenter team mirrors the team of journalists who orchestrate the programme as a whole – in both cases there is a team of two, a man and a woman, and they alternate in presenting items. 'Photocall' and 'Incident desk' give brief accounts of crimes, without filmed re-enactments, and again appeal for audience help. 'Photocall' is built around a set of four photographs of suspects. Each case is briefly summed up by one of the police presenters in voice-over, while images on the screen change according to the following sequence: photograph of suspect; pictures of location of crime, vehicles used, etc.; 'mug shot' of suspect with personal details shown on screen (age, height, build, hair-colour); original photograph of suspect, with a voice-over appeal for help. 'Photocall' ends with a number for people with information to phone. 'Incident desk' differs from 'Photocall' in that the police presenters are on-camera addressing the audience.

The 'Aladdin's cave' of unclaimed and stolen property, the last substantial feature before the end, provides light relief after the catalogue of crimes. This feature evokes a popular television programme, *The Antiques Roadshow,* in which members of the public bring their prized possessions for identification and valuation by experts in antiques. The items of stolen and unclaimed property shown are exclusively (apparent) antiques, and they are displayed as they might be in an antique shop. This feature has its own presenter, who sets himself off from the others both in his appearance (a bow-tie and moustache are antique-dealer style rather than police or journalist style), and by giving what might pass as specialist descriptions of some of the items. For instance:

> well I'm quite taken by these e this pair of glass bon-bon dishes well . not so much the glass dishes but more the silver frames I love this cast swan . and he rests upon a little lion's paw foot . now they've got e: English hallmarks but they they were imported if you're the owner . you'll know where they were imported from

The discourse is sometimes mixed, in that collector's descriptions are sometimes merged with the police identification of distinguishing marks.

The closing of the programme brings in another common *Crimewatch* motif:

> must be said that e: after the grim litany of crimes we've shown tonight it may be worthwhile pointing out the obvious that . most people are decent and . in their hundreds if not thousands . are now calling in to help so if you can't stop up till *Crimewatch Update* please . don't have nightmares do sleep well . goodnight

It is commonly claimed that 'moral panics' about crime are a characteristic of contemporary society – that people's fear of crime is in many cases disproportionate given the actual risks they are subject to. Programmes like *Crimewatch* might be regarded as contributing to moral panics, and such attempts to reassure people indicate sensitivity on that score.

What I have said so far about the structure of this edition of *Crimewatch* gives a preliminary sense of the articulation of voices in the programme, which is, as I have indicated, one of my main focuses. It indicates that voices are not neatly associated with roles – in particular, that the presentation of features is shared between media presenters and police officers, and the presenters are doing police work in, for instance, appealing for witnesses. This fudging of the difference between mediators and public officials is one element in the process I referred to earlier of restructuring of police–public relations in a way that helps legitimize the police, as also is the closing feature which brings to police work the benign and popular resonances of *The Antiques Roadshow*.

I now want to take the analysis further by focusing in on one of the re-enactment features, the Claire Tiltman murder. In terms of the critical discourse analysis framework presented in earlier chapters, the emphasis will be on discourse practice and intertextuality, supported with selective textual analysis. Comments on sociocultural practice will follow later. I shall begin looking at the articulation of *genres* in the re-enactment, then look at how *voices* are combined together, and finally at the main *discourses* that are drawn upon.

Generic analysis

I have indicated that re-enactments in *Crimewatch* are internally complex, involving a diverse set of elements in a predictable sequence:

> Presenter's introduction
> Film ('re-enactment proper')
> Interview between presenter and police officer
> Appeal for audience's help by the presenter

These are indeed the main elements of the re-enactment under scrutiny, but this gives only a rough and inadequate idea of its generic complexity, because the film is itself internally complex. So I shall begin with a fairly detailed summary of it.

The first point to make is that it is not a simple narrative of what happened to Claire Tiltman. The narrative element is preceded and followed by non-narrative elements:

> Fire-fighting sequence
> Narrative of Claire's last day
> Pool-game sequence

The first of these shows Claire (played by an actress) learning about fire-fighting with the fire brigade as part of a Duke of Edinburgh Award scheme, actually using a fire hose on a burning building. The sequence is dramatized, with some dialogue between Claire and a fireman, and a lot of squeals and laughter. Claire comes across as a pleasant and lively teenager. The sequence is accompanied by voice-over from Claire's (real) father and mother – for part of this, the fire-fighting film is interrupted by a close-up photograph of Claire and film of Claire's parents sitting together on a couch – and from the fireman who is a 'character' in the film. The final pool-game sequence is similar – it shows Claire playing very successfully at pool, with an accompanying voice-over from her parents talking about her interest in and skill at the game, during which the picture shifts to Claire's parents again seated together on the couch. The sequence (and the film) closes with an appeal by Claire's mother to the wife, girlfriend or mother of the murderer to come forward. The central and longest part of the film is the narrative of Claire's last day. The main episodes are:

> Claire preparing to go to school
> Claire's journey to school (she arranges to visit her friend that evening)
> Claire taking an examination at school
> Claire back home
> Claire walking to her friend's house
> A witness driving past where Claire was killed seeing a suspect car and a girl (Claire) running out of an alley
> The discovery of Claire's body, attempts to revive her

Apart from the examination, Claire's walk and the witness in the car, these episodes involve dialogue, and most episodes also have elements of 'commentary', mainly voice-over.

Voice-over: generic complexity

I want to focus on the generically diverse roles of voice-over as a way into the generic complexity of re-enactments. Voice-over serves a variety of functions in the film and draws upon a number of genres. The main genres are what I shall call *narrative, biography*, and *public appeal*. Some of this generic diversity is exemplified in the following example of the presenter's voice-over:

> Claire had a mile to walk to Vicky's home . were you driving down the A226 . here called the London Road through Greenhithe Kent between Dartford and Gravesend . it's six o'clock on Monday a month ago Monday the eighteenth of January

The first sentence shows the presenter as narrator, working with the dramatized film narrative to tell the story, in this case providing information important to the narrative which cannot easily be shown in the film. The question which follows (up to *Gravesend*) illustrates voice-over as public appeal for information. Notice the official (police) discourse manifest here in the formal description of location, which is 'person-neutral' in the sense that it makes no assumptions about audience knowledge, and no claims of shared knowledge or co-membership between presenter and audience. The third element of the extract (from *it's six o'clock*) is again narrative, but in this case it has a dramatizing function in marking the onset of the climactic episode of the narrative which culminates in Claire's murder – notice the use here of an 'historic present' tense (*it's*) instead of a past tense. In its specification of date and time, it also shares with the second element the official function of producing a precise person-neutral description of events, though notice that *a month ago* is an imprecise lifeworld temporal specification rather than an official one.

There are several other instances of generically narrative voice-over from the presenter. The following example of voice-over is interesting:

> the exams was the last day . she'd done quite well in them actually coz . she wasn't a . particularly a scholar but . she did work hard . she done very well

It has a partly narrative role, contextualizing the film of the examination hall with the information – actually already given – that this was the last day of the exams. What is noteworthy is that Claire's father is here taking on what is otherwise the presenter's role. But it is also partly what I'm calling biography, it is telling us about Claire rather than about the crime.

In the last three episodes of the narrative of Claire's last day, from Claire walking to her friend's house, we find generically narrative voice-over of a special kind, from three witnesses – the jogger, the driver, and a person identified as Michael Godfrey. I want to draw a contrast between these as instances of *testimony* and the *external narrative* which I have referred to as 'narrative' so far. The difference is one of point of view (Toolan 1988). External narrative tells the story from the point of view of a narrator external to the events themselves who is able to take an overview. The 'narrator' in this case is a production team including a film team, but mainly personalized as we have seen as the presenter. Testimony is the story from the point of view of one of those involved, indirectly involved in this case as a witness of a part of the events. The use of testimony echoes common recent practices in broadcast documentary, allowing ordinary people to apparently 'speak for themselves' (whereas in interview genre their voices are mediated by the presenter) and foregrounding persons and personalities (Tolson 1991).

As the jogger describes what he saw, what he describes is shown in the film. Testimony is typically not just a narrative of what happened, in this case Claire's walk as witnessed by the jogger. The focus is partly upon the personality of the witness, and his/her responses to and evaluation of events. The jogger's account is prefaced with biographical contextualization (*I often go jogging along the London Road*), and ends with a report of what went through his mind (*oh thank you for letting me run in the road*). We might say that this testimony is transformed into the external narrative of the film which accompanies it, with quite a long objectifying shot of the jogger running down the road, and Claire shown actually crossing the road rather than just (as in the jogger's testimony) behaving as if she might. This sets up a tension between testimony and external narrative. But there is also a parallel tension within the testimony, a contrast of styles between the part which describes what the jogger saw, and the reported thought. The latter is conversational and colloquial in using the rhetorical form 'I thought to myself' + direct speech (*I thought to myself oh . thank you for . letting me run in the road*). The former bears traces of written language (e.g. use of *thus* and positioning of *again* before *noticed* – *I again noticed Claire in the distance*), and these features plus the attempt at precise factual description of place and action (e.g. *she walked out towards the main road as if she was going to cross*) evoke the style of formal official (including police) report. Official report is normally associated with external narrative – hence my allusion above to a 'parallel tension'.

Voice-over works in a similar way in the next episode (witness driving past the scene of the crime). Again, this is testimony, and it foregrounds the witness's affective responses. His disgust at the way the car he noticed was parked is expressed both lexically (e.g. *stupid* in *this car that's parked in a very stupid place*) and through expressive delivery. As with the jogger's testimony, the grounding of the account in ordinary experience and sensibility is underscored by colloquial rhetorical forms – 'I remember thinking' + direct speech, and 'it suddenly dawned on me'. While testimony is a public genre in the sense that it is associated with public functions – notably evidence in courts of law – it is essentially the public appropriation of personal experience and of the private-domain genre for recounting personal experience, conversational narrative. Which is why it is normally colloquial and conversational in style. Testimony is a form for linking personal experience and public accountability.

The voice-over from the witness Michael Godfrey is in two parts. The first is another instance of testimony, but the second, while having a narrative function, is different from anything so far:

> I'm sure that . Claire would have sensed . that somebody was with her . in that last moment . I think that's quite important . for her family to know that . that she wasn't on her own

It is not part of the story, part of the account of what happened, but a comment on and evaluation of the story, drawing some comfort from it, and linking the story as past events to the present and Claire's family's continuing grief. Notice the deictic forms here, particularly the verb tenses. The past-tense verbs, but also the demonstrative *that* (*in that last moment*) contrast with the present tenses which anchor these words in the moment of speaking, after the event – *I'm sure, I think, that's quite important*. Although, like testimony, this is the perception and point of view of one witness, it does also have a role in the main external narrative, or perhaps rather it serves to bring the two narrative perspectives together, providing a closure, the sense of an ending.

The *biography* genre is mainly present in the voice-overs in the firefighting and pool-game sequences, which are primarily building a sympathetic and positive picture of Claire. The voice-over from her parents in the opening sequence is a jointly developed account of her interests:

FATHER: she was in the fire brigade . the Duke of Edinburgh
Scheme and ⌈ e:
MOTHER: ⌊ I don't think she wanted a nine-to-five job
she wanted to go in the fire brigade
FATHER: that that was her intention to go in the fire brigade . no
one would change it (laughs) she was a lovely kid you
know s –: it's just such a shame

Notice how her mother cuts into and continues her father's account, and how he then picks up and thematizes 'the fire brigade' (with *that*) from her turn. Notice also how her father's account shifts from talking about Claire in the third-person to talking in her voice, so to speak, in a clause (*no one would change it*) that is marked as free indirect speech by its modal verb (*would*). This is followed by an affectionate laugh and makes a transition from the third-person account of

Claire's interests to her father's explicit wording of the evaluative and moral conclusions the account and the film point to – *she was a lovely kid*, and *it's just such a shame*. The voice-over from the fireman in the opening sequence is generically different: it's a testimonial (different from the 'testimony' I referred to earlier), an evaluation of Claire's performance and potential. The parents' voice-over in the final pool-game sequence is generically similar to their earlier one, a conversational account.

To sum up, then, voice-over indicates that the film is generically complex in being part narrative of events leading up to and following the crime, part biographical portrait of Claire, part public appeal. The biographical element is itself generically complex, including a life-world part, conversational reminiscence, and a more public/official part, testimonial. The narrative too is generically complex, bringing together external narration of events and the personal testimony of witnesses. I now want to carry on investigating the nature of this generic complexity by taking a closer look at the narrative.

Narrative

Police work conventionally makes use of narrative in appeals for help and information from the public. Police officers are sometimes interviewed on news programmes, and give narrative accounts of crimes as a basis for appeals for help. Sometimes the police use a dramatized form of narrative, the reconstruction, which has traditionally involved police officers playing the parts of those involved in crimes. *Crimewatch UK* sees itself as an extension of this: it sees what it is doing primarily in terms of eliciting help from the public in the solving of crimes.

This construction of the programme places it in the domain of fact and information, suggesting a version of external narrative which is focused upon events of and around the crime, and their time and place, and linked to public appeal. But as I have already indicated, what we actually find in re-enactments is part external narrative but also part testimony, and a focus upon personality and character – in this instance upon the personality of Claire herself, her parents, and the witnesses. Films are referred to in *Crimewatch UK* sometimes as 're-enactments' and sometimes as 'reconstructions', and this dual identification perhaps points to their ambivalence: they do have in part a factual and informational character (as reconstructions), but they also have a dramatized and fictionalized entertainment character (as re-enactments). We have in another form the tension between information and entertainment which has been referred to through the book, and it is also in this case a tension between factual and fictional, between public information and drama. It is worth noting in this connection that the sort of crimes that *Crimewatch UK* covers are mainly those which are most obviously open to dramatization – corporate fraud, for instance, is low on the agenda.

Even in conventional police reconstructions, events are dramatized in the sense that people are playing the parts of those involved in the crime. But in *Crimewatch*, these include professional actors as well as some of the people actually involved, but not police. These are professionally produced dramas, even if they are less than distinguished instances. They include extensive dialogue. This, together with other generic elements I have indicated – the biography genres of the opening and closing sequences, and the testimony – contributes to the focusing of character and personality. In fact, one might argue that all of the narrative of Claire's last day before her walk to her friend's house is primarily there to develop character, first and foremost the character of Claire. There is no question of eliciting public information about the events of the earlier part of the day, and a traditional police reconstruction would cover only Claire's walk to her friend's house up to the discovery of her body. This focus upon character and personality which shapes so much of the re-enactment is central to its character as fictionalized entertainment.

A great temptation for journalists with a story of this sort is to play up its sensational potential, the violent, horrific and wanton nature of the attack. *Crimewatch UK* is very restrained in this regard, as it has to be if it is to maintain any credibility for its claim that the programme is primarily about public help for the police. But the actual ambivalence of the programme just referred to does show itself in certain relatively muted ways in which the presenter creates an atmosphere of suspense. Notice, firstly, how the crime is formulated in the presenter's introduction in the three expressions: *another rather grim case that's made national headlines, a killing for the sake of it, she was apparently picked at random*. This is very tame compared with what the tabloid press might make of it, but nevertheless it establishes (in this viewer, at least) an anticipation of horrors to come. Notice, though, that the presenter actually says *another case I'm afraid that seems to be a killing for the sake of it*: this is double-voiced, for it brings together the muted foregrounding of the sensational nature of the story with the programme's commitment (realized in *I'm afraid, seems*) not to contribute to moral panics or sensationalize crime. Later in the presenter's commentary, the background information refers to the *evening without pressure* which Claire was looking forward to. This familiar anticipatory narrative device again builds up suspense for viewers, ironically juxtaposing what Claire hoped for and what we all know is going to happen. A sequence where Claire is offered a lift but refuses it has a similar ironic effect, which is reinforced shortly afterwards by Claire's mother's explanation of why she didn't drive her to her friend's house. I have already referred to the voice-over which uses the historic present to dramatically register the onset of the climactic episode leading to Claire's death.

Voices

I now want to begin shifting the analysis of the discourse practice and intertextuality of *Crimewatch UK* away from genres and towards discourses. I shall do so by looking at the range of voices that are included in the programme, how those voices are distributed within the complex configuration of genres I have pointed to above, and thus what relationships are set up between voices. I will then in the next section look at the relationship between voices and discourses.

The main voices, the main types of social agents, that figure in this programme are the police and other officials (e.g. firemen), ordinary people, and media presenters. Ordinary people include in some cases the victim of the crime (Claire obviously cannot speak for herself, but Muriel Harvey for instance, a rape victim, does), the victim's family and friends, and witnesses.

The feature on the Claire Tiltman murder shows a distribution of voices with respect to genres which is typical for *Crimewatch UK*. The police do not figure in the film; the main account of the crime is mediated by the presenters and by the testimony of ordinary people, but not by the police. The police figure only in the person of Inspector Owen Taylor who is interviewee in the interview which follows the film. This is an instance of what we might call the 'expert interview', in which the interviewee is constructed as having expert knowledge which the interviewer is eliciting on behalf of the audience. The aim of the interviewer is not to probe or challenge, but rather to facilitate communication between expert and audience. The content of the police officer's answers is more or less fully anticipated – and in some cases closely preformulated – in the questions, suggesting that interviewer and interviewee are collaborating in covering an agreed agenda. (Interview genre is presumably preferred to a monologue from the police officer because it breaks blocks of information into more easily digestible chunks.) For example, at the beginning of the interview, the police officer's answer reformulates and slightly elaborates the question:

> PRESENTER: Owen Taylor that must be your fear . this guy's going to do it again
> OWEN T.: yes it is this was a particularly savage attack . Claire was stabbed . several times with a . a large knife and e: I think there's every likelihood this person could strike again

This guy's going to do it again and *this person could strike again* are parallel formulations of the same proposition but in different discourses (a contrast I return to). And again the police officer's *it's not the sort of thing you would normally carry around* closely echoes the presenter's *it's not the sort of knife you would sort of carry*, and *an unusual weapon* echoes *a very unusually large knife*.

Another feature of the questions is the presenter's deference towards the police officer, which is marked in the modality. Two instances use subjective modality to foreground the police officer's judgement – his fears in *that must be your fear*, his opinion in *does he live in the area do you think*. The *must* in the first of these, as well as *presumably* elsewhere, both in declarative questions where the question is in the form of a statement, mitigate the presenter's claim to knowledge by marking it as a presumption which the police officer ratifies in each case. The police officer's answers are a mixture of categorically modalized statements (such as *yes it is, this was a particularly savage attack*) where the basis for speaking authoritatively is implicit, and statements which foreground the police officer's own judgement through use of subjective modalities (such as *I think there's every likelihood this person could strike again*).

The voice of the police here is mainly limited to giving information about the crime and the investigation, but there is an instance of public appeal embedded within one of the answers (*can you honestly live with Claire Tiltman's murder on your conscience . and can you live with the thought that this person may well strike again*). This is not a direct appeal to the audience – the police officer does not look at the camera and speak directly to the viewers, he tells the interviewer what he would 'simply say' to someone who knew who the murderer was. Nevertheless, this indirect appeal *is* in the form of direct speech, in the form of a direct question to the potential witness (compare the option of an indirect question: *I would simply ask that person whether they could honestly live with Claire Tiltman's murder on their conscience*).

But elsewhere in the programme, in the 'Photocall' and 'Inquiry desk' features, police officers take on the role of presenters. The following item from 'Inquiry desk' is presented by a police superintendent:

> first tonight in Incident Desk we need your help to identify this man . who sexually assaulted a motorist on Saturday the seventh of November . the twenty-four-year-old woman was driving along the A323 near Guildford when her car overheated – she was looking under the bonnet of her white Vauxhall Astra when a man stopped . and offered to help her . however his kindness didn't last . he grabbed the woman and dragged her into bushes . she was knocked unconscious and it was an hour and a half later before she managed to raise the alarm . the victim remembered her attacker was smartly dressed . and wore a shiny dark quilted jacket . he was in his early thirties . around six foot . with a strong athletic build . perhaps you saw him driving away in a dark-coloured car . possibly a Sierra or Granada . remember it was the A323 Aldershot Road on Saturday . the seventh of November . if you can help . please call Guildford police station on 0483 31111 . that's 0483 the code for Guildford 31111

Apart from interview, we have here the same range of activities which I described for the presenter in the re-enactment of Claire Tiltman's murder: introduction to the item; narrative of the crime; and public appeal. In addition there is a description of the attacker. Notice that the public appeal is prefaced by two cues for potential witnesses (*perhaps you saw him, remember it was the A323*), both, like the appeal itself, directly addressing the viewer (with *you* and the imperative verb *remember*). Police officers taking on the role of presenter adopt a presentational style and delivery which are very similar to those of professional presenters, though perhaps not as fluent. One might also detect in this example some of the relatively muted journalistic exploitation of the story which I discussed for the re-enactment: why else does the narrative have *he grabbed the woman and dragged her into bushes* rather than just *he attacked the woman*?

In *Crimewatch UK*, the relationship between voices and genres is an open and flexible one. In the case of presenters and police, the flexibility works in both directions. One might see the Claire Tiltman re-enactment in terms of a television presenter taking over a traditional police genre of eliciting help with solving crimes. Actually it is not just the presenter, for while the presenter controls the overall structure of the feature, the main narrative of the crime is jointly developed by the presenter and a variety of ordinary people – the parents, and the witnesses. The police are excluded. Also, it is the presenter who makes the direct appeal to viewers for help. In 'Inquiry desk' and 'Photocall', however, the police not only (as it were) repossess their traditional functions in appeals for public help, they also take over the role of the professional presenter.

A striking feature of the programme is the prominence given to various categories of ordinary people – victims of crime, victims' families and friends, and witnesses. The re-enactments dramatize events in the lives of ordinary people, and the real people figure or are represented by actors in the film and dialogue. The potential relevance of stories to everyday life is a vital factor in their appeal to audiences – the sense of 'it could happen to me' which is accentuated by rooting the stories in ordinary life and experience. Ordinary people also have a major part in the development of narratives in the form of what I've called testimony, and in the biographical parts of the film. I also suggested earlier that Claire's father briefly contributes to the external narrative of events, as well as the biographical element. And ordinary people are also involved in the public appeals, if indirectly as in the case of Claire's mother. So here again, the flexibility of the relationship between voices and genres is striking, with ordinary people overlapping with presenters in narrating crimes, and with presenters and police in appealing for help. Notice, however, that there are limits to the flexibility: apart from the one rather marginal instance of Claire's father, ordinary people do not contribute to external narrative, only to testimony, the narrative of personal experience. They are generally excluded from the overview which the external narrator is endowed with. The programme also draws rather a clear line between those who are explicitly interviewed and those whose voices figure without the mediation of the interviewer: it is the police who are constructed as experts through interview, but not ordinary people.

Discourses: official and lifeworld

I want to focus here on the relationship between two main types of discourses: official discourses, discourses of public life and especially of policing; and lifeworld discourses, discourses of ordinary life and ordinary experience. In *Crimewatch UK* the former are primarily associated with the voice of the police, the latter with the voice of ordinary people, while the voice of the presenter mediates between the two. But the picture is rather more complex in that traces of official discourse are discernible in the contributions of ordinary people, while there are elements of lifeworld discourse in contributions from the police (and the fireman in the Claire Tiltman re-enactment). The mapping of voices on to discourses shows some of the flexibility which characterizes the mapping of voices on to genres. An interesting feature of this programme is the way in which it structures the relationships between official and lifeworld discourses, which is linked of course to the way it structures relationships between voices and the categories of social agent they are associated with.

The discourse of Claire's parents in the firefighting sequence (page 154) is predominantly a lifeworld discourse. Textual indicators of lifeworld discourse include vocabulary (e.g. *a nine-to-five job, go in* rather than, for instance, *join* [the fire brigade]), conversational formulae (*it's such a shame, she was a lovely kid*), and the implicit nature of coherence relations which presupposes that audience members share membership of the same lifeworld, and are therefore able to fill the gaps. Examples are: coherence relations between the two parts of *she was in the fire brigade . the Duke of Edinburgh Scheme*; and coherence relations between the account of Claire's interest in the fire brigade, and *she was a lovely kid*, and *it's just such a shame*. My feeling is, however, that *that was her intention* is a trace of official, public discourse. Ordinary conversation is shot through with such traces, and it is not surprising to find it in experiential talk produced for public consumption on television (though one would need to look at how the editing process affects such traces).

The fireman's testimonial in the firefighting sequence is an interesting mixture. A testimonial is by its nature a public and often official genre, but the discourse here is largely a lifeworld one. One obvious factor is that testimonials are usually written, but this is spoken. Consider, for instance, the beginning of the testimonial:

> Claire . she was a good student . she always used to come to the sessions . she was always the first here

A written testimonial might cover the same ground in something like this way:

> Claire Tiltman was a good student who always attended classes.

Features of lifeworld discourse are the use of first name, the disjunctive structure which places *Claire* initially as a sort of thematic label outside clause structure, the auxiliary verb *used to* which foregrounds the fireman's memories of Claire rather than what, for instance, the course records show. I doubt whether a formal testimonial would include anything equivalent to *she was always the first here* – implicitly conveying a sense of someone's personality in this way is a lifeworld practice, whereas a formal testimonial might refer to her 'enthusiasm'. But there are elements of official discourse here, notably at the end: *possibly be in charge of a fire appliance*.

The dialogue in the re-enactment overwhelmingly draws upon lifeworld discourses, except for the sequence near the end involving Michael Godfrey and the ambulance woman, which includes a stretch of technical medical talk from the former:

> no pulse I've been giving her . CPR . she's not responded . and there's no pulse

CPR (which stands for cardio-pulmonary resuscitation) is obviously a technical expression. But the vocabulary in which treatment (*giving the patient CPR*) and its effects (patients *responding*) are talked about also comes from medical discourse, as does the impersonal way of talking about Claire's pulse (*there's no pulse*). (Compare the ambulance woman's question *has she got a pulse* – interestingly, the lay first-aider talks in a more technical way than the professional medical worker.) The testimony from the jogger, the motorist and Michael Godfrey again overwhelmingly draws upon lifeworld discourse, though as I pointed out earlier there are traces of official report in the jogger's account, in the precise description of place and action, the use of *thus*, and the positioning of *again* before *noticed*.

I suggested above that the presenter mediates between the lifeworld and official discourses. There is some evidence of this in the presenter's contributions to the external narrative during the film. For example, a rather official formulation of the occasion *the final day of Claire's mock GCSE exams* is then translated into the lifeworld formulation *sitting tests*. I mentioned earlier the official police discourse in the presenter's formal description of location. But the mediating work of the presenter is most evident in the interview which follows the film. The police officer is mainly, though not entirely, using official discourse, and in some cases there is a contrast between the official discourse of the policeman and lifeworld discourse from the presenter. I referred earlier in another connection to the relationship between their opening turns – compare the presenter's *this guy's going to do it again*, and the policeman's *there's every likelihood this person could strike again*. Official features of the latter are the carefully formulated probability modality (*every likelihood, could*) and the non-evaluative and gender-neutral term *person*. A rather different feature of official discourse in the police officer's next turn is conjunctions with *or* which ensure that all possibilities are covered – we have two examples here, *the person either lives in the area has got connections in the area . or has lived in the area in the past*, and *someone in that local community . knows who that person is . or suspects who they are*. Presenter mediation takes a different form. The police officer refers to Claire being stabbed with a large knife. The presenter reformulates this as *a very unusually large knife it's not the sort of knife you would sort of carry like a little penknife or anything*. This on the one hand facilitates the police work by foregrounding a detail which might prompt information from the audience, but it also sensationalizes by exaggerating the size of the knife in comparison with the police officer's formulation. Elsewhere the presenter himself talks in the categories of official discourse – *unpredictable violence, outbursts of aggression* – or more exactly in those categories from the specialist discourse of psychology that are appropriated within official discourse. Notice also that there are elements of lifeworld discourse in the talk of the police officer – particularly in his indirect appeal for people to come forward, where he echoes the formulation of Claire's mother (*I don't think I could live with myself*) in *can you honestly live with Claire Tiltman's murder on your conscience . and can you live with the thought that*, using the formula of lifeworld discourse *I couldn't live with X*.

Between state and people

I shall conclude this discussion of *Crimewatch* by considering how the features of discourse practice and text described so far link to the programme as sociocultural practice. I see the programme as an intervention into the fraught relationship in contemporary society between the state and the people. Politicians, governments and institutions of the state have lost much of their public credibility and authority over the last two or three decades. There is a major crisis of legitimacy. In the case of the UK police force, the erosion of a relationship of trust between the public and 'the bobby on his beat' is a matter for endless nostalgia, much of it within the media. Even contemporary police drama series reflect the loss of innocence, focusing upon the fallibility and corruption of the police.

Crimewatch UK can be seen in this context as fighting a rearguard action. But it is not harking back to a golden age of police–public relations, it is reconstructing a relationship of trust and cooperation on a new basis, through a mediatization of police work and of the police–public relationship. The work of policing is transformed in the programme into a joint effort between police, journalists and ordinary people – I noted, for instance, that the policing genre of public appeal for information cuts across these three major voices, so that Claire's mother and the interviewed police officer but especially the presenter all appeal for help with the Claire Tiltman case. This relationship between voices and genres also applies to journalistic work, with police officers sharing the role of presenter (specifically in the 'Inquiry desk' and 'Photocall' features) with journalists. Moreover, the ambivalent mix of reconstruction and re-enactment, and the mixing together of dramatized narrative and public appeal, resituate police work in the familiar and homely world of television entertainment. And the salience of a lifeworld discourse within the re-enactment, in the biographical elements and the dialogue, but also in the actual recounting of events in the testimony of witnesses, links police work with ordinary people and ordinary experience. We have, then, a crossing of boundaries and a merging of voices and practices which powerfully domesticates and so legitimizes police work. Or at least appears to do so: it would be fascinating to know what audiences make of this programme.

Let me link these remarks to the question of how audience members are addressed. Audience address is complex and contradictory. The central contradiction is between the capacity in which the programme purports to address audience members, and the capacity in which it does in effect address them. The programme presents itself as eliciting public help for the police. Audience members are addressed, most obviously in the public appeal and the interview, as responsible citizens who may be able to help. Yet the programme is nationally networked, and only a tiny fragment of the 11 million viewers could conceivably be in a position to help. If the issue is primarily helping the police, why a nationally networked programme, why not use local media?

In fact, it is the address/construction of audience members as spectators of an entertainment that has general relevance for a national audience, articulated as I have suggested above with address/construction of audience members as co-members of the life-world, the world of ordinary experience, to which victims, their families and friends, and witnesses are shown as belonging.

The following entry from the *Radio Times* (17 February 1994) shows in a condensed form the contradiction between real and purported target audiences.

Your help is needed to find an armed gang who robbed a post office van in Burnley, Lancashire, and then shot a policeman in the leg. The villains drove off and hijacked two cars, forcing the occupants out at gunpoint, before finally escaping in a Ford XR3i. If you have any information about this or any of the other crimes featured in the programme, call the studio free on 0500 600600.

Radio Times and similar weeklies play an important part in enticing viewers to watch programmes. We have the usual focus on public help at the beginning and the end, but sandwiched between is a summary of an exciting and shocking story. There is an ethical issue here. It is a commonplace understanding that many people get pleasure from watching violence and horror in films and on television. Perhaps *Crimewatch UK* allows people to do that while comforting themselves that they are doing something else. The ethical issue is whether the BBC should tolerate and sustain the discrepancy – which they surely well understand – between what is claimed to be going on and what is actually going on.

999

Like *Crimewatch UK*, *999* is a prime-time BBC1 programme. It is presented by a well-known television journalist and newsreader, Michael Buerk, and features dramatic rescues usually involving the emergency services. My discussion of *999* will be briefer than the section on *Crimewatch*. My purposes in including it are twofold: first, to show that re-enactments of people's misfortunes using something like a *Crimewatch* formula have a wider appeal in television and do not need the particular justification – public help for the police – that *Crimewatch* claims; second, to show that the sensationalist aspect of such stories and their entertainment value are not always as muted as they are in *Crimewatch*.

Two stretches of voice-over from the presenter during the opening sequence give the flavour of the programme:

all of tonight's rescues are true stories . we've sometimes used actors or stuntmen . but everything you see and hear is based upon the accounts of the people involved . they've helped us to reconstruct events . *as they happened*

tonight on *999* . a daring lifeboat rescue in a storm off the Isles of Scilly . captured . as it happened on video – the three-year-old on an adventure that could easily kill him . and the men who *struggled* for his life

These extracts point to two essential properties of *999* stories: they must be true and based upon authentic accounts of those involved, and they must be good drama. The first of these is made explicit, whereas the second is implicit in the 'headlines' of the second extract. The reserved and muted treatment of the entertainment value of stories in *Crimewatch* gives way here to a foregrounding of drama and suspense and the deployment of various devices for heightening them (see below for examples). The italicized words are all given particular salience in the delivery – *all* is heavily and contrastively stressed, *as they happened* is given emphasis through intonation, loudness and pace of delivery, and *struggled* is heavily stressed and expressively articulated to suggest struggle. The first voice-over is accompanied by the series of dramatic images of rescue which make up the opening visual sequence, and the second by shots of a lifeboat in heavy seas then a yacht capsizing, and a small child walking the streets alone then a man struggling in soft mud to position a car tyre in front of him (to stop himself from sinking). The loud and dramatic theme music continues throughout.

While the programme is characterized by a strong element of voyeuristic fascination with the misfortunes of others, this is mitigated in various ways, so that, as in the case of *Crimewatch* there is an ambivalence of intent and ethos about the programme. In some cases, the moral implications of a story are stressed by the presenter. Some stories provide the basis for educational work – for example, the feature I focus on below concerns a heart attack, and the story is followed by advice for the audience on how to give first aid in the case of a heart attack. Throughout, the presenter's serious and austere tone and expression hovers between highlighting the drama and excitement and deprecating the terrible things that happen to people.

I shall focus on one feature which describes how fire and ambulance services rescued a man who had a heart attack near the top of a 200-foot crane. I shall summarize the main events of the story, indicating points at which tension is particularly built up, and then look in more detail at short transcribed extracts.

A crane operator arrives at work on a building site and chats with his friend the site foreman, telling him he's not feeling too well but will 'be alright'. He starts to climb up to his cab at the top of the crane. Shortly afterwards the foreman tries unsuccessfully to call him on an intercom. He notices a hand waving from high up on the crane, realizes there's a problem, and climbs up to find his friend collapsed on a platform just below the top of the crane. The fire brigade and ambulance service arrive. The ambulance man is terrified at the prospect of climbing up the crane. He controls his fear and starts an agonized ascent. The first drama is when part of his equipment catches on the scaffolding of the crane and pulls him back, so that he seems to be at risk of falling. He at last reaches the crane operator and realizes that he has had a massive heart attack, and tells the fireman and the foreman (who are on the platform with him) that unless the man is got down quickly he will die. Will they make it in time? The fireman proposes to lower him down the inside of the crane in a stretcher, but the foreman says that will take too long if it is possible at all. He suggests winching up a skip to lower the man down in. This is agreed, but tension builds up as vital moments are lost because the man on the ground can't shorten the chains enough for the skip to be winched to the top of the crane. He eventually succeeds, and the skip is winched up. But can the foreman (operating the crane) manage to get it close enough to the platform for the transfer? He does. To lower the crane operator in the skip, he has to be placed horizontally on the stretcher, a dangerous position after a heart attack. Will he suffer cardiac arrest? He doesn't. But can the ambulance man overcome his terror sufficiently to climb from the platform into the skip? With great difficulty he manages to do so, but there is then another drama: can the stretcher be moved across without the skip moving and the man falling to his death? They manage it, the skip is lowered to the ground to the applause of those waiting below, and the man is taken to hospital in an ambulance, where he makes a full recovery. The (real) crane operator praises the ambulanceman and gives his own account of his ordeal, which is interspersed with more video re-enactments. The presenter makes a link from the story to a feature on first aid for heart attack victims.

Here is the presenter's introduction to the feature, delivered on-camera with a building site and a large crane in the background:

> few people would relish swaying about on a crane nearly two hundred feet up in the air . the fear of heights can make you panic . can make you freeze . luckily most of us can avoid the experience . but for members of the emergency services there are times when the job leaves them . no choice they're forced to confront their personal fears and overcome them . for the sake of the people they're trying to help . that's exactly what happened one day on a building site here in London

This introduction first evokes the vicarious experience of danger which is a key feature of the programme through an alarming and exaggerated formulation of the rescue (*swaying about on a crane nearly two hundred feet up in the air*). The presenter's face is serious and indeed grim throughout, and the toughness of the scenario evoked is metaphorically conveyed in a tough, hard, tone – the initial consonants of *crane* and *two* are given a particularly explosive release. Toughness is also conveyed through gesture: a thumb sharply jerked backwards to point to the crane behind the presenter. Both *panic* and *freeze* are heavily stressed, and accompanied by both hands being pushed sharply forward to give further salience to these evocations of danger and fear. The alarming image is made safe (*luckily most of us can avoid the experience*), and the vicarious experience of the audience is contrasted with the real experience of people in the emergency services. The internal struggles and courage of emergency workers (a major focus of this feature) are again visually represented through a gestural metaphor of physical confrontation – the presenter pushes his two clenched fists together in front of his chest. This formulation of the story to follow endows it with a serious purpose and point, a moral, which (as suggested above) mitigates the voyeurism: it shows people confronting their personal fears for the general good.

999 is similar to *Crimewatch UK* in constructing narratives through a combination of re-enactment and dialogue, presenter voice-over, and accounts by the people involved. One difference in the formula is that whereas these accounts are in voice-over in *Crimewatch*, in *999* they are mainly given on-camera. This is part of a more general enhancement of the voices of ordinary people, and an exclusion of official voices: although some of these accounts are given by members of the emergency services such as ambulance workers or firefighters, they generally tend to speak personally as ordinary people, not officially. What tends to be in focus is their reactions and feelings.

Here is an extract at the point where the ambulanceman crosses from the platform into the skip. The alternation between re-enactment and the on-camera account by the ambulanceman in the studio is shown by printing the on-camera account in italics.

PRESENTER: once John was strapped into the stretcher . they came to the most difficult part of the rescue
FIREMAN: okay you go over to the skip first . and I'll pass him to you
AMBULANCEMAN: you just be sure . to hold the skip
AMBULANCEMAN (on-camera): *now . I'm now an absolute nervous wreck . I'm shaking I can't breathe properly I'm . I can't talk properly*
AMBULANCEMAN: just be sure to hold the skip
FIREMAN: I've got it
AMBULANCEMAN: . just hold the skip . okay . ready . okay

AMBULANCEMAN (on-camera): *fear's not the word . I mean I was absolutely petrified*

AMBULANCEMAN: oh Jesus Christ

AMBULANCEMAN (on-camera): *to step off the side of a hundred-and-eighty-foot – (shakes his head) it just sounds crazy to even think about it now . but just to step off the side . a good gust of wind . a-hundred-and-eighty-foot . believe me . it's windy up there . and you can just . be blown away*

FIREMAN: go . you're nearly there

AMBULANCEMAN: got me

FIREMAN: yeah

AMBULANCEMAN: I'm in . I'm in

AMBULANCEMAN (on-camera): *I w– wouldn't do it again . I couldn't do that again . not walk off the side like that*

The frequency of the alternation between re-enactment and on-camera account is striking. A relatively brief episode in the story is stretched over quite a long section of the feature. The camera shot of the actual step from the platform to the skip is itself stretched from *okay . ready . okay* to *I'm in . I'm in*. The first two on-camera accounts make explicit in some detail what is already implicit in what we see and hear in the re-enactment: the ambulanceman's fear. The ambulanceman's first turn (*you just be sure . to hold the skip*) is delivered in a voice that is shaking with fear, and we have a close-up of the man's agonized face. The same is true of his next two turns – indeed his voice breaks on the words *hold the skip*. The extremity of the man's terror is signalled in his blasphemy (*oh Jesus Christ*), which would, I suspect, not lightly be allowed into a script. Notice that the first account (*I'm now an absolute nervous wreck . . .*) uses present tense; it comes across as reliving the experience – the man's voice is actually shaking on the word *nervous*, even though he is sitting in the safety of the studio. The third and longest on-camera account (*to step off the side . . .*) reiterates what is again already made clear in the re-enactment: the enormity of what the ambulanceman did. We have already seen distance shots of the skip floating high up in the air, and of the man stretched between the platform and the skip.

A salient property of this whole extract is repetition. The on-camera accounts repeat the enacted terror of the ambulanceman, and vice versa, and the terror is repetitively enacted in the one and represented in the other. In the re-enactment, *you just be sure to hold the skip* is repeated with minor variations three times. The enormity of the step is repeated visually in the re-enactments and verbally in the accounts: *step* (or *walk*) *off the side* occurs three times, *a-hundred-and-eighty-foot* occurs twice; *wind* is repeated as *windy*; and notice the parallelism at the end between *I wouldn't do it again* and *I couldn't do that again*. Repetition serves to elongate this one short incident in a way that fully exploits its potential as vicarious entertainment.

Although the real people involved and the characters depicted here are an ambulanceman and a fireman, they are not talking in official or technical ways. The dialogue is the sort of talk that forms part of ordinary collaborative action, and the ambulanceman's commentary is about his personal response to the incident. The discourse, apart perhaps from the fireman's *you go over to the skip first . and I'll pass him to you* which hovers between (official) instruction and (lifeworld) suggestion, is a lifeworld discourse. Markedly so in, for instance, the colloquial formula 'x is not the word' (*fear's not the word*), the blasphemous curse (*oh Jesus Christ*) indicative of a loss of control which itself is a marker of lifeworld discourse, the implicitness of coherence relations within the ambulanceman's longest commentary (*to step off the side . . .*), and the formula *I wouldn't (couldn't) do it (that) again* as a coda for a story told in conversation.

Crimewatch UK and *999* manifest in particular forms the shifting and unstable boundary between information and entertainment, fact and fiction, documentary and drama, which I have referred to at various points during the book. In the case of *Crimewatch UK*, the element of entertainment is, as it were, shamefaced, and hides itself under the claim that the programme is about getting the public to help solve crimes. In the case of *999*, the element of entertainment is more open, though even here it is mitigated by some emphasis on the moral implications of the stories, and on how viewers might help people in need.

I have suggested that *Crimewatch UK* is an exercise in legitimation, in rebuilding a relationship of trust between police and public at a time when trust has been seriously eroded. I think we can see *999* in similar terms, but there are important differences. In *Crimewatch UK*, the filmed re-enactments are embedded within substantive studio-based activity, in which, as I argued above, the roles of police and presenter are partly merged. But *999* consists almost solely of re-enactments with linkage and continuity provided only by the presenter, so such a merging of roles is not part of the legitimation process. A key difference between the programmes with respect to legitimation is that *Crimewatch UK* centres upon the police, whereas *999* is at least as much concerned with the fire and ambulance services. Whereas the public reputation of the police has sunk sharply, fire and ambulance workers are still highly regarded. While *Crimewatch UK* is actively restructuring relationships between police and public, *999* is rather consolidating relationships which are already fairly solid.

This contrast shows itself in the discursive practices of the two programmes in the different handling of the voices of police and emergency workers. In *Crimewatch UK* the police present features and are interviewed, but do not figure much in re-enactments and do not provide personal testimony. In *999*, emergency workers figure prominently in re-enactments and dialogue, and also provide testimony which contributes to the narration of rescues. The difference goes along, of course, with a difference in topical focus: *Crimewatch UK* re-enacts crimes, and obviously the police will tend to be involved only at the margins if at all; *999* by contrast focuses upon the activities of the emergency services by re-enacting rescues. But the salience of emergency workers in the provision of testimony (illustrated in the extract from *999* analysed above) is important, because it indicates that the main merging of voices in *999* is between ordinary people and emergency workers. The latter are largely constructed *as* ordinary people, as like 'us' in how they behave and how they react to situations, and, of course, in how they talk. I suspect that this construction is plausible because it corresponds to reality: in real life-world communities, the barriers and suspicions which tend to attach to community members who are police officers do not attach to ambulance or fire workers. The legitimizing agenda of *999* is less problematic than that of *Crimewatch UK*. Nevertheless, both programmes strike me as intervening to legitimize state–public relations.

9

POLITICAL DISCOURSE IN THE MEDIA

Like Chapter 8, Chapter 9 is the application in a particular case-study of the analytical framework introduced earlier. But the approach will be rather different. Recall my argument in Chapter 4 that analysis of media discourse needs two twin focuses – on particular instances, particular texts (communicative events), and on the order of discourse. In Chapter 8 the emphasis was upon particular instances, particular programmes in the *Crimewatch UK* and *999* series. In this chapter, the emphasis will be upon the order of discourse. I shall give an overview of how political discourse is structured in the media – of what I shall call the 'order of mediatized political discourse'.

The decision to place the emphasis on describing the order of discourse in my discussion of politics in the media is partly a response to Bourdieu's critique of a particular sort of discourse analysis as applied to political discourse. Especially given the influence of Bourdieu in contemporary social theory, the critique must be taken seriously. Thompson sums up Bourdieu's position as follows:

it would be superficial (at best) to try to analyse political discourses or ideologies by focusing on the utterances as such, without reference to the constitution of the political field and the relations between this field and the broader space of social positions and processes. This kind of 'internal analysis' is commonplace . . . as exemplified by . . . attempts to apply some form of semiotics or 'discourse analysis' to political speeches. . . . all such attempts . . . take for granted but (fail to take account of the sociohistorical conditions within which the object of analysis is produced, constructed and received.)

(Thompson 1991: 28–9)

The first section of the chapter gives a summary of my analysis in an earlier work (Fairclough 1989) of the political discourse of Margaret Thatcher. That analysis partly meets Bourdieu's critique, and partly does not. I draw upon the Thatcher example through the chapter. In the next section, I summarize Bourdieu's account of the political field, as a preliminary to my main concern in this chapter: the overview of mediatized political discourse, which provides a partial picture of the constitution of the political field. I suggest that part of the analysis of examples of political discourse in the media needs to be placing them within the order of mediatized political discourse, in accordance with Bourdieu's argument. I give most attention in the overview to the classification and articulation of voices, discourses and genres in mediatized politics, with an example from a current affairs programme (on the Parent's Charter). Other facets of the order of discourse are more briefly discussed in the final section: boundaries between mediatized political discourse and other orders of discourse; the production, distribution and reception of mediatized political discourse; the diversity of practices within it; ongoing change in practices; politicians' access to, and training in, the practices of mediatized political discourse. I conclude with a discussion of the relationship between politics and media.

Creating a new political discourse

In an earlier book, I included a chapter on the discourse of Thatcherism (Fairclough 1989, chapter 7, 169–96). This centred upon an analysis of part of a BBC Radio 3 interview with Margaret Thatcher in 1985. It did go beyond the purely 'internal analysis' that Bourdieu is criticizing: it attended to the sociohistorical conditions of Thatcherism, it tried to locate Thatcherism and Thatcher's political discourse within the field of politics, and it considered how Thatcherite political discourse contributed to the restructuring of that field. But the focus was still mainly (in Thompson's terms) on 'the utterances as such', and I want to discuss later how the analysis could be developed to more adequately meet Bourdieu's critique.

I shall begin with a summary of my analysis. Part of the extract which I used in 1989 is reproduced below:

1   MICHAEL CHARLTON: Prime Minister you were at Oxford in the nineteen forties and after the war Britain would embark on a period of relative prosperity for all the like of which it had hardly known but today there are three and a quarter million unem-
5   ployed and e:m Britain's economic performance by one measurement has fallen to the rank of that of Italy now can you imagine yourself back at the University today what must seem to be the chances in Britain and the prospects for all now
    MARGARET THATCHER: they are very different worlds you're
10 talking about because the first thing that struck me very forcibly as you were speaking of those days was that now we do enjoy a standard of living which was undreamed of then and I can remember Rab Butler saying after we returned to power in about 1951–52 that if we played our cards right the standard of
15 living within twenty-five years would be twice as high as it was then and em he was just about right and it was remarkable because it was something that we had never thought of now I don't think now one would necessarily think wholly in material terms indeed I think it's wrong to think in material terms
20 because really the kind of country you want is made up by the strength of its people and I think we're returning to my vision of Britain as a younger person and I was always brought up with the idea look Britain is a country whose people think for themselves act for themselves can act on their own initiative they
25 don't have to be told don't like to be pushed around are self-reliant and then over and above that they're always responsible for their families and something else it was a kind of em I think it was Barry who said do as you would be done by e: you act to others as you'd like them to act towards you and so you do
30 something for the community now I think if you were looking at another country you would say what makes a country strong it is its people do they run their industries well are their human relations good e: do they respect law and order are their families strong all of those kind of things and you know it's just way
35 beyond economics

In the analysis, I suggested that Thatcherism was a radical response from the right to Britain's long-term economic and political decline. It broke with the 'postwar consensus' in British politics after the Second World War which underpinned the welfare state, policies of full employment, and nationalization of utilities and services. It rejected the Conservatism of Macmillan and Heath as decisively as the social democracy of the Labour Party. The break entailed a restructuring of the political field to carve out a space and a political base for Thatcherism. Following analyses of Thatcherism by Stuart Hall and others (Hall and Jacques 1983), I saw this in terms of a new articulation of elements of traditional conservatism, neo-liberalism, and political populism, constituting a political mix which these authors refer to as 'authoritarian populism'. The key point for present purposes is that this articulation is partly brought off by a restructuring of the order of political discourse: a new Thatcherite political discourse is constructed by articulating together elements of conservative, liberal and populist discourses. There is a consequential struggle for hegemony within the Conservative Party, and then within the political order of discourse and the field of politics more generally.

The constitution of a Thatcherite political discourse is illustrated through an analysis of the discourse practice of the radio interview – especially of how these discourses are mixed together – and a selective analysis of features of the text to show how this hybrid discourse practice is realized in a heterogeneous text. The analytical framework will by now be familiar to readers. I focused on interpersonal issues: the construction of an identity (a 'subject position') for Thatcher as a political leader, of an identity for the political public ('the people'), and of a relationship between leader and public. I shall just summarize the main lines of the analysis.

For a new political tendency like Thatcherism to achieve power, it has to carve out a political base, a sufficiently powerful constituency of supporters. Such a political base is partly 'talked into' existence – politicians construct and reconstruct the people, the political public, in their discourse, and a measure of their success is the degree to which people accept, and so make real, these (often wildly imaginary) constructions. In the radio interview, Thatcher frequently talked about 'the British people' (lines 23–29, 32–34, in the extract are examples). Furthermore, she often did so by listing their attributes, as in these cases. What is striking about these lists is that they draw upon diverse discourses and condense these discourses together. In the first extract, for example, she evokes both a liberal political discourse of individual responsibility (*they don't have to be told don't like to be pushed around are self-reliant*), and a conservative political discourse with themes of family, community, and law and order. The links between the elements in such lists are left implicit, which means that the important ideological work of constituting a constituency for this marriage of conservative and neo-liberal agendas is partly done by members of that constituency themselves, in arriving at coherent interpretations of these lists. In saying that Thatcher 'evokes' these discourses, I am suggesting that audience members may bring fuller and richer versions of them to interpretation than the few phrases used here by Thatcher. Audiences can, for this reason, draw out key meanings which are left implicit – for instance, in neo-liberal discourse, people 'don't like being pushed around' specifically by the ('nanny') state, and the trade union 'bosses'.

Thatcher was faced with the unprecedented problem of constructing a plausible identity for a woman political leader, and moreover a woman leader of a tough and resolute right-wing tendency. Available models for such a leader had strongly masculine resonances, so she had the dilemma of needing to appropriate masculine models without compromising her femininity (Atkinson 1984). She has taken a great deal of professional advice on the construction of her identity over the years, for instance lowering the pitch of her voice and slowing her speed of delivery to make herself sound more statesmanlike, but also more feminine and more sexually interesting (with her 'husky' voice), and to overcome being perceived as 'shrill', which has dangerous stereotypical connotations of a woman emotionally out of control. She is very much a product of the technologization of discourse, of the engineering of discursive practices to achieve institutional objectives. Her dress and hair style are also carefully managed to highlight her womanliness. Her language is a mixture of elements which further contribute to ensuring her femininity is beyond question, and elements which appropriate 'masculine' practices of authoritative and even tough talk. Look again from this point of view at the list in lines 22–29. Ostensibly this is a quotation from some unspecified source (*the idea*, line 23), but Thatcher herself often talks in this way. *Look* as an imperative verb form is interesting because it connotes toughness and straight-talking in ordinary life. Thatcher uses it a lot. And the claims that are made about the British people in the list are made authoritatively, using categorical modalities.

The question of how Thatcher is constructed of course slides over into the question of what relationship is set up between her and 'the people' – a person is always constructed in relation to others. So Thatcher's authoritativeness in this extract is obviously a matter of her relationship to 'the people' in the particular local form of the Radio 3 audience (though the particular nature of the audience may well affect how that relationship is constructed). I have suggested a tension between ('masculine') authoritativeness and femininity, but there is also another tension between an authoritative relationship with the audience and 'the people' and a relationship of solidarity. This shows itself in the mixing of traditional political discourse with lifeworld discourse, discourse of ordinary experience. Pronouns are worth looking at in this regard. The pronoun *we*, used for example in lines 11–17, is sometimes used 'inclusively' to include the audience and people generally (e.g. *we do enjoy a standard of living which was undreamed of then*) and sometimes 'exclusively' (e.g. *after we returned to power in about 1951–52*, where *we* identifies the Conservative Party), and sometimes ambivalently (e.g. *if we played our cards right* – is this the Conservatives? the government? or the nation?). Inclusive uses of *we* are a common feature of political discourse. On the one hand they claim solidarity by placing everyone in the same boat, but on the other hand they claim authority in that the leader is claiming the right to speak for the people as a whole. Vagueness about who exactly *we* identifies, and the constantly shifting reference of *we*, are important resources in political discourse. *You* as an indefinite pronoun (in lines 28–31 in the extract) – meaning people in general – also claims solidarity, but it is not authoritative: *you* is a colloquial form in contrast to the mainly written *one*, it belongs to a lifeworld discourse, and its use claims membership of a shared lifeworld. It also can be vague and shifting in who it identifies – see Fairclough 1989 for examples. (Claiming solidarity with ordinary people was not, however, something that Thatcher was good at: her appearance and communicative style were too emphatically those of the middle class and shire counties.) So, the mixing of *we* and *you* here is one manifestation of the mixing of political discourse and lifeworld discourse.

Bourdieu: the field of politics

In the tradition of the German sociologist Max Weber, Bourdieu sees the emergence of modern society in terms of a differentiation of fields: the economy, the state, the legal system, religion, culture and the arts emerge as separate fields which are partly autonomous though intricately linked. Each is marked by its own particular form of institutionalization. The field of politics has undergone a process of

professionalization such that 'political capital', the means for producing political policies and programmes, is increasingly concentrated
amongst professionals. To become an actor in the political field, any
class or group of people must find professional politicians to represent them, which means, according to Bourdieu, that they must para-
doxically become politically dispossessed in order to be politically
represented. Professional political organizations acquire a life of their
own and become increasingly cut off from the people they claim to
represent. A key element in the training of politicians is acquiring a
sense of the overall structure of the field of political discourses, a
sense of the range and relationships of actual and possible political
stances, a feel for the political game; a political 'habitus', in Bourdieu's terminology. An important insight in Bourdieu's analysis
which I develop below is that the discourse produced by professional
politicians is *doubly determined*. On the one hand it is internally
determined by its position in the increasingly autonomous and rare-
fied field of politics, on the other hand it is externally determined by
its relationship to the world outside politics, and particularly to the
lives and struggles of the people whom politicians represent, whose
trust and support has to be won and sustained.

Let me add to this brief sketch of the political field a few more of
Bourdieu's observations about political discourse. Political discourse
provides the clearest illustration of the constitutive power of
discourse: it reproduces or changes the social world by reproducing
or changing people's representations of it and the principles of
classification which underlie them. It also clearly shows the insepar-
ability of ideational and interpersonal processes in discourse: it can
reproduce or change the social world only in and through reproducing and changing social classes and groups – it works simultaneously
on representations and classifications of reality, and representations
and classifications of people. The power of political discourse
depends upon its capacity to constitute and mobilize those social forces that are capable of carrying into reality its promises of a new
reality, in its very formulation of this new reality.

As I indicated earlier, my analysis of the Thatcher interview did
roughly locate the discourse of Thatcherism in the field of politics and
political discourse, did comment on its conditions of production in
terms of the state of British politics, and did indicate its effect in
restructuring the field of politics and political discourse. What it did
not do was provide the systematic account of the field of political
discourse that Bourdieu's approach would require. Bourdieu's thesis
of the double determination of discourse is a useful basis for

developing the analysis. And it can be accommodated within the critical discourse analysis framework introduced in Chapter 4.

The concept of 'order of discourse', and the distinction I drew in Chapter 4 between internal relations within an order of discourse and external relations between orders of discourse, allows us to focus upon the field of politics in its discursive aspect. On the one hand, we might describe the order of discourse of professional politics, political communication and struggle between professionals, as it manifests itself in, for example, Parliament, party conferences, political meetings and discussions. One concern here would be to specify the structured set of political discourses, so that one could see more clearly how, for instance, the discourse of Thatcherism was located within the internal relationships of the order of discourse. On the other hand, we might describe external relations between the political order of discourse and other orders of discourse. This would allow a focus on communication between politicians and publics, as well as on discursive aspects of interfaces between politics and the economy, law, religion, and so forth.

A key external relation is between the political order of discourse and the order of discourse of the mass media. Communication between politicians and publics is the second of Bourdieu's twin determinants of the discourse produced by politicians. Since it is now so heavily concentrated in the mass media, it makes sense to foreground the relation between politics and media in investigating this second determinant, and I shall do so below in my discussion of mediatized political discourse. Much critical work on mediatized politics has stressed complicity between the media and politicians, but it is also important to be alert to tensions, contradictions and struggles in the relationship between the political order of discourse and the order of discourse of the media. Surprisingly, the mass media is in fact virtually absent from Bourdieu's account of political discourse, which is a major weakness. Note that the distinction between an internal description of the political order of discourse perhaps with an emphasis on parliamentary discourse, and an external description of the interface between political and media discourse, should not blind us to the fact that much political discourse is now open to being reported and represented in the media, so that politicians even in their parliamentary discourse are partly addressing the public in anticipation of mediatization, as well as addressing each other. The televising of Parliament has aggravated this tendency.

Another important omission in Bourdieu's account of political discourse is genre. Even in internal analysis of relations between discursive practices within the political order of discourse, genre has to be taken into account. Politicians never articulate their various discourses in a pure form, their talk is always situated, always shaped by genres such as political speech making, parliamentary questions and answers, debate, or negotiation. The point is always significant, but becomes crucial when mediatized political discourse is in focus. The genres of the mass media do not at all neatly correspond to the genres of politics, and this lack of fit is a source of constant tension and difficulty for politicians. An account of the contemporary field of politics which omits this tension cannot be satisfactory. My analysis of the Thatcher interview did allude in passing to this tension, but it did not give sufficient weight to the fact that this is Thatcherite political discourse within a particular media genre with its own expectations and assumptions which are not the politician's. I shall develop the analysis in this direction below.

Bourdieu describes political discourse as a field of struggle, internal struggle to produce and sustain a coherent political discourse within the current structured set of political discourses, external struggle to constitute a political public and a base of support and trust for that political discourse and the institution and charismatic individuals associated with it. These processes of struggle can only properly be appreciated through fine-grained analysis of texts. This is where critical discourse analysis can supplement Bourdieu's rather more abstract analysis. Just as Bourdieu's analysis is an analysis of discourses but not genres, it is also an analysis mainly of choice or paradigmatic relations between discourses rather than the chain or syntagmatic relations of political texts constituted within particular genres.

Although it is not the focus of his concerns, Bourdieu does allude to the reception of political discourse by its publics, and especially to apoliticism and antagonism towards professional politics and its performances. Bourdieu attributes this phenomenon to the political impotence of ordinary people and the monopolization of politics by the professionals. As recent work in media sociology has shown, the analysis of reception has to be a significant element in analysis of mediatized political discourse. (One clear limitation of my Thatcher study was that it ignored this issue.)

The order of mediatized political discourse

My aim in this section is to begin to give a broad overview of the order of mediatized political discourse. I will continue the overview in the next main section, after discussing an example. This is one part of the approach I suggested in the last section; the other would be a similar overview of the (non-mediatized) order of political discourse, in Parliament and so forth. This is an initial attempt to map out a complex area of practice, and much of the detail would have to be worked out through closer studies of particular parts of the area (e.g. political interviews, or party political broadcasts). Needless to say, the map is a tentative one, which should be regarded as a suggestion for readers to check out, modify and argue with. I shall sometimes refer to the Thatcher example as a point of reference, suggesting how the analysis might be developed.

We need to specify the repertoire of voices, discourses and genres within the order of mediatized political discourse, the relationships of choice and alternation within each of these repertoires, and how particular voices, discourses and genres are articulated together in different types of media output. Let's begin with voices. A first step here is to identify the main categories of social agent that contribute to political discourse in the media. We can initially distinguish five: political reporters (journalists, correspondents, radio and television presenters, etc.); politicians, trade union leaders, archbishops, etc.; experts; representatives of new social movements; and ordinary people. There are two important questions about voices. One is to specify in more detailed terms which voices figure in mediatized politics, given the obvious but important point that it is not just professional politicians who produce media political discourse. The other is to show how the various categories of voice are structured in relation to each other in mediatized political discourse – who, for example, tends to have the last word?

The politicians who feature in the media are for the most part leading members of the main parliamentary political parties (government ministers, MPs, MEPs, etc.), but members of smaller extra-parliamentary parties and groups, as well as local politicians, do sometimes figure. We can also include other groups who sometimes feature in their capacity of significant actors in political life – trade unionists, representatives of religious organizations, members of the royal family, and so forth. Experts include political commentators and analysts, and experts in various fields of social policy and so forth, who are often academics.

Representatives of the new social movements are a significant contemporary addition to the range of political voices in the media. These include green organizations like Friends of the Earth or Greenpeace, Shelter (an organization which supports homeless people),

Oxfam, or various 'single-issue' organizations representing, for instance, single parents (National Council for One-Parent Families), deprived children (e.g. the Child Poverty Action Group), or former prisoners. The prominence of these voices in contemporary mediatized politics (McRobbie 1994) reflects their increasing influence and support, and the relative weakening of traditional political parties. McRobbie points out that effective media opposition to the government's scapegoating of weaker social groups such as single mothers often comes from articulate, media-trained representatives of these organizations rather than from opposition political parties.

Another major political voice is the voice of ordinary people. Ordinary people have featured for a long time in news and documentary programmes as 'vox pop', edited and circumscribed extracts from interviews with ordinary people which incorporate an element of popular reaction into reports on political and social issues. More recently, ordinary people have started to play a more active part in political conversation and debate in talk shows and especially audience discussion programmes such as the *Oprah Winfrey Show* or (in the UK) *Kilroy* and *The Time, The Place*, and the audience-discussion format seems to be having some influence on news and current affairs broadcasting more generally (Livingstone and Lunt 1994). The hallmark of such programmes is that ordinary people are involved on a relatively equal footing with experts (sometimes politicians) in unrehearsed and virtually unedited discussions on topical issues, loosely managed by a media 'host', in which the experiences of ordinary people often have a higher status than the expertise of the experts, undermining the conventional status of the latter in the media (though recall my analysis of an extract from the *Oprah Winfrey Show* in Chapter 7).

These major categories of voice are distinguished at a high level of generality, and each of them is internally diverse. Amongst professional politicians, for example, there is a structured complex of voices categorized according to political party and according to tendencies within political parties – individuals who figure in the media are standardly identified as Conservative, Labour, etc., and more specifically as, for instance, Thatcherite, 'pro-' or 'anti-European', and in the Labour Party as 'traditionalist' or 'modernizer'. Note that media categorizations of professional politicians may be rather different from categorizations within the world of professional politics itself or within academic analysis. One issue worth attending to is the social class, gender and ethnic distribution of the range of voices within mediatized politics. There has been a significant increase in the salience of women's political voices in the media. In particular, many representatives of new social movements are women, though women are still very much in the minority overall, certainly amongst professional politicians, political analysts and presenters. An interesting question is how those women who figure prominently in the media, for instance, Virginia Bottomley in the Major government, are constructed – sheer presence is not in itself a straightforward measure of greater equity. Virginia Bottomley, for instance, who is very good at taking and holding the floor in interviews, is commonly referred to as 'unstoppable' or something equivalent, evoking stereotypes of women as tending to talk too much. Black and brown faces and voices, on the other hand, are still very unusual in television politics (the television newsreader Trevor Macdonald is the notable exception). Working-class voices are quite common amongst ordinary people who figure in programmes, though hardly in proportion to the overall composition of the population, but are relatively rare otherwise. Again, construction is a key issue: Ken Livingstone and Dennis Skinner are examples of working-class politicians who have been demonized in the media.

The relationship between voices and discourses is often far from simple, and cannot be taken for granted. For instance, the relationship between discourses, political parties, and positions and tendencies within political parties, is a variable and shifting one. The link between a voice in the political field and a political discourse is not as inherent and essential as it might appear. Groups and individuals change their discourses in response to changes in the political field, one consideration being to sustain their relationships of similarity to and difference from other groups and individuals. The political discourse of a political voice is in this sense always relational and relative (Bourdieu 1991). For example, in the mid-1990s leading Labour politicians draw upon discourses which would have been 'Thatcherite' fifteen years ago, and with the election of Tony Blair as Labour leader, a preoccupation in the Conservative Party is establishing 'clear water' between Conservative and Labour.

A major opposition in mediatized political discourse is between the professional political discourses which derive from the field of politics, and lifeworld discourses which are based in ordinary experience. While professional political discourses are mainly drawn upon by politicians and lifeworld discourses mainly by ordinary people, the picture is rather complex. On the one hand, ordinary people may draw upon professional political discourses to varying degrees. On the other hand, it is a striking feature of contemporary mediatized politics that lifeworld discourses are appropriated, again to varying degrees, by politicians and media reporters. Another issue is what discourses are brought into the political domain by the new social movements – ecological and feminist discourses are obvious examples. Discourses may be 'drawn upon' in various ways. They can simply be unselfconsciously used, they can be self-consciously deployed for rhetorical purposes, or they can be contested, undermined and struggled against. See below for an example of the latter.

In the mapping of voices on to discourses, it is sometimes difficult to determine what is collective and what is individual. There is, for instance, an unclarity in my analysis of the Thatcher interview: is the discourse that I describe the discourse of a collective voice (the Thatcherite political tendency), or of an individual voice (Margaret Thatcher)? It seems to be a bit of both. The merging of conservative and neo-liberal discourses is a general feature of Thatcherism, whereas the way in which Thatcher manages her self-positioning as a woman political leader is obviously a matter of her individual style. But I am not sure where exactly to draw the line between general and individual features in the analysis. To do so would require a fuller investigation of the discourse of Thatcherism and a comparison between Thatcher and other leading figures within the tendency (such as Sir Keith Joseph in the earlier part of the Thatcher period, or John Major at the time of writing). Be that as it may, individual identity and charisma (Atkinson 1984) is an essential part of politics, and the analysis therefore needs to attend to distinctive individual voices and styles of political discourse as well as to the discourse associated with collective voices at various levels of generality.

Much of contemporary political discourse is mediatized political discourse. Its major genres are no longer just the traditional genres of politics, they are also the genres of the media. Traditional political activities and their genres – parliamentary debates, party conferences, international conferences – carry on, but they too are represented in the media. And they are represented within the formats and genres of the media – news, documentary, and so forth – so that their representation is always a selective recontextualization (see Chapter 6) according to the requirements of these formats and genres. At the same time, genres for political discourse that the media themselves generate are increasingly important for politicians – most notably the political interview, but also, for instance, phone-in programmes. Also, the boundaries between professional politicians and other media voices are increasingly blurred, with politicians appearing, for instance, on chat shows along with other celebrities such as pop stars, or presenting or 'hosting' programmes like journalists (e.g. Robert Kilroy-Silk, the host of *Kilroy*, is a former Labour MP – see Livingstone and Lunt 1994). An example is a two-part television documentary in 1993 called *Tomorrow's Socialism* which was presented by the former Labour Party leader, Neil Kinnock. An account of the order of mediatized political discourse would need to specify the range of genres where political discourse appears, and the roles that various political voices have within them.

Genre is the point of intersection between choice relations and chain relations. Genres have structure, constraints on syntagmatic organization which I discussed in Chapter 5 in terms of 'activity types'. A fruitful line of analysis is to look at the ordering which these activity types impose upon political voices and political discourses. For example, the genre of political interview can be seen as a device for articulating together the voices of the professional politician and the radio or television reporter. Political interviews are not, of course, private conversations, they are interactions with audiences. The orientation to audience is evident in the discourses that are drawn upon. Reporters justify the adversarial nature of many contemporary political interviews and their challenging and even aggressive questioning of politicians (Bell and van Leeuwen 1994) by claiming to speak on behalf of the ordinary people in their audiences. Sometimes they draw upon lifeworld discourses, simulating the talk of ordinary people. But politicians also often claim their credentials as representatives of ordinary people by drawing upon lifeworld discourses, so that many political interviews are an amalgam of the discourses of professional politics and ordinary life. Recall, for instance, the discussion of extracts from the BBC Radio 4 *Today* programme in Chapter 7.

While much media output draws upon established genres in rather conventional ways, some is more creative, generating novel genres through innovative combinations of established ones. Livingstone and Lunt (1994) see audience discussion programmes as creative in this sense, evolving a genre which combines three established genres of debate, romance and therapy, with the debate element itself involving a configuration of different genres of dialogue – quarrel, debate proper, critical discussion, inquiry and negotiation. An important consequence is that the main voices that figure in audience discussion programmes – television reporters, experts, politicians, and ordinary people – are themselves complex configurations of roles, given that each different genre which contributes to the mix is likely to ascribe a particular role to these voices. For instance, the generic ambiguity is clearly seen in the role of the host: is he or she the chair of a debate, the adored hero of a talk show, a referee, a conciliator, a judge, the compere of a game show, a therapist, the host of a dinner party conversation, a manager or a spokesperson? At times, the host plays any one of these roles, thus altering the roles of other participants and listeners.

(Livingstone and Lunt 1994: 56)

Combinations of genres may be simultaneous in the sense that even a short sequence from a programme may be generically hybrid. But programmes also combine together different genres and multiple instances of the same genres sequentially, producing complex articulations and orderings of voices. I shall illustrate this in the next main section.

Although the focus in my analysis of the Thatcher interview was on Thatcher's political discourse, I did give some peripheral attention to questions of genre which might fruitfully be developed. The media genre here is a form of celebrity interview: the programme was one of a series of in-depth interviews with prominent figures in various walks of public life. This genre is associated with particular expectations about the construction of the interviewer–interviewee relationship and the interviewee–audience relationship, and about the nature of and relationship between questions and answers. Questions are designed to probe the personality and outlook of the interviewee, and answers are expected to be at least to some degree frank and self-revelatory. Audience members are constructed as overhearers listening in on a potentially quite intense interaction between interviewer and interviewee. The programme should at once be educative and entertaining.

Thatcher, however, handles the interview in part as if it were a political interview and also an occasion for political speech making, treating the audience rather than the interviewer as addressee, and constructing the audience as a mass audience rather than purporting to address audience members individually as broadcasters normally do. The speech-making element is evident, for instance, in the listing structures I referred to earlier, such as lines 23–29 in the extract (page 178). The tension between the two participants' assumptions about genre – the tension between the practices of political discourse and the practices of media discourse – is evident in the uneasy relationship between the interviewer's questions and Thatcher's answers. Thatcher behaves as she might in a political interview, using the questions as opportunities to say what she wants to say without trying to compliantly answer them. Thatcher does not, for instance, really answer the question in the extract. Moreover the questions, in accordance with the interviewer's assumptions about genre, are asking for a level of reflection and self-analysis which the answers do not give; the discourse of the questions is studiously avoided in the answers. This is particularly clear when Thatcher is asked (not in the extract) about her 'vision of Britain', 'what is it that inspires your action'; Thatcher's answer avoids the self-analytical discourse of the question. While the interviewer is trying to get Thatcher the person to *reveal* herself, Thatcher the politician is intent on *constructing* herself, and her public. A later question tries unsuccessfully to engage Thatcher in theoretical debate, referring to Thatcherism as 'radical' and 'populist'; Thatcher says she 'wouldn't call it populist' but then talks (in a populist way) of 'striking a chord in the hearts of ordinary people', and uses the word 'radical' in a common-sense way but not the semi-technical political sense intended by the interviewer.

The tension indicated here between traditional practices of political discourse (including practices of political interview which originate in the media but have now become naturalized as part of the tradition), and the media practices which constitute the frames within which politicians are now required to operate, are I suggest a rather general feature of mediatized political discourse. From a media perspective, Thatcher's performance in this instance is not awfully successful, and indeed failure on the part of politicians to successfully negotiate the demands of the new and for many of them unfamiliar field of politics is quite common, despite increasing attention to media training (Franklin 1994). How audiences might react to a performance of this sort requires separate analysis. My analysis of the Thatcher interview in effect abstracted the political discourse of Thatcherism from the media genre in which it was located. I would now argue that the question of what sort of political discourse politicians produce in mediatized politics cannot and should not be divorced from the question of how politicians reconcile their traditions with the unfamiliar and shifting demands of media practices and genres.

An example: the Parent's Charter

I want now to show how complex sequences of genres within a programme can impose orderings upon voices and discourses, and to illustrate again the tensions that can arise between political discourse and media formats. I shall refer to an edition of the BBC1 current affairs programme *Panorama* which was devoted to the Citizen's

Charter, a government initiative associated especially with Prime Minister John Major and designed to give people redress in cases where public services fail to meet designated standards. One of the reports which made up the programme dealt with the Parent's Charter, the part of the Citizen's Charter that applies to schools. My focus will be on how professional politicians are positioned and isolated in this part of the programme.

The report has three main stages – introduction, story, and analysis; an introduction by the presenter, which also effects a transition between this report and the previous one; a story, about children who have been left without places in secondary schools in the outer London borough of Bromley, and in particular about one such child, Helen; an analysis stage, in which the Parent's Charter and especially its claims about parental choice are analysed. A variety of source materials are deployed including several interviews and films. These are heavily edited, with short sequences being spliced together, and different sequences from the same interview or film being placed at different points in the report. Several different genres are drawn upon: interview, presenter narrative, political commentary and analysis, political speechifying, expert opinion, and ordinary conversation and conversational narrative.

I shall begin with a summary which indicates some of the articulations of genres, voices and discourses. This report immediately follows an extract from an interview with William Waldegrave, Cabinet Minister with responsibility for the Citizen's Charter in which he gives an account of its objectives. In the introduction, the presenter, in making the transition from this to the Parent's Charter report, gives a contrary and critical account of the Citizen's Charter as *part of a Tory strategy to pursue private-sector methods while holding the public purse strings tightly.*

The story opens with film of a public meeting and the angry voices of parents whose children are without a place at secondary school because the government's strategy of 'parental choice' – a focus of the Parent's Charter – has led to local schools being over-subscribed. Voice-over commentary from the presenter formulates the situation as *one person's choice has become another's denial.* The presenter then quotes from and critically analyses the Parent's Charter, and narrates the case of Helen, who has no secondary school place to go to. Like most of the presenter's contributions, this is in voice-over. There follow extracts from interviews with her mother, then her father, then Helen. The presenter goes on to talk about the school Helen wanted to go to. There is an interview with the headteacher, the presenter describes Helen's 'painful' position of being excluded while most of her friends were given places, and there is then more interview with Helen. The next sequence deals with Helen's second-choice school. The presenter describes the school, there are further extracts from the Parent's Charter, and an interview with the headteacher. There is then a sequence focusing on the local education authority, opening with film of the town hall and voice-over from the presenter which refers to officials' apprehension about the public meeting, and shifting to more shots of the meeting with the voices of angry parents and the headteacher of Helen's first-choice school. The presenter announces that Helen has now at last been allocated a place, and there is an interview with her mother which closes off the story stage.

The analysis stage opens with extracts from an interview with a local Conservative councillor who resigned her position as chair of the Education Committee in disgust at the chaos in secondary school admissions. This is juxtaposed with further extracts from the interview with William Waldegrave. The presenter then comments that the Citizen's Charter is *not about rights but about remedies*, and the feature closes with a snatch of interview with the Treasury Minister Francis Maude, which appears to confirm that conclusion.

The main voices, then, are those of the presenter, ordinary people (Helen, her parents, people at the meeting), the headteachers (experts of a particular sort), and the politicians (the local councillor, the government ministers). Particular voices are associated with particular genres. The presenter narrates, analyses and comments. The headteachers give expert opinion. The ordinary people in the reports converse, but so too does the local councillor. Waldegrave, the government minister, by contrast makes a political speech. The report is organized in a way which sets up an opposition between the generally discredited genre of political speechifying used by Waldegrave, and the other genres. Particularly striking, given that they are both Conservatives, is the juxtaposition of the conversational language of the local councillor and the political rhetoric of the minister:

CONSERVATIVE COUNCILLOR: I blame the government . I . I feel . that if . I – I very much support this Citizen's Charter I think it's about time . the ordinary citizen had the right to take public authorities to task . if they don't deliver what they what they ought to I – I very much support that I think it's a great idea . a lot of people who are in favour of market market forces say no that's wrong market forces must be an absolute thing . but . in the case of choice it can't be absolute can it it can't be . absolute for everybody . I mean these parents who are . milling about . so unhappily now . they won't feel that they've had wonderful choice

WILLIAM WALDEGRAVE: now we're enabling parents to make a . a real fuss . a fuss that means something . saying we've compared schools we actually like . these ones we want more of these now I don't I'm of course not welcoming the fact that not all getting their first choice . now . but

PRESENTER: it's not that they're not getting their first choice (Waldegrave: right) they're saying you can't go to any school (in the borough)

WALDEGRAVE: well they want to g– they want to go to schools like those provided in Bromley . they want more schools . like that . and they're going to push to get em . now in the old days they would have just had to take what they were given . by local education authorities following guidelines from the department . but that's what's turning round it's rather a good example of how we want to . get the energies of citizens . to to work f– for themselves but also . for the standards which will then spread across the country

Panorama, 18 May 1992

There is a widely noted ambivalence about the Citizen's Charter which allows it to be read in terms of either a discourse of citizenship or a discourse of consumption. The issue is whether it seeks to enhance citizens' rights, or is solely concerned to subject public services to market pressures from consumers. The formulation of the Citizen's Charter given by William Waldegrave immediately before the Parent's Charter report (*getting quality into public service*) draws upon the discourse of consumption, as does his first contribution in the extract above in foregrounding parental (in effect, consumer) pressure as a mechanism for raising standards. There is a market-oriented metanarrative underlying the government's political discourse around the Citizen's Charter: the Charter will give people rights of redress for poor service and will thus stimulate consumer pressure which will push up standards. Maude, at the end of the feature, explicitly denies that the Citizen's Charter has to do with citizens' rights, and formulates it in consumer terms as *making sure the citizen gets a good deal for the money that the government spends on the citizen's behalf*. But notice that although he is referring to people as consumers he uses the word *citizen*, articulating together the discourses of consumption and citizenship.

Apart from the voices of government ministers, a discourse of citizenship predominates. The focus is upon the right to parental choice which the Parent's Charter seems to embody: *You can choose the school you would like your child to go to.* The report is a problematization and elaboration of this aspect of the political discourse of the Citizen's

Charter, and it is noteworthy that all categories of voices – ordinary people, experts (headteachers) and the presenter as well as politicians – speak politically and engage in a struggle over the discourse of choice. Let me list in order some of the formulations used. Presenter: *the question is whether all this choice will really make the difference in hospitals schools*. Parent in meeting: *it strikes me that it's the schools that have the choice and not the parents*. Presenter: *in Bromley one person's choice has become another's denial*. First headteacher: *if you have the . a vast amount of choice you've also got the responsibility of coping with that choice and that may mean encouraging a child to understand that she's got to wait*. Presenter: *like the Parent's Charter's promise of choice . the music department Helen fancied was just wishful thinking*. Second headteacher: *Bromley parents have less choice now than they did before*. Parent in meeting: *I feel you've taken my decision-making away from me*. Presenter: *a government that has promised them a right to choose whichever school they want to go to and yet the Council can't deliver*. Conservative councillor: *in the case of choice . it can't be absolute can it . it can't be absolute for everybody . I mean those parents who are milling about so unhappily now . they won't feel they've had a meaningful choice*. Waldegrave's only mention of choice differs significantly from all these in limiting and relativizing choice: he refers to parents' *first choice*.

In addition to these various formulations, justifications and contestations of the political discourse of the Charter, a number of other political discourses briefly surface in the feature. The presenter draws upon a left oppositional discourse early on, and actually gives this discourse the status of truth: *the Charter has to be seen for what it is . part of a Tory strategy to pursue private-sector methods while holding the public purse strings tightly*. There is also a snatch of cynical lifeworld discourse about politicians from a parent in the film of the meeting: *it's because of this meeting I reckon they got them out quick*. And the last contribution from Helen's mother draws upon a discourse of grassroots political campaigning:

PRESENTER: are you going to continue this process to see it doesn't happen again
MOTHER: oh absolutely until every child this year is settled into school and then we shall continue until we make sure it never . ever . happens again

The mother's contribution is striking in its delivery, drawing upon a non-professional political rhetoric which is manifested in a slow emphatic delivery of *absolutely* and the last four words (*never . ever . happens again*).

The isolation of the government ministers (Waldegrave in particular) is terms of genre and discourses is underscored by the positioning of their voices in the report. There is a broad movement up a chain of responsibility within the report, from the voices of ordinary people (the meeting and the case of Helen), to the experts (headteachers), to the local councillor, and finally to the government ministers. The voices of the two government ministers are cut off from the others in being located peripherally at the end of the feature (there is also the Waldegrave interview extract that immediately precedes the feature). There is an element of drama here, with the ministers being confronted with an alliance of voices, discourses and genres which is built up in the main body of the report, especially in the story. The sense of Waldegrave being confronted by this chorus of critical voices is accentuated by the juxtaposition already noted between his contribution and that of the highly critical councillor, the fact that she is also a Conservative underscoring the clash of positions.

The reading of this report which I have been foregrounding is one which emphasizes tension and struggle between the media and professional politicians, seeing the presenter in this case as orchestrating and contributing to an oppositional alliance drawing together voices from the lifeworld, the professions, local politics, and journalism. The professional politicians are edited into a corner, as it were. According to this account, using the media as a way of communicating with the public is no simple matter for contemporary politicians. The terms on which the media can be so used are often demanding, and in some cases the media seem to be able to dictate them (though less so for a powerful politician like Thatcher).

However, a very different reading of reports of this sort is possible, according to which the difficulties and challenges facing politicians are mainly there to give an impression of the autonomy of the media and the answerability of politicians, while at a deeper level there is complicity and cooperation between journalists and politicians to sustain the status quo. Waldegrave and Maude may be isolated and confronted at the end of the report, but the emphasis they clearly want to put on quality and value for money in their account of the Citizen's Charter is allowed to stand as the last word, and the political discourse of the professional politicians is given the legitimacy of providing closure for the feature. Moreover, the oppositional voices and discourses with which the ministers are confronted are very limited, with notable absences. For the most part, it is accepted that citizens' rights in the domain of education are appropriately formulated in terms of the consumerist discourse of choice; people do not challenge 'choice', they merely argue that 'choice' isn't working. This is linked to the programme's selection of the white, middle-class, Conservative borough of Bromley; the ordinary people who figure do not include people of colour, or working-class people. Their predominantly middle-class nature is visually obvious, as well as indicated by the language they use. If the programme had set out to seriously challenge and corner ministers, it could have brought together far more damaging voices and discourses. Voices and discourses which, especially since the retreat of the official opposition Labour Party to safe middle ground, are rarely seen or heard at all in the mainstream media. These two alternative readings suggests an ambivalence in the relationship between politics and the media which I return to in the final section of the chapter. In certain cases, it may seem that the media control the politicians, in others that politicians manipulate the media in complicity with journalists. In many cases, as here, the relationship is ambivalent.

Mediatized political discourse: further considerations

So far, my overview of the order of mediatized political discourse has focused upon the identification of repertoires of voices, discourses and genres, and the shifting configurations/articulations which they enter into. But there are a number of other considerations which are relevant in characterizing the order of mediatized political discourse. I shall discuss some of these rather briefly in the final section. The issues I take up here are: boundaries between mediatized political discourse and other orders of discourse; the production, distribution and reception of mediatized political discourse; the diversity of practices within it; ongoing change in practices; politicians' access to, and training in, the practices of mediatized political discourse.

The issue of boundaries or frontiers between orders of discourse has in fact already been quite extensively discussed above, in that mediatized political discourse has itself been presented as an area of intersection and tension between the orders of discourse of professional politics and of the media. However, there are other frontiers, also areas of intersection and tension, which need to be attended to. There is, for instance, the ill-defined frontier between political discourse and the discourse of government (the state, administration, bureaucracy), which is of current concern given the dramatic increase in government and local government advertising in the media and accusations of the politicization of public information (in, for instance, campaigns to encourage people to buy shares in privatized public industries such as Gas and Water). There is also an important frontier area between mediatized political discourse and academic discourse, the discourse of various types of experts in and around the political arena, including the discourse of the 'think tanks' which have become a major element in the contemporary political process. These and other examples underline the view that the field of political discourse must be seen as an open field, where frontiers with a range of other fields are constantly being negotiated.

An adequate account of the order of mediatized political discourse would need to incorporate accounts of its key processes: the production, distribution, and consumption/reception of mediatized political texts. In Chapter 3 I discussed in general terms the importance of attending to all three processes in analysing media discourse, and I shall not repeat that argument here. The discussion above of voices, discourses and genres has focused upon the processes of production, though without going systematically into the practices and routines of production. Political discourse gives rise to particular issues of distribution and reception. With regard to distribution, one issue is what one might call the 'trajectories' of different types of political discourse: their varying distributions across discursive practices and domains within the order of discourse of the mass media and within other orders of discourse (such as those of government, or education), the intertextual chains (see Chapter 4) they enter into, and the transformations they undergo as they move along these chains. Some types of political discourse – for example a major speech by a leading politician – have highly complex trajectories, entering into many domains of reception, which will to a degree be anticipated in the way in which they are produced. Part of what is involved here is a complex process of recycling within the media: an interview with a politician on a breakfast television show can become a lead item in both newspapers and broadcast news programmes, and a topic for editorials, current affairs programmes, and phone-in programmes. Mediatized political events often themselves constitute the main political news.

The consumption/reception of media discourse raises a number of specific issues. One is the general question of how political discourse impacts upon people's lives – what wider influences and ramifications it has beyond the portions of people's lives that they devote to watching, reading or listening to the news and other political material. One way into this difficult question is through discourse analysis of the ways in which people talk about mediatized politics, focusing specifically upon the question of what parts of their discursive repertoires they draw upon in doing so, and how the political discourse of the media is recontextualized and transformed in their talk, and articulated with elements from other discoursal sources. For example, in an article in *Discourse and Society* (Fairclough 1992b) I suggested that people taking part in a reception study of Israeli political television were drawing upon the discursive practices of ordinary life ('the life-world') in talking about mediatized politics – recontextualizing that political discourse within everyday experience. A related issue discussed briefly in that paper is whether and to what extent audiences critically analyse and 'deconstruct' mediatized political discourse (see Liebes and Ribak 1991, Livingstone and Lunt 1994). A more general issue is the worrying alienation of people from party politics in a number of western democracies. Analysis of consumption/ reception of mediatized political discourse should be able to throw some light upon this very significant development. (See Livingstone and Lunt 1994 for a discussion of the related issue of increasingly critical responses by audiences to experts on television.)

A danger in giving an overview of the complex field of mediatized political discourse is that the diversity of practices will be lost sight of. A fuller description would need to go into differences between types of media (television, radio, press), differences between outlets in each type (between television stations, between radio stations, between newspapers), and diversity within particular outlets. For example, practices of political interview even within a single television station such as BBC1 are not homogeneous – they vary between programmes, but even within programmes according to the models preferred by particular interviewers and editors. The picture is one of considerable diversity, instability and change. Practices like political interview are sensitive barometers of wider processes of social and cultural change, showing subtle shifts in, for instance, the construction of the identities of both politicians and journalists, and in social relationships between them, and between them and audiences (Fairclough 1995). Relationships between diverse practices may be relationships of struggle, with particular practices coming to symbolize wider positions and interests within media institutions which in turn may be linked to wider social struggles. The order of mediatized political discourse, like other orders of discourse, can usefully be regarded as a domain of cultural hegemony which is constantly open to hegemonic struggle, a struggle for power within media institutions which will relate, if in possibly complex and indirect ways, to struggles for power in the wider society.

The picture, then, is a very complex one, and we need to beware of easy simplifications.

Another issue is the issue of access to mediatized political discourse. This partly overlaps with the discussion earlier of the range of voices within the order of discourse, and the relationships that are constructed between the voices (e.g. between professional politicians and ordinary people) in particular types of output. There is also the increasingly important matter of the apparatuses which political parties have developed to train their members in using the media, to prepare and groom them for media appearances (often radically changing their appearance, clothes, and communicative style), to set the agenda of political news, and to optimize the media exposure of their members.

The emergence of mediatized politics is sometimes seen as the colonization of politics by the media, and sometimes seen as the colonization of the media by politics. Certainly the energy and resources that political parties and national and local government are now putting into their information and communication departments indicates a major effort on their part to control their relationship with the media – to 'package politics' as the title of a recent book on the subject puts it (Franklin 1994). Yet if we consider the relationship between politics and media from the perspective of discursive practices, it is clear that it has required more concessions and adaptations from politicians than from the media. One indicator of this is what has happened recently to politicians who are exceptionally gifted in the traditional discursive practices of politics – the great political orators. They have become marginalized, have lost their public visibility, and have even become figures of ridicule. Michael Foot, a former leader of the Labour Party, is a good example. If the political apparatuses do largely dictate the agenda of mediatized politics, they do so only at the price of a radical mediatization of the internal practices of politics which has profound implications for the viability and legitimacy of the political public sphere. But the settlement that has been arrived at between politicians and the media is not a stable one. It is a relationship of complicity and mutual dependence which is constantly unsettled by its contradictions, for the agendas of politics and media are not in the end the same. Oscillation between harmony and tension, trust and suspicion, are inherent. The order of mediatized political discourse is itself, therefore, an essentially unstable one.

10

CRITICAL MEDIA LITERACY

In the course of this book, I have emphasized the importance of the media and of media discourse in wider processes of social and cultural change, and in wider power relations and ideological processes in society. The media, and media discourse, are clearly a powerful presence in contemporary social life, particularly since it is a feature of late modernity that cultural facets of society are increasingly salient in the social order and social change. If culture is becoming more salient, by the same token so too are language and discourse. It follows that it is becoming essential for effective citizenship that people should be critically aware of culture, discourse and language, including the discourse and language of the media. As a conclusion, I want to draw together some of the issues and analytical methods dealt with in this book in the form of questions that someone who is critically literate in the language of the media ought to be able to answer about a media text – a newspaper article, a programme on television, or a radio programme. Critical media literacy is not just a matter of awareness of media discourse (Luke 1994) – it also includes, for instance, awareness of the economics of media and production processes within the media – but critical awareness of language and discourse is an important part of it (Fairclough 1992c). What follows can be regarded as a tentative agenda for teachers.

I suggest that it ought to be an objective of media and language education to ensure that students can answer four questions about any media text:

1. How is the text designed, why is it designed in this way, and how else could it have been designed?
2. How are texts of this sort produced, and in what ways are they likely to be interpreted and used?
3. What does the text indicate about the media order of discourse?
4. What wider sociocultural processes is this text a part of, what are its wider social conditions, and what are its likely effects?

These are of course very general questions, which can be developed into more specific ones. Notice that the book has not dealt equally with all of them: there is more material appertaining to 1 and 3 than to 2 and 4. I shall discuss them in turn.

1. *How is the text designed, why is it designed in this way, and how else could it have been designed?*
This question highlights the idea that texts are based upon choices, and that alternative choices might always have been made. Sometimes the question will direct attention to the variation that currently exists in media practices – for instance, the sort of variation in radio science that was brought out in Chapter 7 in the comparison between *Medicine Now* and *High Resolution*. Sometimes the question will suggest that current practices are shaped by (and help shape) current social and cultural circumstances – and that things might be (and perhaps once were, and will be) different.

The question of how texts are designed has received more attention in the book than any other. I have provided a 'metalanguage' for talking about the language and intertextuality of texts. Such a metalanguage is essential for a critical literacy of media language, but developing a metalanguage which can be made generally accessible through the educational system is a formidably difficult problem which I have not addressed in this book. Let me summarize as a further and more specific series of questions the main forms of analysis introduced in the book. I also include some of the types of linguistic and textual analysis used in connection with each group of questions.

(a) Intertextuality
• What genres, voices and discourses are drawn upon, and how are they articulated together?

– direct and indirect speech, generic structure or 'staging', narrative analysis (story, presentation), conjunctions, collocations

(b) Language

i. Representations
- What presences and absences, foregrounding and background-ing, characterize the text?
- What process and participant types are there? How are processes and participants categorized and metaphorized?
- What relationships are set up between propositions (clauses) in texts?

– presupposition, process and participant types, nominalization, agency and voice (active and passive), categorization and wording, metaphor, main and subordinate clauses, theme, local and global coherence relations

ii. Relations and identities
What are the participants (voices) in the text, and how are they con-structed?
- What relationships are set up between participants – specifically between:
    - media personnel (journalists, presenters) and audiences/readerships
    - 'others' (e.g. experts, politicians) and audiences/readerships
    - media personnel and 'others'
- Are constructions of participants and relationships simple, or complex/ambivalent?
- What relative salience do institutional and personal identities have in the construction of participants?

– oral delivery, body movement, key (serious or humorous), con-versationalization, vocabulary, mood, modality, interactional control features, lists

iii. Image and text
- In the case of television, how are visual images constructed, and what relationships (e.g. of tension) are set up between language and image?

2. *How are texts of this sort produced, and in what ways are they likely to be interpreted and used?*
This question relates to some of the issues dealt with in Chapter 3, but of course neither processes of production nor processes of consumption have been major concerns of the book. With respect to production, it is

important to be aware that what we read in a newspaper or see on the television screen is not a simple and transparent representation of the world, but the outcome of specific professional practices and techniques, which could be and can be quite different with quite different results. It is also important to be aware that the practices which underlie texts are based in particular social relations, and particular relations of power. With respect to consumption, important issues are the diversity of practices of reading, listening and viewing (and their social conditions), and the potential for divergent interpretations and uses of any given text by different sections of a readership or audience.

3. *What does the text indicate about the media order of discourse?*
Part of critical media literacy is an overall sense of the practices of media and of the media order of discourse, and a sensitivity to significant tendencies of change. This question assumes that any given media text will shed some light upon these issues, in that it will be a product of a particular state and evolution of the order of discourse. Particular questions here include:

- Is the text indicative of stable or unstable relationships, fixed or shifting boundaries, between discursive practices within the order of discourse, and between the media order of discourse and socially adjacent orders of discourse?
- What particular choices (inclusions/exclusions, of genres or discourses) is this text associated with?
- What chain relationships across the media order of discourse and/or socially adjacent orders of discourse is this text situated within?
- What particular tendencies of change (e.g. commodification or conversationalization of media discourse) does this text exemplify?

4. *What wider sociocultural processes is this text a part of, what are its wider social conditions, and what are its likely effects?*
This question brings into the picture wider social conditions (including economic and political ones) which constrain media discourse and media texts, and their social effects – in terms of systems of knowledge and beliefs (and ideologies), social relations of power, and the positioning of people as social subjects. It also draws attention to changes in society and culture which frame the sort of changes in the media order of discourse alluded to in question 3 above. The three-dimensional framework for critical discourse

analysis introduced in Chapter 4 is relevant here: the analysis of any media event links together statements about:
- the text and its linguistic properties
- the discourse practice – processes of text production and consumption (recall that intertextual analysis links text to discourse practice)
- the sociocultural practice which the discourse practice and the text are embedded within

We might add to the four questions so far a fifth question suggested in Luke *et al.* (1994):

5. *What can be done about this text?*
The point of this question is to highlight the status of media texts as a form of social action which can be responded to with other forms of social action. These may be other texts – letters of congratulation or complaint, reviews, discussions – or nontextual forms of action. Some media texts, for instance, can stimulate public campaigns, meetings and demonstrations. One example is the widely noted influence in 1989 of media representations of struggles within the former socialist countries of Eastern Europe upon the development and spread of those struggles. Another is a powerful documentary produced by John Pilger for Channel 4 in 1994 on the genocide practised by the Indonesian government against the people of East Timor. One effect of this question, within a programme of critical literacy awareness, may be to encourage people to move beyond reception of media texts to action in response to those communicative events.

BIBLIOGRAPHY

Abercrombie, N. 1991: The privilege of the producer. In Keat, R. and Abercrombie, N. (eds), *Enterprise culture*, Routledge.

Allen, R. C. 1992: Audience-oriented criticism and television. In Allen, R. C. (ed.), *Channels of discourse reassembled*, 2nd edn, Routledge.

Althusser, L. 1971: Ideology and ideological state apparatuses. In Althusser, L., *Lenin and Philosophy*, New Left Books.

Atkinson, J. M. 1984: *Our masters' voices: the language and body language of politics*, Methuen.

Atkinson, J. M. and Heritage, J. 1984: *Structures of social action*, Cambridge University Press.

Austin, J. L. 1962: *How to do things with words*, Oxford University Press.

Bakhtin, M. 1981: *The dialogical imagination*, trans. Emerson, C. and Holquist, M., University of Texas Press.

———. 1986: *Speech genres and other late essays*, ed. Emerson, C. and Holquist, M., University of Texas Press.

Barthes, R. 1977: *Image–Music–Text*, Fontana.

Beck, U. 1992: *Risk society: towards a new modernity*, trans. Ritter, M., Sage Publications.

Bell, A. 1984: Language style as audience design. *Language in Society*, 13 (2): 145–204.

——. 1991: *The language of news media*, Blackwell.

Bell, P. and van Leeuwen, T. 1994: *The media interview: confession, contest, conversation*, University of New South Wales Press.

Benjamin, W. 1970: The work of art in the era of mechanical reproduction. In Benjamin, *Illuminations*, Jonathan Cape.

Bernstein, B. 1990: *The structuring of pedagogic discourse*, Routledge.

Blackwell, T. and Seabrook, J. 1993: *The revolt against change: towards a conserving radicalism*, Vintage.

Bourdieu, P. 1977: *Outline of a theory of practice*, trans. Nice, R., Cambridge University Press.

——. 1991: *Language and symbolic power*, Polity Press.

Brown, G. and Yule, G. 1983: *Discourse analysis*, Cambridge University Press.

Brown, P. and Levinson, S. 1978: Universal in language usage: politeness phenomena. In Goody, E. N. (ed.), *Questions and politeness*, Cambridge University Press.

Bruck, P. 1989: Strategies for peace, strategies for news research. *Journal of Communication*, 39: 108–29.

Brunsdon, C. 1990: Television: aesthetics and audiences. In Mellancamp, P. (ed.), *Logics of television*, Indiana University Press.

Button, G. and Lee, J. 1987: *Talk and social organisation*, Multilingual Matters.

Cardiff, D. 1980: The serious and the popular: aspects of the evolution of style in radio talk, 1928–1939. *Media Culture and Society*, 2 (1).

Cope, B. and Kalantzis, M. 1993: *The power of literacy: a genre approach to teaching writing*, The Falmer Press.

Corner, J. 1991: The interview as a social encounter. In Scannell, P. (ed.), *Broadcast talk*, Sage Publications.

Corner, J., Richardson, J. and Fenton, N. 1990: *Nuclear reactions: form and response in public issue television*, John Libbey.

Dews, P. 1987: *Logics of disintegration*, Verso.

Ellis, J. 1982: *Visible fictions*, Routledge.

Enzensberger, H. 1970: Constituents of a theory of the media. *New Left Review*, 64.

Fairclough, N. 1988: Discourse representation in media discourse. *Sociolinguistics*, 17: 125–39.

——. 1989: *Language and power*, Longman.

——. 1991: What might we mean by 'enterprise discourse'? In Keat, R. and Abercrombie, N. (eds), *Enterprise culture*, Routledge.

——. 1992a: *Discourse and social change*, Polity Press.

——. 1992b: Discourse and text: linguistic and intertextual analysis within discourse analysis. *Discourse and Society*, 3 (2): 193–217.

——. (ed.) 1992c: *Critical language awareness*, Longman.

——. 1993: Critical discourse analysis and the marketisation of public discourse: the universities. *Discourse and Society*, 4 (2): 133–68.

Fairclough, N. 1994: Conversationalization of public discourse and the authority of the consumer. In Keat, R., Whiteley, N. and Abercrombie, N. (eds), *The authority of the consumer*, Routledge.

———. 1995: Ideology and identity change in political television. In Fairclough, N., *Critical discourse analysis*, Longman.

Featherstone, M. 1991: *Consumer culture and postmodernism*, Sage Publications.

Fiske, J. and Hartley, J. 1978: *Reading television*, Methuen.

Forgacs, D. 1988: *A Gramsci reader*, Lawrence & Wishart.

Foucault, M. 1972: *The archaeology of knowledge*, trans. Sheridan-Smith, A. M., Tavistock Publications.

———. 1978: *Discipline and punish: the birth of the prison*, trans. Sheridan-Smith, A. M., Penguin Books.

Fowler, R. 1987: Notes on critical linguistics. In Threadgold, T. and Steele, R. (eds), *Language topics: essays in honour of Michael Halliday*, John Benjamins.

Fowler, R. 1991: *Language in the News: discourse and ideology in the press*, Routledge.

Fowler, R., et al. (eds) 1979: *Language and control*, Routledge.

Franklin, B. 1994: *Packaging Politics: political communication in Britain's media democracy*, Edward Arnold.

Fraser, N. 1989: *Unruly practice: power, discourse and gender in contemporary social theory*, Polity Press.

Freire, P. 1972: *Pedagogy of the oppressed*, Penguin.

Garfinkel, H. 1967: *Studies in ethnomethodology*, Prentice Hall.

Garnham, N. 1986: The media and the public sphere. In Golding, P., et al. (eds), *Communicating politics*, Leicester University Press.

Gee, J. 1990: *Social linguistics and literacies: ideology in discourses*, The Falmer Press.

Giddens, A. 1991: *Modernity and self-identity*, Polity Press.

Goffman, E. 1969: *The presentation of self in everyday life*, Penguin.

———. 1981: *Forms of talk*, Basil Blackwell.

Gramsci, A. 1971: *Selections from the prison notebooks*, trans. Hoare, Q. and Nowell-Smith, G., Lawrence & Wishart.

Greatbatch, D. 1986: Aspects of topical organisation in news interviews: the use of agenda-shifting procedures by news interviewees. *Media Culture and Society*, 8 (4): 441–55.

Habermas, J. 1984: *Theory of Communicative action* vol. 1, trans. McCarthy, T., Heinemann.

———. 1989: *The Structural Transformation of the Public Sphere*, trans. Burger, T., Polity Press.

Hall, S. 1977: Culture the media and the ideological effect. In Curran, J., et al. (eds), *Mass communication and society*, Edward Arnold and the Open University Press.

Hall, S. and Jacques, M. 1983: *The politics of Thatcherism*, Lawrence & Wishart.

Hall, S., *et al.* 1978: *Policing the crisis: mugging, the state, and law and order*, Methuen.

Halliday, M: 1978: *Language as social semiotic*, Edward Arnold.

——. 1985: *Introduction to functional grammar*, Edward Arnold.

——. 1989: *Spoken and written language*. Oxford University Press.

Halliday, M. and Hasan, R. 1976: *Cohesion in English*. Longman.

Hartley, J. 1982: *Understanding news*. Routledge.

Heritage, J. 1985: Analyzing news interviews: aspects of the production of talk for overhearing audiences. In van Dijk, T. (ed.), *Handbook of discourse analysis*, 3, London: Academic Press.

Heritage, J. and Watson, D. 1979: Formulations as conversational objects. In Psathas, G. (ed.), *Everyday language: studies in ethnomethodology*, Irvington.

Herman, E. and Chomsky, N. 1988: *Manufacturing consent: the political economy of the mass media*, Pantheon Books.

Hodge, R. and Kress, G. 1979: *Language as ideology*, Routledge.

——. 1988: *Social semiotics*, Polity Press.

——. 1992: *Language as ideology*, 2nd edn, Routledge.

Hutchby, I. 1991: The organization of talk on talk radio. In Scannell, P. (ed.), *Broadcast talk*, Sage Publications.

Inglis, F. 1990: *Media theory: an introduction*, Blackwell.

Kellner, D. 1992: *The Persian Gulf television war*, Westview Press.

Kress, G. 1989: History and language: towards a social account of language change. *Journal of Pragmatics*, 13: 445–66.

Kress, G. and Threadgold, T. 1988: Towards a social theory of genre. *Southern Review*, 21: 215–43.

Kress, G. and van Leeuwen, T. 1990: *Reading images*. Deakin University Press.

Kristeva, J. 1986: Word, dialogue and novel. In Moi, T. (ed.), *The Kristeva Reader*, Basil Blackwell.

Kumar, K. 1977: Holding the middle ground. In Curran, J., *et al.* (eds), *Mass communication and society*, Edward Arnold and the Open University Press.

Labov, W. 1972: *Language in the inner city*, University of Pennsylvania Press.

Labov, W. and Waletzky, J. 1967: Narrative analysis: oral versions of personal experience. In Helms, J. (ed.), *Essays on the verbal and visual arts*, University of Washington Press.

Lakoff, G. and Johnson, M. 1980: *Metaphors we live by*, University of Chicago Press.

Lash, S. 1990: *Sociology of postmodernism*, Routledge.

Leech, G. N. 1966: *English in advertising*, Longman.

——. 1983: *Principles of politeness*, Longman.

Levinson, S. 1979: Activity types and language. *Linguistics*, 17: 365–99.

——. 1983: *Pragmatics*. Cambridge University Press.

Liebes, T. and Ribak, R. 1991: A mother's battle against TV news: a case study in political socialization. *Discourse and Society* 2 (2); 203–22.

Livingstone, S. and Lunt, P. 1994: *Talk on television: audience participation and public debate*, Routledge.

Luke, A., O'Brien, J. and Comber, B. 1994: Making community texts objects of study. *The Australian Journal of Language and Literacy*, 17 (2): 139–49.

Luke, C. 1994: Feminist pedagogy and critical media literacy. *Journal of Communication Inquiry*, 18 (2): 27–44.

McRobbie, A. 1994: Folk devils fight back. *New Left Review*, 203: 107–16.

Mancini, P. 1988: Simulated interaction: how the television journalist speaks. *European Journal of Communication*, 3 (2): 151–66.

Mardh, I. 1980: *Headlinese: on the grammar of English frontpage headlines*, CWK Gleerup.

Martin, J. R. 1986: Grammaticalising ecology: the politics of baby seals and kangaroos. In Threadgold, T., *et al.* (eds), *Language semiotics ideology*, Sydney Association for Studies in Society and Culture.

Media Literacy Report 1993 (draft): WIR Industry Research, Sydney.

Mishler, E. 1984: *The discourse of medicine: dialectics of medical interviews*, Ablex Publishing Corporation.

Montgomery, M. 1988: DJ talk. In Coupland, N. (ed.), *Discourse Stylistics*, Croom Helm.

———. 1990: *Meanings and the media: studies in the discourse analysis of media texts*. PhD thesis, University of Strathclyde.

———. 1991: 'Our Tune': a study of a discourse genre. In Scannell, P. (ed.), *Broadcast talk*, Sage Publications.

Montgomery, M., Tolson, A. and Garton, G. 1989: Media discourse in the 1987 general election: ideology, scripts and metaphors. *English Language Research*, 3: 173–204.

Norris, C. 1992: *Uncritical theory*, Lawrence & Wishart.

Pêcheux, M. 1982: *Language, semantics and ideology: stating the obvious*, trans. Nagpal, H., Macmillan.

Pilger, J. 1992: *Distant voices*. Vintage.

Postman, N. 1987: *Amusing ourselves to death: public discourse in the age of show business*, Methuen.

Quirk, R., Greenbaum, S., Leech, G. and Svartvik, J. 1972: *A grammar of contemporary English*, Longman.

Richardson, K. 1987: Critical linguistics and textual diagnosis. *Text*, 7 (2): 145–63.

Sacks, H., Schegloff, E. and Jefferson, G. 1974: A simplest systematics for the organisation of turn-taking in conversation. *Language*, 50: 696–735.

Scannell, P. (ed.) 1991: *Broadcast talk*, Sage Publications.

Scannell, P. 1992: Public service broadcasting and modern public life. In Scannell, P., *et al.* (eds), *Culture and power*, Sage Publications.

Silverstone, R. 1985: *Framing science: the making of a BBC documentary*, British Film Institute Publications.

Sinclair, J. 1992: Trust the text. In Davies, M. and Ravelli, L. (eds), *Advances in systemic linguistics*, Pinter Publishers.

Straumann, H. 1935: *Newspaper headlines*, Heinemann.

Stubbs, M. 1983: *Discourse analysis*, Basil Blackwell.

Swales, J. 1990: *Genre analysis: English in academic and research settings*, Cambridge University Press.

Talbot, M. 1990: *Language, intertextuality and subjectivity: voices and the construction of consumer femininity*. PhD thesis, Lancaster University.

Thompson, J. B. 1984: *Studies in the theory of ideology*, Polity Press.

——. 1990: *Ideology and modern culture*, Polity Press.

——. 1991: Editor's introduction to Bourdieu 1991.

Threadgold, T. 1989: Talking about genre: ideologies and incompatible discourses. *Cultural Studies*, 3 (1): 101–27.

Tolson, A. 1990: *Speaking from experience: interview discourse and forms of subjectivity*. PhD thesis, University of Birmingham.

——. 1991: Televised chat and the synthetic personality. In Scannell, P. (ed.), *Broadcast talk*, Sage Publications.

Toolan, M. 1988: *Narrative: a critical linguistic introduction*, Routledge.

Trew, T. 1979a: Theory and ideology at work. In Fowler, R., *et al.* (eds), *Language and control*, Routledge.

——. 1979b: 'What the papers say': linguistic variation and ideological difference. In Fowler, R., *et al.* (eds), *Language and control*. Routledge & Kegan Paul.

Trudgill, P. 1986: *Dialects in contact*, Basil Blackwell.

Tuchman, G. 1978: *Making news: a study in the construction of reality*, New York: Free Press.

van Dijk, T. (ed.) 1985: *Handbook of discourse analysis*, 4 vols, Academic Press.

van Dijk, T. 1988a: *News as discourse*, Erlbaum.

——. 1988b: *News analysis*, Erlbaum.

——. 1991: *Racism and the press*, Routledge.

van Leeuwen, T. 1984: Impartial speech: observations on the intonation of radio newsreaders. *Australian Journal of Cultural Studies*, 2 (1).

——. 1987: Generic strategies in press journalism, *Australian Review of Applied Linguistics*, 10 (2): 199–220.

——. 1991: Conjunctive structure in documentary film and television. *Continuum*, 5 (1): 76–114.

——. 1993: Genre and field in critical discourse analysis. *Discourse and Society*, 4 (2): 193–223.

Wernick, A. 1991: *Promotional culture*, Sage Publications.

Williams, G. forthcoming: *French discourse analysis*, Routledge.

Williams, R. 1975: *Television: technology and cultural form*, Shocken Books.

——. 1981: *Marxism and literature*, Oxford University Press.

Wodak, R. 1990: *Wir sind alle Unschuldige Täter. Diskurshistorische Studien zum Nachkriegsantisemitismus*, Frankfurt-am-Main: Suhrkamp.

INDEX